The Fight for Food

Titles of related interest

The farmer as manager
Tony Giles and Malcolm Stansfield

Interpretations of calamity
Edited by Kenneth Hewitt

Perspectives on drought and famine in Nigeria
G. Jan van Apeldoorn

The
Fight for Food

Factors Limiting Agricultural Production

Harold E. Croxall   Lionel P. Smith

London
GEORGE ALLEN & UNWIN
Boston   Sydney

George Allen & Unwin (Publishers) Ltd,
40 Museum Street, London WC1A 1LU, UK

George Allen & Unwin (Publishers) Ltd,
Park Lane, Hemel Hempstead, Herts HP2 4TE, UK

Allen & Unwin Inc.,
9 Winchester Terrace, Winchester, Mass 01890, USA

George Allen & Unwin Australia Pty Ltd,
8 Napier Street, North Sydney, NSW 2060, Australia

First published in 1984

British Library Cataloguing in Publication Data

Croxall, H. E.
    The fight for food.
1. Agricultural productivity
I. Title   II. Smith, L.P.
338.1'6   HD1415
ISBN 0-04-630011-2
ISBN 0-04-630012-0 Pbk

Library of Congress Cataloguing in Publication Data

Croxall, H. E.
    The fight for food.
Bibliography: p.
Includes index.
1. Agricultural productivity.   2. Food crops.
3. Food supply.   I. Smith, L. P. (Lionel Percy),
1914– . II. Title.
S494.5.P75C76 1984   338.1'4   84-6413
ISBN 0-04-630011-2
ISBN 0-04-630012-0 (pbk.)

Set in 10 on 11 point Baskerville by Computape (Pickering) Ltd.
and printed in Great Britain by Richard Clay (The Chaucer Press) Ltd,
Bungay, Suffolk

Preface

> Nothing must be accepted as true till it has been clearly recog-
> nised as being so; which means that every care must be taken to
> avoid haste and prejudice.
>
> *Descartes*

Although responsible civilised nations are now urgently trying to
devise policies to solve an energy crisis arising from the diminishing
supplies of fossil fuels, inadequate attention is still being given to the
fact that civilisation as we know it, and even the survival of the human
species, basically depend not on fuel for machines but on fuel for
mankind – in other words, food.

It is not surprising that Western European nations, at a time when
the financial solvency of their Common Agricultural Policy is threatened by surpluses of food and wine, tend to regard malnutrition and
starvation as problems of only the 'Third World', despite the fact that
cases of inadequate diet still occur among the underprivileged min-
orities of most of the affluent nations.

A wider and less myopic vision would suggest that in the face of an
ever-increasing world population (the control of which seems to be
beyond the power and sense of humanity) plus an understandable
demand from the underdeveloped countries for a higher standard of
living, complacency about food supplies cannot be justified any more
than it can be about future energy resources. We do not propose to sit
in judgment over the Malthusian doctrine but, with occasional food
surpluses and long-lasting food deficiencies co-existing in different
parts of the world, we think it may be relevant to identify and discuss
all the numerous factors which influence agricultural production and
productivity.

We shall restrict this discussion to agricultural production from the
land. This does not mean that we underrate the importance of the
water areas of the world as a source of food. Indeed, as knowledge and
skill increase on the use of these vast resources in the best non-
destructive manner, they may become increasingly significant in the
provision of food, but this is an aspect of the subject beyond our
competence to explain or examine.

Even with the omission of mariculture, the factors governing
production from the land will provide more than enough problems
and complexities. We shall also restrict the discussion to the pro-

duction of essential food crops. Ornamental crops and luxury foods are important aesthetically (and, to their producers, economically), but they are concerned with the quality of life and are not essential to the sheer survival of mankind.

There is often a tendency in many quarters to hope and even believe that the problems of food supply have simple solutions. Thus, in 1983, a Member of Parliament for one of Britain's most important agricultural constituencies (with an acute mind trained in legal matters) seriously proposed that all forms of support for agriculture should be diverted to more deserving industries which would generate enough wealth to purchase ample food supplies on world markets. This simplistic solution was warmly acclaimed by another intelligent parliamentarian who was diverted into politics from a brilliant career as a classical scholar, a provenance which, over the ages, has many times been a source of over-confidence and scientific ignorance.

Yet everyone who follows Voltaire's advice to cultivate his garden knows by experience, if not by reason, that any production from the land is at the mercy of a whole range of conflicting factors, and that there are no perfect, permanent answers to the questions posed. The gardener is well aware that climate, soil and situation place limits on the range of biological species that can be successfully produced, and that this success can only be achieved by a constant struggle against pests and weeds. The gardener is also conscious of the need for expertise and for making the right decisions on the adoption of new techniques and improved varieties. Privately, if not publicly, it is also conceded that the monotonous regularity with which the prizes for roses at the local horticultural shows go to Mrs Smith, those for beans to the Reverend Jones, and for onions to Mr Robinson is not entirely due to chance and biased judges.

The form and design of the garden are also dictated by economic and social pressures, and the time and money which can be expended upon it have a great influence on its composition. When money is short, a rose bed may have to give way to vegetables to feed a hungry family; in more affluent circumstances, the orchard may be displaced by a tennis court or swimming pool to facilitate the mating rites of the adolescents. There is thus an infinite diversity of garden use, and although planners and architects conspire to build quasi-identical housing units in equal-sized plots, no one is surprised when such attempts at uniformity and egality are destroyed by no two of the adjacent gardens being exactly alike.

To a large extent, the garden is a microcosm of the wider agricultural scene. A number of the factors causing diversity in design and variability in results are precisely the same on both scales. This is especially true in regard to the effects of climate, weather, soil and situation, although the response of the gardener may be different from that of the farmer. The economic and social pressures may differ a great deal in both nature and extent, but they have a common modifying effect on the plans for a large commercial farm or for a small garden plot.

It is our intention to try to identify these factors more precisely and to illustrate how they operate. This attempt is not intended to be confined to conditions in any restricted geographical area. Although examples will be quoted mainly from the temperate climatic regions and from the British Isles in particular, attention will be concentrated on the principles involved so that the arguments arising are applicable to any agricultural location with suitable changes in the weighting of the various factors. Food-producing areas anywhere in the world are subject to the same diversity of influences, but these influences vary in strength from place to place, from year to year, and from farm to farm.

We will attempt to simplify a complex set of problems by first examining the factors over which man has little or no control, then those over which he can exert a significant influence, and finally those of which he is the arbiter. As already explained, all farmers and gardeners are aware that success is largely, and sometimes entirely, determined by the critical weather, over which they have no control. Climate limits the choice of what should be grown, and weather determines the reward, in terms of yield, of any particular growing season.

Therefore, it seems logical to consider first the limitations of climate and weather and then the problems of soil and situation, which, together with the weather, produce the environment in which the farmer has to work. We have virtually no control over the existence of pests, diseases and weeds, although we can try to overcome their worst effects on food production. Such attempts will be the next aspect of the subject to be considered.

Account must then be taken of the husbandry techniques and technological innovations which are the tools of the trade available to the farmer, enabling him to make the best of the conditions under which he has to raise his crops and rear his livestock, taking advantage of favourable conditions and trying to counteract the adverse factors.

Problems of manpower and equipment play a large part in the economic factors. The costs of production matched against the returns obtained from the sale of produce have a very direct effect on productivity; a farmer is not a philanthropist. Production costs are partially within human control; prices paid to food producers are almost entirely decided by the actions of man, although their effect on productivity is not necessarily either direct or simple.

There are other important social and political factors which are man made, particularly the competition for land use, the size of farms, land structure, and the conflicting reactions between urban and rural populations. Any compromise solution to such problems must concern itself with an assessment of the use of available energy and resources.

Finally, we have to discuss the most difficult and crucial problem of how all the various factors interact with each other, and how their combined effects determine the decisions which the farmer has to make. It is the rightness or wrongness of these decisions, the human factor, which ultimately controls the levels of both production and productivity and the amount of food available for human consumption.

Before starting on this difficult exercise, perhaps we should define productivity, or at least indicate the sense in which we intend to use the word. Too often it is loosely used as a synonym for output. Different economists try to measure it with a degree of precision in various ways, as the value of output per unit area of land or unit of stock: as the profit per unit of capital invested, as the output per man engaged, and so on. All such methods may be useful in the making of comparisons in a particular set of circumstances, but none gives absolute and indisputable values.

We prefer to regard productivity as the difference between the total costs of production and the income realised by the sale of the end-products. We do not claim that this is any better than any other definition, but it is how most farmers regard the term. If costs exceed returns, then their scale of activity will be reduced and they may finally have to give up farming. On the other hand, if their margin of income over cost rises, then they not only become more prosperous, but they tend to expand their farming business, and often in such expansion they become more efficient producers.

We do not intend to fill the pages with specific numerical examples, which can be found in profusion elsewhere with varying degrees of clarity and exactitude. A working solution to a farming problem in one area in one set of circumstances may not be applicable with the same hope of success elsewhere, and any particular quantitative explanation is unique to the case being studied. Tribal customs, however good, are not universal laws, a fact which is often forgotten by those involved in giving technical assistance or advice in countries not their own.

The best solution to any farming problem is the one which takes due account of all the fundamental issues, and it is those issues and limiting factors which we are now attempting to explain, indicating the ways in which they can operate, singly and in combination. It would be an impossible task to give a comprehensive account of the infinite number of permutations which are possible. We thus can give only a review of the broad principles involved, with examples mainly drawn from countries such as Britain with a temperate climate and a democratic political system. This is the type of area in which we have the most personal experience and for which reliable information is available.

If we chose examples with other types of climate or under other types of government, then the factors we describe would have a different impact. Yet we believe that the fundamental approach to the problem of improving productivity is the only one which will enable us to arrive at the correct solution in any situation or under any regime.

It is always essential to identify the nature and intensity of the individual factors which influence the decisions of the farmer and, through him, affect agricultural productivity. In a world of increasing specialisation, it is even more important to try to understand the effects of the interactions of these factors on each other and on the response of the farmer. Without this comprehensive perspective the importance of separate individual factors may be given a false importance, and if they are allowed to dominate the actions of farmers without any curb, then, instead of progress, the net result may be chaos.

Many attempts have been made to analyse the prospects of food production with respect to separate limiting factors. We hope that this book will help towards the consideration of the problem in its entirety. There is little hope of finding the correct answer to a complicated question unless its full complexities are understood. There is even less hope of winning the fight for food unless such answers are found.

H. E. Croxall
L. P. Smith
August 1983

Contents

Introduction

The types of limiting factor

'A field requires three things, fair weather, sound seed, and a
good husbandman.'

Anon.

Translated into modern terms, this old adage can be amplified in the
following manner.

The weather can be termed the meteorological factor; it is probably
the most variable element of all from place to place and from year to
year. In many ways it is the dominating influence in the growth of
crops and in the proliferation of the enemies to production. It is very
difficult to influence and almost impossible to control.

The field itself represents the soil (or edaphic) factor, involving the
nature, quality and quantity of the land. This was recognised in
pagan times by use of the term Earth Goddess. The greatest natural
variations in soil are from place to place; the variations with time are
slow, but are accentuated by interactions with current weather. It is
difficult to make significant improvements in soil quality, although
certain ameliorations are possible; it is all too easy to cause major and
often irreversible changes in quantity by erosion. The potential
productivity of a farm is largely determined by the soil and climate.

The genetic quality of the crop seeds and the farm stock can be
termed the biological factor, which man is constantly striving to
improve. Also under this heading can be included the unwanted
weeds, pests, parasites and diseases which man is striving to suppress.
Although conspicuous improvements have been made in relatively
recent years, these struggles to improve the friends and defeat the
enemies are a continuing battle, carried out by both farmers and
scientists.

The husbandman epitomises the human factor, but he is by no
means the only type of human being involved. It is true that he makes
the operational decisions, but he is affected by the aims, intelligence,
ability and honesty of many others, including politicians, administrators, advisers, customers and a host of other interested parties.
His operating powers are limited, not only by his own ability and by
that of his workforce, but also by the facilities and power at his
disposal.

These four different types of factor can be discussed separately, but none can be considered in isolation as all are interactive and inter-dependent. The process of collation and combination of their effects could be thought of as a kind of jigsaw puzzle in many dimensions with some of the pieces missing, some undecipherable, and some of ever-changing shape. It is not exactly surprising that perfection is rarely attained, and yet the comforting fact is that reasonable answers to such difficult questions are so often found by the majority of the farmers in many nations.

A partial explanation for this 'better than chance' state of affairs is that many of the critical decisions are made on the farm itself by someone closely involved in the whole process of production. Another helpful reason is that farming has traditionally inclined towards a 'fail-safe' technique, thus largely avoiding wholesale failures. Centrally made, high-level decisions are magnificent when they are correct, but they can cause widespread disasters when they are wrong.

A sensible aim, and indeed the aim of this book, is to improve the standard of decision making at all levels. To do this it is necessary to try to understand the influence of the several factors and their relative importance regarding the problem under consideration. In so doing it has to be appreciated to what extent the numerous factors can be controlled, influenced or merely accepted.

It is difficult to make any major progress in increasing food production and raising productivity unless all the people involved are at least aware of the difficulties faced by the various sections of the agricultural industry. Even if it is impossible to solve other people's problems, there is no excuse for not knowing that they exist.

Part I

The meteorological factor

1

Climate and the effects of weather

Climate controls the way we live, and especially the crops we can grow; it exercises this control through the effects of weather.

The weather is the description of the physical environment at a particular moment at a particular place, a scientific snapshot of the conditions at one instant of time. The amalgamation of a succession of these meteorological events leads to the weather of a day, a month, a growing season, or a year.

As the length of time increases beyond a year, this weather description changes almost imperceptibly into a description of climate. The climate of any place is the summary of all the weather conditions that have been experienced over a period of time, usually a period of years.

An account of any climate should not only include information about the average weather, but also details of the variations about such an average, both in frequency and in extent. Essentially, climate is a précis of information about past weather events, neither more nor less.

The limitation of such climatic data is that no matter how carefully the past weather has been measured and observed, despite the care that has been taken in analysis and presentation, the past climate is still no certain guide to future weather conditions.

Climates are continually changing, albeit slowly and by small amounts. In some circumstances even small changes can have a serious effect on an industry such as agriculture. Nevertheless, the past climate is the only meteorological reference available to a planner, and this future uncertainty makes it all the more important to understand the links between weather and the biological factors, so that the implications of climate and its possible changes can be put into the correct perspective.

The elements of weather

The weather has an important, and sometimes a dominant effect on almost every agricultural operation and biological process. This effect may be direct, in that the weather controls an activity, or it may be indirect, in that circumstances are created which interact with other factors. Examples of such indirect effects are the condition of the soil, the incidence and intensity of pests and disease, or the liability of the soil and air to pollution; these will be discussed later.

Sometimes only a single weather factor, such as temperature, is involved. More often, a combination of several weather factors, and occasionally a sequence of weather events, have to be taken into consideration so as to understand the full influence of the physical environment and be able to explain the consequences.

The important weather elements which must be considered can be listed as follows.

(a) The length of day, or length of night, which provides a reliable form of clock or calendar in any one area.

(b) The temperature, both of the soil and of the air, which affects the length of time available for the growth of plants and the speed of some processes; it can also act as a kind of clock or calendar.

(c) The sunshine, which is a measure of the energy input. The heat balance, both of plants and animals, is of prime importance in regard to both growth and yield. Although such features are often discussed in terms of temperature, it is the disposition of energy which is important.

(d) The rainfall (and snowfall), the input factor in the soil-water balance. The maintenance of adequate soil moisture is essential for good crop growth, especially at certain critical periods. It is the correct assessment of the heat balance and water balance that provides the key to understanding the effects of weather on yields.

(e) The transpiration and evaporation, which have to be included in the water balance as the output factor.

(f) The humidity, which is a factor in the transpiration process and which is often of critical importance in problems of plant or animal disease.

(g) The wind, another transpiration factor which is also very important in questions of plant growth or animal exposure. It is often the controlling agent in the transfer and spread of pathogens or pollutants.

(h) Weather hazards, of which frost is the most obvious, but which also include gales, thunderstorms, hail, snow and floods.

It is not only the outside weather which is important, but also the conditions inside buildings such as those used for the growing of protected crops, for the storage of food, and for the housing of livestock. Such indoor weather is greatly influenced by the external weather as well as by the construction, design and control facilities of the structure.

When considering the weather factors which limit production, it is necessary to know the range of conditions which are likely to be experienced. This range indicates the chances of the best conditions and also the risks of unacceptable adverse conditions. Risks have to be taken in all types of farming, but any operation undertaken against the climatic odds can only be justified if the potential rewards make it worthwhile.

The effects of temperature

Initial attempts at agroclimatological analysis often suffer from the fact that temperature is a very obvious weather factor and that temperature data are the easiest to acquire. As a result, many explanations of crop distribution and performance are expressed in terms of temperature alone, when in fact there are other more logical and more effective weather parameters which also should be used.

It cannot be too strongly emphasised that temperature is not a form of energy: temperature is *not* heat. Temperature has no dimensions, it is only a condition which is reached as a result of the heat balance of a particular subject. Usually in meteorology the subject is the sensor of a thermometer in a white louvred box, known as a screen.

This temperature measurement gives a close approximation to the true air temperature in shade at a particular height; great care has to be taken in the exposure of the thermometer. Such an 'air' temperature may be only a guide to the surface temperature of a leaf, and can be appreciably different to the soil-surface temperature or the temperature at seed depth. Conventional air temperature measurements, made under standardised conditions, should always be thought of as reference levels, not as absolute values for any particular biological event.

Probably the most dependable applications of temperature data are in relation to the limiting factors for plant growth and for establishing relationships with crop phenological stages. Setting apart the damaging effects of frost, temperature levels can be specified between which the growth of various plants can be expected to take place. Temperatures between these limits are necessary for growth but not sufficient in themselves, as other meteorological factors have to be considered.

Some published material fails to specify whether the temperatures referred to concern the air or the soil. Even if soil temperatures are quoted, the all-important depth below the surface may not be stated, any diurnal variations tend to be ignored. Fortunately, the mean 24-hour air temperatures and the mean 24-hour soil temperatures in a shallow root zone are very similar, so that no major errors are introduced by this uncertainty, although soil character has a recognisable effect which cannot always be ignored. Again, temperature is being used as a reference point, not as a basis for precise biological interpretation.

The air temperature regime is all too commonly expressed in terms of day-degrees or accumulated temperatures (often inexcusably termed 'heat-sums'), which represent the extent of the temperature above (or below) a certain threshold value multiplied by the length of time concerned. For example, a mean day temperature of 20°C would contribute to accumulated temperatures above 10°C a value of (20 − 10) × 1 = 10 day-degrees.

This concept has been used with more enthusiasm than success in a large variety of agrometeorological problems, but it does have some value in analysing the effect of air temperature on various stages of plant development. Accumulated temperatures can never be used to obtain reliable relationships of weather with crop yields with any great hope of success. Accumulated soil temperatures at seed depth have proved to be useful parameters in regard to germination times, provided that soil moisture was also taken into account.

Another reason why standard air temperatures should only be regarded as reference values is that there can be a very large variation in temperature within the biosphere, the realm of the plant from root to tip. The largest day to night variations in temperature occur at the soil surface, which tends to be hottest at midday and coldest at the end of the night. This range decreases upward in the air and downward in the soil.

Air temperature data can thus be used for some specific problems with some success. In others, it can be used to provide general guidance but cannot supply a full explanation, and so may be inadequate for accurate purposes.

Considerable use may be made of soil temperatures if data are available. They are slightly easier to measure than air temperatures because there are fewer problems of direct solar radiation which affect the exposure, but they are more subject to sampling errors. Air is subject to an almost constant mixing process; soil is not.

The diurnal variations of soil temperature decrease rapidly with depth, and it is found that the 30-cm (1-foot) depth offers a sample temperature which provides useful information in regard to growth seasons. The temperatures of soil at this depth tend to smooth over the more rapid day-to-day or hour-to-hour changes which occur at shallower levels and in the air above, and they hence become more reliable as indicators or reference values of generalised conditions.

Soil temperatures at this depth can certainly be used to define the effective growing seasons of a major crop such as grass. They can also be used as reference temperatures, giving some indication of seed germination conditions, but for more precise analysis the temperatures at the appropriate seed depth must be considered.

The length of a growing season, its mean value and the variations from year to year that can be expected about such an average, are very important agroclimatological factors for consideration of the potential production of an area. Soil temperatures should always be preferred to air temperatures for this purpose, especially when there are changes in height above sea level to be taken into account. In areas exposed to strong winds, such as hills and mountains, air temperatures can give a misleading overestimate of the potential growing season. Estimates in coastal areas can also be similarly affected.

Effects of radiation from the Sun

Temperatures, in one form or another, may thus be used to some effect to express the length of the growing season or the duration of plant growth stages, but the extent of green matter production during this period is largely dependent on incident energy.

Such energy is provided by the daily sunshine, and even on a cloudy day an appreciable amount of the radiant heat from the Sun reaches the surface of the Earth (the short-wave radiation). Throughout the 24 hours of day and night, the Earth and everything on it is radiating some heat back into space (the long-wave radiation). The temperature of the air is a result of such an exchange of heat energy, conditioned by its initial level of temperature, which depends on its area of origin and thus on the wind direction; air arriving from a cold source must be colder than air arriving from a warmer source.

The total incoming radiation, direct and diffuse, bears a close relationship with the hours of bright sunshine, and may be estimated to a fair degree of accuracy, provided that latitude, time of year, slope and aspect of the land are taken into account. Illumination, or the energy available within the visual spectrum range, is also closely related to sunshine duration.

The summation of this incident solar energy over the growing season gives a good indication of the growth potential of any area, provided that soil moisture and fertility conditions are suitable. In general, it may be said that the greater the available incoming energy at the critical time, the larger is the potential yield of the growing crop, especially within the temperature ranges usually prevailing in the middle latitudes. Nearer the Equator, other factors come into play, but with a crop like rice, for example, yields are still strongly related to the total incoming energy.

Certain crops require good sunny conditions at critical growth stages, such as the ripening phase. On the other hand, strong incoming radiation may encourage rapid growth but may impair quality. The environmental conditions required for maximum quantity and optimum quality are rarely satisfied simultaneously under natural conditions, and care must be taken not to confuse these qualities. A good taste or flavour, or the presence of a desirable constituent for processing is often associated with relatively slow or poor growth. The best wines are not made from grapes grown on the richest soils. The too rapid growth of grass in ideal weather conditions may lead to an imbalance in constituents, leading to nutritional disorders in animals grazing the otherwise excellent crop.

Good sunshine is also important at harvest time, especially during the hay harvest. It helps to lower the moisture content of grain crops and so reduce the costly need for artificial drying before storage. The sunshine requirement for a farm is tied to a very precise and demanding timetable.

Long hours of sunshine are closely associated with high day temperatures in summer, and it is often difficult to separate the two effects. Direct sunshine, especially in light winds, will raise surface temperatures above those in the surrounding air. In a growing leaf, this rise in surface temperature is counteracted by cooling due to the evaporation of water by transpiration, but if the plant stomata close and transpiration decreases, then wilting may result.

Animals can move into shade to avoid the stress of strong sunshine, but plants have no such mobility and have to react to the dictation of the weather. In climates with long seasons of uninterrupted sunshine it is very difficult to grow food crops without the intensive use of irrigation.

Sunshine data are not so widely available as temperature data in meteorological records. Furthermore, the accuracy is less, and although temperature records are usually compatible on an international basis, the same cannot always be said of sunshine measurements; the theoretically more precise radiation data may be even more unreliable.

Many empirical formulae have been proposed to convert sunshine hours or measurements of cloudiness into estimates of incoming solar radiation, each suited to the climatic conditions prevailing in the area of origin. Values of the mean radiation obtained in this manner are usually of acceptable operational accuracy, but errors have to be expected in the estimation of individual or daily values.

The acquisition and application of radiation data are thus by no means easy processes, and this partly explains why so much investigational work in the past has made the maximum use of temperature data. Nevertheless, until radiation is given accurate and adequate consideration, little real progress can be expected in either agrometeorology or agroclimatology.

Effects of rainfall and transpiration

Plants cannot grow without water, and they do not grow to their full potential without easily available water. At the other extreme, they cannot thrive with an excess of water in the soil because their roots also need oxygen, although some food plants (such as rice) are adapted to growth under conditions of excess water. Adequate rainfall is thus needed, but persistent rains imply continual cloud cover and a deficiency of sunshine, and, as already explained, the plant needs this solar energy.

The ideal climate for primary production thus involves a very delicate balance between too little and too much as far as both radiation and soil moisture are concerned. The words 'primary production' are not just a turn of phrase, for it is very important to understand that plant photosynthesis is a form of production which is the nearest approach to a real addition to the worth of the world. Most other 'production' processes are either a form of transformation from one asset to another, or, more extravagantly, a form of irreversible consumption, such as the use of hydrocarbon fuels.

It has been well said that the most important question in the world today is 'Will it rain tomorrow?', for if it does not rain on some tomorrow, then crops will not grow and there will be no food to eat for animals or men. A reliable balanced rainfall is essential for successful agriculture.

For the ideal soil-moisture balance, the daily input of rainfall would closely equal the daily output of evaporation from the soil and transpiration from the living plants. This would ensure that the available moisture in the soil within reach of the plant roots, the 'current account' of the soil bank, would always be adequate for growth and never in excess.

In the controlled climate of a glass- or plastic-covered structure, this ideal can theoretically be achieved. In the open field, reliance has to be placed on the distribution of daily rainfall, which can only be supplemented by skilled irrigation practice when water is available and when the extra cost is covered by extra profits. In some areas of the world where the growing season is dry, irrigation is the only answer to the problem.

One of the redeeming features of a temperate maritime climate (such as that of the British Isles) is that it approaches an ideal rainfall climate in most years. Few other parts of the world have annual average rainfalls which are almost equally distributed throughout the months of the year, although even in Britain the winter months in upland areas are appreciably wetter than those of the summer.

If there were more summer rain in this kind of climate, it would involve more clouds and less sunshine. If there were fewer winter rains, then there would be insufficient water to be made available for domestic and industrial use. Such areas are 'temperate' in more ways than one. Dry periods occur but they rarely last long enough to qualify as droughts on a world aridity scale. Even so, dry periods in a normally reliable rainfall area can cause serious drops in yields.

Although in a temperate area the input of rain is often fairly balanced throughout the year, there is a marked annual change in output due to evaporation and transpiration, which are greatest in high summer and very little indeed in mid-winter. This results in a seasonal excess of input over output in the winter half of the year which is essential to restore the soil to field capacity after it has been dried out by the extraction of water by the roots of summer crops, and to provide runoff, drainage and deep seepage water which fills the rivers and reservoirs and recharges the underground aquifers.

In the summer growing season the output can often be greater than the input, leading to deficiencies which need not be serious to plant growth if there is a reserve of moisture in the soil available to the roots. The extent of the reserve depends on the nature of the soil and the depth of the roots. For very shallow-rooted plants or crops growing on thin soil, such as rough upland grazing, this reserve is quite small. It may not exceed some 50 mm (2 in), which is equivalent to the plant water needs of a dry summer fortnight. For deeper, richer soils and for plants whose roots penetrate deeper into the earth, such as cereals and trees, the reserve is greater. There are few occasions when trees in Britain suffer from a major deprivation of soil moisture, the summer of 1976 being a rare example of such a shortage. Cereal yields are not often affected by summer rainfall deficiency, and 'drought never brought dearth in England'.

To avoid temporary checks to growth due to soil-moisture deficits, the summer rains have to fall with sufficient regularity to prevent the exhaustion of these soil reserves. Therefore it is the distribution of rainfall that is important in any climatic representation. The practice of using an annual average rainfall statistic to represent the moisture climate is far too simplistic. The critical factor is the frequency of serious soil-moisture deficits or damaging excesses. Furthermore, rainfall cannot be analysed by itself, but only in relation to the potential transpiration: it is the water balance involving these two factors which is important.

It is therefore far more useful to consider the moisture climate in terms of soil-moisture deficits (the amounts withdrawn from soil reserves) in summer. In winter, when input exceeds output, attention should be concentrated on excess rainfall. Details are required (for both seasons) of the average conditions and the variations about such averages which are liable to occur in a succession of cropping years.

As the variations in potential transpiration from place to place and from year to year are smaller than the similar variations in rainfall, the latter is still the dominant variable, but the critical agricultural implications cannot be defined without the use of the output factor. The type of soil and the type of crop must also be considered in any reliable analysis being prepared for the purpose of selecting the best type of farming and the most suitable crop for a given soil-moisture climate.

The soil-moisture regime is also important in relation to soil cultivations, especially when heavy farm machinery is being used. When the soil contains all the water it can hold against the pull of gravity, it is said to be at field capacity. If additional rain falls on soil in this state and drainage is slow, then the passage of heavy vehicles over the surface can do lasting damage to the soil structure.

The bulk of the autumn cultivations have preferably to be carried out before the date when the soil returns to field capacity, and the average date when this occurs is a critical factor in planning for an arable rotation. Later in the farming year, spring cultivations may be held up if the soil has not begun to dry out. The old weather lore concerning 'the peck of March dust' and its value to the farmer emphasises this soil-water balance factor.

Incidentally, the phrase 'soil humidity' often occurs in scientific papers which have been translated into English from another language. This expression means 'soil moisture', and does not refer to the humidity of the air in the soil. Much effort has gone into the introduction of a standard set of units in scientific papers for international use; a sometimes greater cause for concern is the lack of universal technical terms which are not open to misunderstanding, especially in a developing science.

Effects of humidity

Humidity can be a confusing word, often because of a lack of understanding as to how it is expressed. It is usually described in terms of relative humidity, as a percentage, indicating the ratio of how much water vapour the air actually holds with respect to the maximum amount it is capable of holding. This maximum holding capacity varies with temperature and increases as the temperature rises. The actual absolute amount of moisture in the air does not vary much in the course of a day, but the relative humidity falls as the temperature rises, and *vice versa*.

The lowest relative humidities experienced in a temperate climate are those inside a heated building in winter. The actual water content of the cold outside air is small, and when this air enters the building it is heated, and its relative humidity can fall to below 30 per cent, thus entering the range of dryness which would be expected by day over desert areas. Conversely, if cold air is let into an animal house, where the air is warmer than outside and contains a great deal of water vapour, then the much-praised ventilation which is supposed to cure all ills will in fact increase the interior relative humidity as the cold air cools the inside atmosphere. If air is cooled sufficiently until the moisture present equals the maximum holding capacity at that level, then the 'dew point' is reached, with 100 per cent relative humidity; further cooling will result in condensation.

Average humidities can be misleading, and the annual average relative humidity is not a convenient agroclimatological parameter; the duration of high or low humidities is far more significant. The humidity regime is of considerable importance, not only in relation to transpiration and evaporation, to the curing of hay or the moisture content of harvested grain, but also in regard to the incidence of diseases which require moist surfaces for infection and spread.

The relative humidity calculated from wet and dry thermometer measurements in a standard meteorological screen can only be a guide to humidities elsewhere, but it can be very useful on occasion. For example, if the relative humidity in the screen remains above 90 per cent after rain, it is a fair assumption to make that all leaf surfaces in the open are still wet.

Instruments which use a humidity-sensitive element such as human hair (blondes are preferred) can be unreliable for continuous measurements; adequate maintenance to obtain consistent records is a difficult problem. Humidity probes do not always attain the accuracy desired, and the monitoring of humidity probably presents more trouble to the instrument designer and to the observer than any other element.

Effects of wind

The effect of wind on plants and animals is often ignored, or at least underestimated. Britain is a windy country, especially near the west and north coasts. Average winds are stronger over the British Isles than over any other European country, with the exception of Iceland and Norway. Tree shelterbelts or hedges can effectively reduce the strength of the wind blowing over the crops, but recent increases in field size over arable England have tended to remove such ameliorating effects, and the results, although more convenient for the use of large farm machinery, have not been entirely favourable for plant growth.

Other European countries, such as the Netherlands, Denmark and Germany, with less serious problems of strong wind incidence have paid far more attention to the provision of shelter for crops and animals. On the American continent, shelter has been found to be beneficial for grain crops in the central plains of Canada and the United States, areas well away from the stronger coastal winds. In the Southern Hemisphere, New Zealand is a country where considerable attention has been paid to the problem of carefully designed shelter.

Wind causes structural damage and brings about the lodging of grain crops or shedding of the ears, and, on a less obvious but possibly more important scale, it retards the efficiency of the photosynthetic processes, possibly because it causes a partial closure of the stomata. Windy areas are thus not climatically suitable for optimum growing conditions, and in extreme cases some crops may not be able to grow at all. It is extremely difficult to establish trees on the windy islands of the North Atlantic such as Iceland, the Faroes, Orkney and Shetland. The northern forests of Scotland and Scandinavia make less growth than would be expected from their conditions of temperature and radiation, and the cause is probably the excess wind.

Animals also react unfavourably to strong winds, which cause a greater loss of body heat so that they need a larger food input to compensate for this loss of energy. If the external conditions are harsh and food is scarce, they lose condition rapidly, especially during the gestation period. Despite the fact that spring upland growth is almost certainly earlier on the southwestern slopes of a hill, free-ranging flocks of mountain sheep will often seek the more sheltered northeastern slopes where the exposure to the prevailing wind is less, even though food supplies in the more sheltered area are less freely available.

Wind is also a major factor in soil erosion, as anyone who has seen a 'blow' on light sandy or peaty soil will readily understand. The wind erosion in the 'dust-bowl' areas of the United States was one of the major ecological disasters in that country. Such weather effects can be very serious indeed because the topsoil removed by the wind can often never be replaced.

It is not easy to obtain a clear picture of the wind climate of an area because there are so many local variations due to that largely indefinable factor known as 'exposure'. Every site has to be considered on its own merits and judged accordingly. The removal of shelter is all too easy to accomplish; its replacement may be costly and time consuming.

Transparent low cover for crops is another form of shelter. The improved plant growth under glass or plastic is often explained in terms of the change in radiation balance. The transparent cover admits the incoming short-wave radiation by day and reduces the outgoing long-wave radiation from the soil and crop; the equally important effect of wind reduction, decreasing the advective heat loss, is often ignored.

The surface soil warms up in the daytime, especially in direct sunlight; it then heats the air above it and, if this air is stationary or only moving very gently, much of the heat gained from the Sun is retained by the surface soil and adjacent air. In a wind, this soil-warmed air is carried away and replaced by cooler air, so that much of the incoming heat is dissipated. Soil temperatures under transparent cover are much warmer by day than those in the open field. This gain of daytime heat by the soil helps to offset the night cooling. Low crop cover is thus a transparent windbreak.

In previous centuries, wind was an important source of energy on the farm, turning windmills which were then used to grind corn or to pump water. If the world energy shortage continues to become more serious, there may still be a need for a partial return to wind power to provide supplementary energy for an agricultural community.

Effects of frost

Frost incidence is an obvious limitation to crop growth, especially in regard to tender fruits and similarly sensitive horticultural plants. It is very local in its effects, and large variations in frequency and intensity can be found over relatively short distances. The local topography and the nature and condition of the soil are other important influences as is the current weather situation.

Frosts are always likely to be more severe over dry soil, and some of the most serious spring frosts will occur over a peat soil when the surface has become dry. The use of mulches also increases the severity of frost. An idea of the general liability of an area to the dangers of late spring frost can be assessed after due consideration of the site factors, but needs special care and attention to detail, and tests of sample night minimum measurements should be made.

There are several cultural practices which can reduce the frost risk. These include special allocation of irrigation water supply to keep the soil moist, as is done in the fruit areas of Australia, orchard heaters and wind machines. Complete and successful frost prevention on each and every occasion can be a very costly procedure. It is cheaper and more satisfactory to avoid the frost-prone areas. Care must also be taken to avoid creating artificial frost traps by bad design of holdings; cold air forming over the site at night must be given the opportunity to drain away and not collect in pools over the susceptible crops.

Certainly no new project for the use of a new area to grow a frost-susceptible crop should be undertaken without some attempt to understand the degree of frost risk involved. It can be a very costly business to find this out by experience. The principles governing frost incidence are well known, it is their interpretation in terms of operational risk that is difficult.

The most severe frosts occur during winter, but few crops are at risk in this season and little damage is done. Indeed, some crops need winter cold to complete their growing cycle. Overwintering crops covered by snow can escape serious damage despite very low air temperatures above the snow cover; a severe winter frost over bare ground causes greater crop damage and soil heaving, which can effectively uproot a plant.

It is the late spring frost which can result in disastrous losses of yield. Plant growth at this season is far more susceptible to low temperature, and crops such as fruit or vines can be completely wiped out. The weather of one night can be critical, a meteorological incident leading to a horticultural disaster.

Effects of fire

Countries with a favourable rainfall climate (such as Britain) do not run the major dangers of prairie or bush fires, except on a minor scale when heather or stubble burning gets out of control. The fires that used to be common on fields beside the railways vanished when the steam engines departed. Some forest and heath fires do occur, but they are nowhere on the same scale as those in countries such as Canada or the United States, and not as threatening to life and property as those in the South of France or in Australia. Lightning can start such fires, but most of them are the result of man's incautious actions. The chief part played by weather in such disasters is the creation of dry conditions in the undergrowth and surface plants, which render them very liable to combustion.

Fires are often most likely to occur at the end of a dry spell in spring when forest litter is decayed and dry, but a hot dry summer is obviously a time of increased fire risk. The areas most likely to be threatened by wild fires are those which are most liable to long rainless spells, but in an exceptional summer even wetter areas may be at risk.

In forestry, fire is a major hazard and a major problem, because it is difficult to anticipate, prevent or stop. Weather not only contributes towards the risk of a fire, it also plays a part in the difficulties of firefighting. A change in wind direction might help to bring the fire under control, but it could also increase the threat of spread. Heavy showers do more to stop a fire than any effort of man.

Grain crops are most at risk to fire immediately prior to harvest, although the practice of stubble burning brings its own problems. Grassland areas have fewer fire hazards unless a badly made haystack overheats and bursts into flames. In upland areas, heather is sometimes subjected to a 'controlled burn' to encourage young growth, and this may be a difficult operation if the weather changes. The use of fire in land management is a subject for ecological debate, but it is certain that no fire should ever be started without due consideration of the weather prospects.

The increased use of forested areas for recreational purposes, such as camping, has increased the fire risk in some areas. The most important weather factor is the conditions prevailing over the recent past. These are known, cannot be altered, but can be assessed in terms of fire risk; special precautions and public warnings can be advised if the fire risks are high.

Effects of floods

There are three main causes for the flooding of farm land: very heavy local storms, prolonged periods of rainy weather, and snow-melt.

Summer floods are generally the result of a very heavy thunderstorm falling over a small area. The effects can be devastating, but the chances of it happening on one farm in one lifetime are very low. Such storms cannot be foretold, except by the use of radar at short notice, and there is little that can be done in the way of taking precautions. The greater part of the damage caused by these heavy and rapid rainfalls is water erosion, the carrying away of topsoil and the crops growing therein, and the blocking of drains, ditches and roads by the ensuing debris.

Summer floods tend to be local in character, but the floods of autumn or winter are more widespread and are often the result of a long period of rainy weather, not an intense sudden fall. When the soil is below field capacity, it is capable of absorbing much of the falling rain like a giant sponge. Once the soil has reached capacity, the danger of flooding increases because the rain is falling faster than the water can percolate downwards in the soil and reach the drains which could take it away. Surface runoff will increase, the drains will be running at their full capacity, and the ditch, stream and river system may be inadequate to take away the volume of water involved, which will overtop the banks and flood the surrounding land.

Areas liable to flooding are well known from previous experience, but their risks may have been increased by more efficient and more rapid drainage of upland fields in the catchment area upstream. A badly drained area would, in its unimproved state, take several days to deliver its excess rain through the inefficient drainage system, but once this removal of water from the land has been accelerated, the watercourses have to deal with a much larger volume of flood water (or 'spate'). Bank erosion may occur, and fields downstream in the river valley will be flooded, especially if the final outflow of the river to the sea is held up by high tides or upstream wind.

The dangers of such autumn flooding increase appreciably after the soil has returned to field capacity. This return date can be estimated with a fair degree of accuracy by the use of standard meteorological data, both for the current year and also in the form of a climatic average. Thus, unlike the sudden summer storms, the flooding can be anticipated, warnings can be issued, and farm stock can be moved to safer pastures.

Some of the worst flooding of farmland can occur after the rapid thawing of a deep snow cover. The threat is obvious, the rough timing of the thaw is not very difficult once the onset of warmer weather is identified, but there is little that can be done beyond the taking of simple evasive action.

If the thaw takes place slowly, brought about by the arrival of warmer air, floods may be avoided. Late winter Sun is too weak to cause much thawing, and in any case much of its heat is reflected from the snow surface. The real danger comes from warmer weather with rain, which will both add to the amount of water and melt the snow because of its relatively large heat content.

If crops are flooded by fresh rainwater or melted snow, their growth will be checked, but they can recover from this unless the submergence is prolonged and the roots begin to rot. More serious effects are caused when the crops are flooded with salt sea water. Sea floods are usually due to a combination of adverse meteorological circumstances. The wind must be blowing at gale force or more in an on-shore direction at the time of high tides, especially at spring high tides as neap high tides are lower, and the rivers must be flowing at near their peak outflow.

The net effect is that the land defences are breached by the rise of the level of the sea to well over its normal maximum height. Once this occurs, major flooding will be caused inland in those areas which are near, or even below, sea level. In Europe the areas most at risk are the Netherlands and the eastern counties of England. These districts around the southern North Sea are in greatest danger because the North Sea is both narrower and more shallow at its southern end. A northerly or northwesterly gale in the rear of a depression between Scotland and Norway is thus forcing the sea water into a diminishing space. Sea levels can rise by force of such winds at any state of tide, but the coincidence in time and space of wind thrust and high tide is the critical factor in major flooding.

The magnitude of the threat dictates the defence policy. In the Netherlands, with far more at stake in lives and land, very large sums of money have been spent to combat the sea invasion, and major engineering projects have been and are being undertaken. The British, with far less at risk, spend far less money on sea defences and seem prepared to accept the damaging consequences when, every hundred years or so, such action is found to be less than adequate for the protection of farmland. London, however, has been protected by the building of the new Thames Barrage in the estuary, and seems now to have reasonable defences, which is more than can be said of Venice. If the general sea level rises following the increased melting of ice at the poles, and if gales from critical directions become more frequent, then many countries may face a greatly increased danger of sea flooding in the low-lying coastal areas.

Effects of snow

Long before the problems of a thaw flood, heavy snowfall can be disastrous to a livestock farmer, especially in the hills and uplands. Snow may do little harm to growing crops, which are in fact safer under snow than exposed to hard frosts. Livestock, principally sheep, can be buried under deep snowdrifts and have to be rescued before they suffocate. Once rescued, they have to be fed; fodder may be hard to find and harder still to transport. The major effect of snow to all farmers is a breakdown in power supply or communications, and especially an interruption in the delivery of food supply.

Snow does not fall to a uniform depth; drifts will form behind any obstacle, such as a boundary hedge or a wall, and will build up to a far greater depth than snow over level unobstructed ground. This means that places which are normally sheltered from the wind will have the greatest depths of snow and become danger zones for stock. Sheep will huddle together behind a stone wall and be covered by the snowdrift.

Roads bordered by hedges or walls will quickly be filled with deep snow because of the effect of the boundary shelter. A possible defence is the erection of open meshed snow fences on lines parallel to the road some distance back along the adjacent fields, so that the snow collects behind these temporary obstructions and leaves the road relatively clear.

Winter snow regularly occurs in northern continental countries, but in maritime areas such as the British Isles, the severity of its incidence can vary greatly from year to year, although the upland areas of Scotland are clearly those at maximum risk. In addition to the possible loss of stock, the fodder problem is crucial, especially in a prolonged cold snowy spell, when the local stores of animal foodstuffs may be inadequate.

The forecasting of snow is difficult because the borderlines between rain, sleet and snow are minute and not easy to identify. A very small change in air temperature can cause all the difference, and the problem is complicated because the heaviest snowfalls are those which occur at temperatures just below freezing point close to the rain/snow borderline. The forecasting of changes in winter climate or increased liability to heavy snowfalls is even more difficult, especially in an area such as the British Isles where small decreases in winter temperatures or increases in the frequency of northerly winds would lead to large increases in the number of days with snow cover.

If a region experiences moderate to heavy snowfalls every winter, then farming practice will have adjusted its winter programme accordingly. Snowfall is certain; the only remaining problems are how soon will it arrive and how long will the winter last. It is always possible to make plans to cope with a known danger or a regular occurrence.

In areas where heavy snowfalls only occur one year in five or ten, or perhaps only once a lifetime, the effective impact of a severe winter may be much greater because no precautions will have been taken. Furthermore, with modern transport facilities offering an apparently rapid and reliable supply of food or fodder at short notice, there is likely to have been far less stockpiling on the farm. Farmers of the last century in an area liable to snow would never have been able to expect emergency airlifts of food by helicopter; they would have made the necessary preparations to fend for themselves.

Snow is welcomed in some grain-growing areas (such as the USSR) because it protects the crops from hard frost, and when it melts it provides the bulk of the soil-moisture reserves which are necessary to keep the crop growing through the dry months up to harvest. The absence of adequate snowfall is thus a danger and can lead to serious decreases in yield and an urgent need for imported grain.

Effects of storms

The most violent storms with the strongest winds are virtually non-existent in the temperate latitudes. The tropical revolving storms, hurricanes or typhoons, are most frequent in the late summer in the southern parts of the oceans of the Northern Hemisphere. They form over the sea, but when they move towards land they can cause enormous damage, both by the strength of the wind and by the consequent flooding on coastal areas. The parts of the world which are most at risk are in south-east United States, the West Indies, the

Indian subcontinent and the China Seas. One such disaster in recent years almost totally wrecked the town of Darwin in Northern Australia. The effective agricultural damage can be most serious when a small island lies in the path of such a storm, but fortunately such catastrophes are not common.

Even stronger winds than those in a hurricane are met with in tornadoes, very intense, revolving, funnel-shaped storms which occur over land in summer, chiefly over the southern states of the USA. Although the area affected is very much smaller than that for extensive hurricanes, the damage to buildings and crops along the tracks of tornadoes is always severe and they present an annual threat to production.

Thunderstorms and hailstorms are far more widespread in incidence over the world, although each individual storm is local in character. The worst of such storms occur in hot weather, so that they are least frequent on northern and western coasts of the Northern Hemisphere, but such areas are more liable to winter hailstorms. The conditions leading to heavy storms can be foreseen, but the precise location of the storm seems to be almost a matter of chance, and can only be foretold shortly before the occurrence by the use of special weather radar. The widely held belief that there are regular 'hail tracks' always taken by storms is difficult to justify, although it is true that some of the worst crop damage from hail is often experienced on slopes facing the travelling storm.

Some crops, such as fruits and vines, are very susceptible to hail damage, and one storm can ruin the entire production of a year on individual holdings. Glass or plastic houses can also be extensively damaged, and the cost of repair can be considerable, in addition to the loss of the 'protected' crops. Agroclimatological planning to avoid the risk of hail damage is not easy, as the areas most liable to hail are often those most suitable for the growing of the susceptible crops.

Over the centuries, many attempts have been made to ward off the hailstorms, from the ringing of church bells to the use of modern ground-to-air missiles. Although many optimistic claims have been made, it is very difficult to prove that any method has been successful. The use of nets to cover tender crops during the danger period appears to have some use, but obviously the whole countryside cannot be covered in this way.

In a thunderstorm it is the heavy rain, with large raindrops and rapid rates of fall, that causes the most damage to standing crops. The violent downdraughts of air, common to severe storms, also help to lodge a grain crop, especially at times close to harvest when the heads are heavy with the prospect of a high yield. Heavy rain can also cause grain shedding from the ears, and a very wet period of weather after a crop has been lodged and is lying on the ground will cause the grain to sprout before it can be gathered in. A summer with a series of heavy thunderstorms can be a calamity to an agricultural community. It is thought by some historians that the start of the French Revolution was finally brought about by a disastrous summer of heavy storm damage to the crops.

Lightning strikes rarely cause major loss to crops, unless they start a fire. With stock it may be serious. Sheep in particular tend to herd together in a storm, often in the apparent shelter of trees. If the tree is struck by lightning, then experience has shown that many of the sheep in the vicinity of the trunk will be killed. There are many other causes of livestock loss, but none so dramatic.

The effects of weather on plants and animals

The effect of weather on life and growth is so complex and comprehensive that in order to understand the precise details reference has to be made to specialist publications. In any general survey, however, it is essential to be aware of the general principles.

The total loss of a crop due to extreme weather conditions is immediately obvious. What is far less obvious is the loss in production caused by less than optimum weather conditions occurring at any time in the growing or farming cycle. All plants react to the weather, which determines the physical conditions surrounding their leaves and roots at all stages from germination to harvest. These reactions are not simple to understand or explain, but a simple concise summary might suggest the following:

- Temperature and day-length affect the development of a plant, telling it *when* and *how* to grow.
- Sunshine energy controls *how much* growth can be made.
- Soil moisture determines *if* a plant can grow.
- The exact environmental requirements for optimum growth vary according to the type and variety of plant and its stage of growth.

Harvest does not mark the end of possible weather effects. Some of the yield can be lost in storage or in transport prior to consumption. Such storage losses, which are mainly due to pests and diseases occasioned by the physical conditions, are rarely below 10 per cent; in some countries and climates, the storage losses can amount to as much as 50 per cent of the originally harvested food. This liability to loss is reduced if the storage time is short, or if great care is taken over the storage conditions. The storage time is nil if the crop is consumed as and where it grows, as when forage crops are grazed by farm animals.

The quantity of fodder crops depends on the weather, but so does the quality in terms of nutrient content and digestibility. Growing conditions often make it difficult to obtain a crop that has both quantity and quality, and one of the arts of husbandry is to obtain the most of one without losing too much of the other. This calls for continual experienced judgement in the decisions which have to be made by the farmer. Correct timing is essential, and a mistake made one week cannot be put right by action a week later.

Grazing by stock can only take place during the growing season and for a restricted time thereafter; for the rest of the year, the food for farm animals has to be conserved on the farm or bought in from elsewhere. The conservation of grass by the making of hay has always been a difficult problem for a farmer. His farm must be situated in a fairly wet climate suitable for the good growth of grass, but he still needs a period of sunny days to make good hay. Good quality hay can be made in a matter of days if the weather is suitable; if the weather is wet, bad hay will take weeks of hard labour to bring in, and it will then be hardly fit to eat. Good hay is cheap; bad hay is expensive. When good hay is scarce, it can be very expensive to buy. A change in farming practice to silage making has eased some of these problems, but the process is not an easy one and good timing in relation to the weather is still needed.

The length of the grass-growing season, determined by the weather conditions of temperature and soil moisture, is a very critical factor in considering the balance between grazed and conserved fodder. A decrease in the growing season will inevitably mean an increase in the period for which stored food is required, and the ratio between these two periods can change appreciably. For example, a 40:12 week ratio could be changed to a 36:16 week ratio by a spring which was 2 weeks late and winter which was 2 weeks early. In the first case, only one-third of the summer growth would have to be conserved for self-sufficiency; in the latter case, almost one-half would be needed.

A long growing season may itself present problems if it contains long dry periods. Grass growth will decrease and even cease altogether as soil-moisture reserves are exhausted. Food set aside for winter consumption may have to be fed to stock to maintain milk yields. Water supplies may run short as streams and ponds dry out. Weather which is good to the holiday-maker may be bad for the livestock farmer.

The effect of weather on the supply of food for farm stock is only part of the problem. The general weather conditions also help to determine what use the animals make of the ingested food. The basic problem is one of energy balance. The input of food energy has to keep the animal fit and well, permit it to grow and also to provide by-products such as milk and wool. External conditions which cause heat loss, such as low temperature, wind and rain, or which cause other stress conditions in an animal will inhibit this energy conversion and restrict production.

The time when weather conditions can have their greatest effect on livestock production is during the reproductive phase. The losses involved in failure to conceive, in abortion, or in deaths of young animals shortly after birth are far greater than is usually realised outside farming circles. Many of these losses are due to weather-induced food deficiencies or to external physical stress caused by inclement weather. Such losses can theoretically be reduced by good husbandry, but in some years the adverse weather conditions are very difficult to combat, especially if stock have to give birth in open fields, and young lambs are particularly at risk.

Farm animals, given the opportunity, are mobile and thus can, to some extent, minimise the effects of harsh weather by seeking shelter or shade, or by ranging in search of food. There is little doubt that the provision of housing during extreme conditions of summer or winter would improve the environment for the animals, but the cost may be prohibitive.

Intensive housing may not be an unmixed blessing. When a large number of animals are confined within a relatively small area, correct design, siting and management are essential. If mistakes are made, then conditions may be created which will encourage the introduction and rapid spread of pests and diseases, which will be very difficult to control. The larger the livestock unit, the greater is the penalty for any errors. A computer-controlled environment is not automatically an improvement on good stockmanship.

To a certain extent, a farmer can, by skilful choice and timing, dictate conditions to his crops; livestock tend to dictate conditions to the farmer. Nevertheless, the weather can make a mockery of the hardest worker and the best laid plans. The unkindest cut of all is when the conditions are universally favourable so that there is a production surplus and prices fall to the exclusion of any profit, which is a poor reward for success. This has always been so, and it was Shakespeare's farmer who was said to have hanged himself in expectation of plenty.

Effect of weather on pests and diseases

Generally speaking, the smaller a biological entity, then the more it is dependent on weather conditions. It is therefore no surprise that the incidence and extent of pests and diseases are closely related to such conditions as temperature, humidity, moisture, sunshine and wind.

The precise nature of this pathogen–weather link varies

throughout the life cycle, dominating the timing of phases and the final population density. It sometimes happens that one critical stage in the life cycle is strongly dependent on one type of meteorological event. If this is so, then the identification of this significant weather and the knowledge of its occurrence can provide essential information for use in the war against the unwanted organism.

Typical examples of such critical physical factors are the duration of leaf wetness required for infection by many fungal diseases, and the soil temperature and moisture necessary for the development of soil-borne pests. In areas where attacks from such enemies may be expected every year, the meteorological assistance is concentrated upon the indication of the correct timing of protective or curative measures based on observations of the critical weather.

In areas where serious attacks do not occur every year, an assessment of the weather conditions can tell the farmer or his adviser whether such control measures are likely to be needed or be commercially worthwhile in any particular year. Relevant climatic data can also indicate whether certain areas are likely to be suitable for the establishment of any new pest or disease for which the weather requirements are known.

As many pathogens can now be kept in check by the sensible use of modern chemicals, it is theoretically possible to reduce production losses, but only at a cost. Precautions against loss can be expensive in manpower and in materials, and they can be ineffective if they are not timed or applied correctly. It is therefore important that the maximum use is made of any knowledge of the weather factor. The critical weather which controls infection cannot be prevented, but the understanding of its effects and the translation of such knowledge into improved farming practice offer the promise of scientific control and reduced loss.

The weather may also dictate the number of days, if any, which are available for the efficient application of spray treatment. It also influences the efficiency of the method employed, especially in regard to the wind conditions during spraying and the effects of subsequent rainfall on the spray deposit. It is the timing of the counteractive measures that is important, and this is more related to the weather than to the calendar, even the crop calendar or phenological stage. Correct early action can preclude the need for later expensive action when the epidemic may be beyond effective control.

The indirect effects of weather are also important. A slowly growing plant in weak condition always seems to be more susceptible to attack, while, on the other hand, rapid new growth unprotected by a recent spray is obviously at risk. This secondary effect is even more important in the case of animals. Stock in 'bad fettle', undergoing a physical stress, are more likely to succumb to an additional stress from any pathogen. This additive effect is most important during pregnancy, but cannot be ignored at any period in the life of a farm animal.

Good stockmen understand this, which is the reason why good husbandry is such an important factor in farm production. Old and tried methods may not be perfect, but new ideas may introduce new mistakes. A new building of the best modern materials may be placed conveniently out of sight to placate the planning authorities, only to find after erection that it has been sited in a frost hollow and is quite unsuitable for some young stock because of the low night temperatures.

Physical stress can be cumulative, as in the example of a long hard winter. Even a milder winter, but one with long periods of rain and wind, may bring problems for stock kept out of doors with little natural shelter. The animals have to use energy to keep themselves dry and warm and cannot thrive under such conditions. The full meaning of the term 'exposure' and its expression as a function of weather are only just beginning to be appreciated, although hill farmers have known their importance for generations.

A short-term physical stress can also be significant, especially if it coincides with a pathogenic stress. Such a coincidence in time and place may indeed be the key to many epidemiological problems. The possible need for a multiplicity of stresses may explain why diseases do not occur more often. The puzzle to the investigator is often why a disease does not occur, rather than why an outbreak does occur.

If the conditions are such that they provide a succession of multiple stresses, then a local outbreak may develop into a major epidemic. The interval between such coincidental stresses might have to be related to the develoment time or incubation period of the pathogen. This rather precise requirement of relatively rare occurrence would explain why major outbreaks are so infrequent. The reasons why an epidemic dies down are just as important as the reasons why it starts.

The extent of the airborne spread of pests and diseases is not always appreciated, especially when the pathogen is too small to be seen by the human eye. When it is realised that locusts have been carried by air currents from North Africa to England, that butterflies or moths have made the West–East Atlantic crossing, and that it is suspected that coffee berry disease may have crossed the South Atlantic from West Africa to South America by wind, then the problems of the long-range transport of pests and diseases deserve close consideration. Over recent years, rapid progress has been made in the investigation of the meteorological conditions under which such travel can take place, one example being the spread by airborne virus of foot-and-mouth disease. It is no longer necessary to invoke the movement or migration of birds as a necessary requisite for disease transmission.

The weather determines the conditions of the release of a pathogen into the air, the uplift into the higher levels, the subsequent speed and direction of movement, the continuance of viability, the descent to the surface, the chances of infection of a new host, and the subsequent spread. Unless the weather conditions are favourable at each and every stage of this long process, the airborne invasion will fail, and it is just as well for food production that this is so. Nevertheless, the risk is always present and cannot be ignored. Pathogens do not carry passports; ground hygiene controls at ports and airfields are essential to maintain a degree of quarantine, but they can be evaded if the weather is suitable for this unseen air traffic.

Short-range transport over distances of metres or kilometres demands similar but less stringent meteorological conditions. Problems of uplift and survival become less important, the precise track is less critical and the probabilities of successful movement become greater. The wind can leap barriers, it can ignore the restrictions placed on the movement of men or vehicles made in an attempt to halt the disease spread. Detailed examination of several foot-and-mouth epidemics in England showed that in the period before the statutory movement restrictions were brought into force (between the initial outbreak and its recognition), over 90 per cent of the spread occurred in a downwind direction. This does not mean that the regulations are useless, but that they have to be reinforced by careful considerations of the conditions favouring airborne spread. This is now being done with appreciable operational success.

The modern farming tendency towards large areas of monoculture and the grouping together in large units of farm animals has considerably increased the dangers from airborne spread. The infection sources are greater and there are far more chances of subsequent infection sites within smaller distances. The meteorological requirements for spread are less demanding, and the chances of disease progress are increased.

Plant and animal health regulations at frontiers are essential and must be rigorously enforced, but if the weather is unkind, these defences can be breached.

Effects of weather on pollution

Another airborne threat to food production is that of pollution. The harmful pollutants may be in the form of a gas or may be fine particles suspended in the atmosphere with little or no terminal velocity, so that they do not fall to the surface under the force of gravity to any great extent. Larger particles tend to fall out on to the soil or crops in the immediate vicinity of the pollution source. High smoke stacks, while protecting the surrounding area from some of the pollution, in the end only succeed in spreading the possible dangers over a wider area. The wind direction and speed, and the turbulence and convection characteristics of the air, are of critical importance in determining the final destination of the airborne pollutants.

Small pollution particles can be washed out of the air by rain and, more efficiently still, by snow. There are thus two main forms of land and crop contamination: dry deposition and wet deposition. Both types of pollution are now being extensively measured by special instruments, and in this way more knowledge is being obtained of this threat to production, especially in regard to what is known as 'acid rain'.

A raindrop (originally almost distilled water) can, by a chemical reaction with gaseous or solid airborne pollutants, become a dilute solution of acid. This 'acid rain' can have very adverse effects on crops and forests. Much attention has been paid to this problem in recent years, especially in Scandinavia, an area wich seems to be on the receiving end of much of the pollution. It is ironic that this should happen in the days of smoke abatement and a very large reduction in the numbers of coal-burning industries and domestic houses which used to fill valleys and cities with 'smog'. It would be most unfair if, in attempting to clear the air of visible pollution, one of the side-effects would be an increase in invisible pollution.

Pollution on a small scale may be deplored, but it can be tolerated. The most dangerous forms are those which involve cumulative poisons, such as lead or mercury. It is no longer advisable to grow crops for human consumption in close proximity to a busy road or motorway, because of the danger of contamination from the lead in vehicle exhausts. Mercury pollution is more likely to be waterborne from industrial waste effluents.

Weather conditions have a lesser part to play in water pollution than in air pollution, but even so they cannot be ignored. The leaching of chemicals from the soil by excess winter rainfall is a consequence of the water balance. The full understanding of the problems of water pollution needs careful detailed consideration. It is all too easy to blame the farmer for polluting the rivers by overuse of chemicals, forgetting that no farmer uses more fertilizer than his crops need. Facts, however, have never deterred the committed.

The effects of the deposition of airborne material need not always be adverse. Land in some areas benefits from the addition of sulphur or nitrogen compounds. In suburban gardens, the sulphur in the atmosphere used to keep certain diseases in check, providing a free protective spray against, for example, black-spot of roses.

Apart from such exceptions, cleaner air has brought many advantages to agriculture and horticulture. The hours of bright sunshine, particularly in the winter months, have increased. It is now easier to keep clean the glass or plastic used for protective cropping. Crops in fields to the lee of large towns or cities are less liable to contamination.

Once any form of pollution has become airborne, its final destination is solely determined by meteorological factors. This destination may be the sea, the land, or the upper layers of the atmosphere. It is the last-named destination which may yet give rise to the most problems. The continual rise of carbon dioxide in the air may produce results of the greatest significance to food production in the next century.

Effects of weather on erosion

Pollution may poison the land; erosion will remove it altogether. The weather elements which accelerate soil erosion are mainly wind and rain. Wind can blow away the topsoil when it is dry and not held together by the roots of a crop or covered by a mulch. Rain can wash the soil away in a variety of ways, taking it in suspension down the streams and rivers into estuaries or even into the sea. Much of the soil in the Netherlands has been augmented by water erosion along the valley of the Rhine.

The second type of factor causing erosion is man's use, or rather mis-use, of the land. The third factor is the soil itself, its type and structure, and this will be discussed in greater detail in Chapter 4.

2

Cumulative effects and consequent problems

Reference has already been made to the importance of effects which coincide in time and place; it is now necessary to consider the effects of sequences of weather, usually referred to as seasons. The effects of the weather of one season do not end when that season is over; the problems of the following seasons are influenced by what has happened before. It is thus difficult to define a precise end of a farming year, but for many farmers it is when the major summer crop is finally harvested. Michaelmas Day, at the end of September, is the traditional quarter-day when changes of farm ownership or tenancy took place. This was also the time of the hiring fairs when farm staff sought new employment or farmers new staff. Such fairs were often the opportunity for farm labourers to find their marriage partners, and one such festival, modernised but still recognisable, survives to this day at Lisdoonvarna in County Clare, in west Ireland.

The autumn season

Once a late crop, such as sugar beet, has been harvested and the ground cleared, the main activities on an arable farm at this season are autumn ploughing and the sowing of winter cereals. The ease with which such work can be done depends greatly on the weather and the type of soil; some rain is needed but not too much because the soil must not be too dry or too wet. In a very heavy clay with difficult working properties, the sequence of weather and the intervals between rainy days can be very critical indeed.

Autumn work can be a race against time, for the weather is 'closing in' in more senses than one. If the autumn soil preparation and sowings are delayed by the weather, a crop production loss may be incurred which cannot be recovered at a later stage in the growing season, because the maximum potential yield has already been determined by the emergence date of the seedling crop.

Autumn may be said to end when crop growth slows down and stops, and this is largely determined by the soil temperatures, which can be depressed by a series of frosts leading to an early winter.

However, frost over land which has been ploughed can be an advantage because it breaks up the large clods of earth and helps to provide a good tilth. Most farmers would prefer an 'open' autumn with mild temperatures and little rain, but this weather combination does not occur very frequently. The choice is usually between weather that is cold and dry or mild and wet. In general, this season is one in which every opportunity must be taken to get through with the essential work on the land – winter always comes early to the inefficient.

The winter season

The adverse effects of a wet autumn are compounded if this type of weather persists into the winter months. Excess rain during the winter half-year cannot be retained in the soil without waterlogging. With adequate drainage, this excess moves downward through the soil carrying with it lime and plant nutrients such as nitrogen, a process known as leaching. The removal of necessary fertilizers by leaching must be compensated by fresh applications in the spring, otherwise yields will suffer. Even if the nitrogen has not been removed entirely by the drainage water, it may have been moved to layers of soil out of reach of plant roots.

Traditionally, farmers in north-west Europe appear to welcome a cold winter, preferably setting in after Christmas with snow in January. A mild January meets with their special disapproval, and there are many old adages in several countries which bear this out. In the drier areas, rain or snow in February is needed to 'fill the dykes', or, more correctly, to bring the soil back to field capacity. A dry zone in the subsoil at the end of winter is a poor start to the growing year.

The arable farmer, once his autumn crops are sown, prefers snow to hard frost over bare soil; what he does not want is a winter which is cold at both ends and very mild in the middle. He looks forward to dry spells late in the winter to enable him to start his spring ploughing and seed-bed preparations. Winter is also the time when many maintenance jobs are carried out on the farm, including repairs to hedges and ditches. The crops may be inactive, but the workers are not idle.

A whole set of new problems arises in climates which do not experience a cold winter. The crop pattern changes and timing is more dependent on the incidence of rain than on the threat of cold.

The spring season

To a farmer, spring is not a fixed date on the calendar, but the time when growth is revived in his crops. In the British Isles this start of growth can vary some 30 days or so either side of the average date, making a big difference to the length of the growing season. An early spring is welcomed, but it must be a true spring and not a false start in which the weather can be warm for a few days and bitterly cold a little later.

False springs are quite a common feature of the coastal lands of northwestern Europe, and the British Isles are very liable to experience this change from winter to spring and back again. Neither farmers nor their crops respond well to a series of starts and stops. In continental Europe, spring tends to be later than in areas further west, but when spring reaches such areas it tends to stay, hence the belief 'a late spring never deceives'.

To ensure the highest yields from a spring sown crop the farmer needs a very exact sequence of weather. He first needs a drying soil to enable him to carry out the necessary soil cultivations. He then needs warm soil with sufficient moisture at seed depth to provide good germination; and then periods of light rain or showers after emergence to enable the shallow-rooted young plants to grow without check. A late sowing almost certainly means a reduced yield. A dry spell after sowing can be very serious and may even necessitate a second sowing. Excesive rain and waterlogged soil can be equally damaging. The traditional April weather, 'rain and sunshine, both together', is by no means a bad recipe and would cause few complaints.

In a year when the weather is favourable, and when it does everything right in the correct sequence, then all farmers will benefit from the kindly helpful season. In years when it seems that the weather has gone mad, it is only the very skilled and experienced farmer who will finish with top yields at harvest time, but he will still need to have been able to call on sufficient manpower and machine power to make the most of the limited opportunities.

The effect that weather has on the incidence of pests and diseases is a major worry throughout the life of a crop. Chemical crop protection is expensive, and may be a waste of money if action is taken too late or was not needed anyway. Early action, if and when needed, is of prime importance, and this must be based on regular close inspection of the crop, and preferably helped by identification of the significant weather which is favourable for infection or infestation and the subsequent spread of unwanted organisms.

The summer season

In summer and in the weeks leading up to harvest, the weather is still important. Optimum amounts of rain and sunshine are required for maximum growth, and temperature factors can be critical in marginal areas. Although it is not always the case, warm weather is often dry, and cool weather is often wet, so that again it is difficult for the months to be 'all in tune'.

Most cereals have a deep root system, but shallow-rooted crops can soon be retarded in growth by lack of soil moisture, and a check of this kind is rarely fully compensated by subsequent rain. Irrigation can overcome a rainfall deficiency, but in areas where it is most needed, water supplies are limited, and in any case irrigation is expensive in terms of men and equipment.

A soil-moisture shortage within root range is a danger to all crops in the initial stages, but once a cereal crop has been established it does not suffer much from a partial drought, although it welcomes rain as the grain begins to fill. A variable summer with warm dry periods interspaced with rainy weather may even be the best weather for high cereal yields as, indeed, appeared to be the case in England in 1982.

A cool summer brings the biggest threat to areas which are on the fringe of suitable climate conditions for a particular crop. Not only will there be a reduction in the length of the growing season, but the development stages will be extended, and maturity may not be attained before the season is over. It is the northern countries which are most at risk in a cool summer. The introduction of new cereal varieties has enabled cereal crops to be grown in higher and higher latitudes, both in Canada and in Northern Europe, but fringe areas such as these are always at risk from the effects of a small climatic change.

A very hot summer is almost certain to be dry except for the occasional thunderstorm, when hail damage could be serious in limited areas. Such conditions are often favourable for the rapid multiplication of crop pests; wet mild summers are more suitable for infection by disease.

An occasional crop failure due to extreme summer weather has to be accepted as an unavoidable farming risk, but two such failures in successive years are a danger signal no farmer can afford to ignore, even if the losses have not crippled him financially. It is perhaps fortunate that European summers tend to follow a biennial pattern (a good one following a poor one) rather than in sequences of summers with similar weather. An illustration of this can be traced in the vintage wine charts. Random climatic variations are tolerable, but a climatic change giving a preponderance of unfavourable years is a serious threat.

The harvest time

The critical weather period for all crops is at the time of harvest, and unless conditions are favourable, a year's work may be set to naught.

Although modern equipment has enabled a farmer to bring in his harvest in a far shorter time than could his father or grandfather, with far less need for supplementary workers, he still needs the right weather at the right time. Damp moist weather can force him to harvest grain with far too high a moisture content, so that it needs expensive drying before it is fit to market or store. Continual rains can cause lodging or sprouting in the ear; even in dry weather a heavy dewfall can cause delays.

Although rainy weather is the worst enemy of any harvest, a long dry spell can cause difficulties in the lifting of root crops because the ground will be too hard for machines to operate. In general, weather extremes of all kinds will cause problems, and it is not surprising that harvest festivals and harvest suppers still celebrate the end of a difficult farming operation.

Few years bring favourable weather at every stage of crop growth, and few types of weather are equally suitable for all types of farming. A farmer with a large area of a cereal crop to harvest would want dry weather at the same time that a grassland farmer would need rain for renewed growth. Earlier in the summer a spell of fine weather would be ideal for haymaking, when cereals might profit from extra soil moisture. If the climate of the area has little variation about the mean, the choice of farming system is adjusted to these contradictory needs, but in areas where summers vary considerably from year to year there can be no pleasing all the farmers all the time.

Livestock farming

The weather requirements of a livestock farmer differ from those of a mainly arable farmer, which is why their farms are situated in different climatic areas separated by an intermediate zone of mixed farming. The cattle and sheep are an essential link in the human food chain, in that they convert grass, which cannot be eaten by man, into products which form part of the human diet. If grass or similar fodder crops are the most suitable type of growth in an area, then farm animals must form part of the food production system.

This state of affairs introduces a double set of weather-sensitive problems. One concerns the effects of weather on the animals, the other the effects on the crops grown for their consumption. The farming year in livestock production falls into two sections: the period when animals can graze the growing food, and the period when such growth has stopped and they have to be supplied with conserved fodder.

The start of spring growth is therefore a critical time of the year in areas with a cold winter. Provided that the fields are not too wet and so liable to 'poaching' or 'pugging' by the tread of hooves, stock can then be turned out to graze. A late start to the grazing season can place a large strain on the stocks of conserved fodder, and prices for bought-in animal food can be high. Grass growth is usually earliest in the west and south, and latest in the north and east. It is also very dependent on the height of ground above sea level: in early spring areas, the delay of grass growth with height can be as much as one day for every 6 or 7 metres increase in height; in later spring areas, the delay with elevation is less.

Although an early spring is always welcome to the livestock farmer, there is always a danger of a swing back to winter conditions. If sheep have been turned out onto upland fields and there is a return to winter conditions, snowfall can cause heavy losses. Unless the climate of the area is very reliable in timing, decisions at this time of the year are always difficult to make.

Except for the dairy herds which use a system of autumn calving, spring is also the time when most animal birth takes place. Favour- able weather at this period, at a date determined by the time of conception several months earlier, is of the greatest importance for a sheep farmer. Losses at birth (many of which are due to inclement weather) cannot be replaced until the next generation. The tendency to twinning in ewes, however, is affected by the weather of the previous late summer prior to tupping.

Cows attain their maximum milk production soon after calving. If good grass is plentiful at this time, the initial peak production will be high and this will influence the potential of milk production throughout the lactation period. To maintain this potential, the dairy cow will need good food at all times, and a check in production due to absence of palatable fodder is not easy to recover; the fall in milk yield can be checked but the lost milk cannot be replaced.

A year that is good for grass is said to be good for nothing else, mainly because grass thrives on regular rainfall to keep it growing to the fullest extent, a deficiency of sunshine being more tolerable than a deficiency of soil moisture. Insufficient rain will soon check grass growth and present the farmer with management problems. He may have to use fields for grazing which he would prefer to shut up for production of hay or silage. Excess rainfall will create wet pastures and the risk of poaching, a problem more common in spring or autumn than in summer.

Even a perfect summer rainfall distribution which would ensure maximum grass growth will produce problems because it will encour- age soil-borne parasites (such as liver fluke) which affect farm animals. Heavy thunderstorms will help the spread of diseases (such as dermatitis) which spoil the fleece of a sheep and halve the price of the shorn wool.

Plant diseases tend to occur shortly after the critical weather, but the incidence of many animal pests often depends on specific weather which occurs at a much earlier stage in a longer life cycle. The degree of danger can therefore be identified at an earlier stage and enable warnings to be issued concerning the possible intensity of a future attack.

The grassland farmer has one further very important weather requirement which is hard to satisfy in the normal run of meteorological events: he needs frequent rain to grow plenty of grass up to and after the period of harvest, but when the grass is of optimum quality and fit to cut, he needs a dry sunny period to make hay.

The timing of the hay harvest (or of the making of silage) is always difficult. If grass growth is slow due to a late spring, cold weather or a lack of soil moisture, the farmer will delay cutting in the hope of getting a heavier crop. In so doing he is sacrificing the hay quality, which is decreasing with each succeeding week. The later the grass is cut, then the poorer is the nutritional value of the crop for winter keep.

Good haymaking years, when the weather is favourable at the right time for cutting, are by no means frequent in the wetter climates. When they do occur, all farmers can make good quality hay, and a plentiful hay crop may provide food for more than one winter ahead. In most years the process is difficult, especially if the good weather occurs just before the crop is ready. Good hay is cheap to make when conditions are suitable; bad hay is always expensive.

Some small farmers may not be able to take advantage of suitable haymaking weather because they have other urgent work to do. In some areas there used to be an age-old custom for small farmers to band together to bring in the hay, but this inevitably meant that some of them did not get the ideal weather. Modern machinery has helped to reduce the time taken to cut, dry and store hay, but small farmers cannot always afford such luxuries.

With the climatic odds against the making of good hay, it might be thought that the answer lies in more silage and the use of forage harvesting machinery. The climatic risks are reduced but greater investment is needed, and, for reasons difficult to specify, silage has never become a popular winter feed for stock with the conservative farmer.

A late season shortage of good grazing is a disadvantage to sheep farmers because (as mentioned earlier) if the ewes are eating on a rising plane of nutrition when they come to the ram, there is a far greater chance of twins being conceived. On the other hand, if the weather is too wet in late summer and early autumn, some poaching and sward damage is likely. Once again, the farming weather requirements are neatly balanced, and nothing fails like excess.

Every year the end of the grazing season is more often a result of wet weather rather than cold weather. The grass may still be growing slowly despite the fall of soil temperatures, but the pastures are too wet to use. Early winter cold spells are important to dairy farmers. Unless their herds are brought in under cover at night just before this time, the milk yields will drop considerably and it will be difficult, if not impossible, to bring them back to the expected level of production once the herd has finally been brought into winter quarters.

The difficult decisions of spring, when to stop supplementary feeding and start grazing, now have to be met in reverse; when to stop grazing. Stock grazing a water-saturated pasture may damage more grass than they eat, but the livestock farmer has to face the problem of how much fodder must be kept for the winter days ahead, and he often tries to keep his animals out until the last possible moment.

This worry as to whether enough animal food is being kept in reserve explains why the length of winter is more important than its severity. Stock reared for meat production often put on very little weight during this period, even if well fed, and in the poorer areas they lose condition, and upland stock were often wintered in lowland farms to avoid this. The longer the period that conserved fodder has to be supplied, then the lower will be the ultimate profit.

The dangers of heavy snow and possible animal deaths have already been mentioned. A cold and wet winter will also tend to cause pregnancy toxaemia in ewes, with a consequent drop in lambing percentage. Incorrect winter feeding can induce a copper deficiency causing a disease known as 'swayback', but this tends to be absent in hard winters because there is more hand feeding of better quality food. In general, it may be said that livestock farmers have their worst weather worries in winter, arable farmers in summer.

There is no such thing as a perfect climate for any type of farming, except on paper. It could be theoretically specified but it is rarely likely always to occur. All that can be done in practice is to take a sensible assessment of the weather risks. There is always some aspect of a year which causes a check to production in one or other type of farming; in a bad year there may be many such drawbacks.

Protective cropping

With the weather offering apparently nothing better than a series of headaches, it is not surprising that for high-value crops, growers seek some form of protected environment. This involves the use of glass or plastic structures, often with further environmental control including air and soil heating, automatic irrigation and artificial light. This type of land use and production represents the greatest investment of monetary capital per unit area. The expenditure of large sums of money can only be justified by assured high yields and by high prices for the product. Less justifiable is the use of considerable amounts of irreplaceable energy to create the artificial climates needed to produce the luxury crops. This input of energy in an environmental control system is very sensitive to the external weather, especially sunshine, temperature and wind.

Such structures must be designed and sited to admit the maximum heat and light from natural sources; they must also be such that the heat loss from the building must be at a minimum. In some areas, on the other hand, there is the high summer problem of too much heat from the Sun and unacceptable high temperatures within the protected area. Methods have then to be devised to keep the environment cool, at the level of temperature required by the crops.

A careful choice of site for such capital-intensive systems is very important. It is too late to discover that the area is climatologically unsuitable after large sums of money have been spent. Ideal sites are not easy to find, because an area with a good sunshine record may be subject to strong winds, and a climatically suitable site may be far from the nearest markets.

Under cover, the vagaries of rainfall can be ignored, but the supply of water to the soil must be carefully controlled. This requires knowledge and skill, and adds further to the running costs. All forms of control of interior climate involve careful coordination of the meteorological factors, light, day and night temperature regimes, humidity and soil moisture. Pest and disease control must attain a high level of efficiency. It is difficult to alter one physical variable without altering another, so that the grower has two problems: to establish what is the ideal climate for the growth of his crop and to use his controls to produce such a climate. The process is difficult and expensive, and the exterior weather is not always helpful.

The meteorological problem

The farmer faces the problems of his meteorological environment on two timescales: the long-term scale of climate and the short-term scale of weather. The former determines his strategy (or what he is trying to do), the latter his tactics (or how he can do it).

By careful appraisal of the climate he can form an opinion of the type of farming most suited to his area, and an estimate of the weather risks involved. In so doing, he has to assume that the climate based on past weather is a fair guide to the weather of the future. If he is in the centre of a climatic area suitable for a particular crop, he has little to fear from climatic variations of the type usually met with over a lifetime. If he is on the fringe of such an area, then a slight variation from the climate average by the weather of the next decade may be far more critical for his enterprise.

Such minor climatic variations are only to be expected, but a period of major climatic change is potentially far more serious. There have been occasions in the past when such changes have occurred and no doubt there will be more in the future, with or without the changes prompted by the activities of mankind. It is only to be hoped that such changes will take place slowly enough to allow systems of food production to be adjusted smoothly to the new weather patterns. It is arguable that the farming pattern is more sensitive to change than are books of climatic averages, which tend to lag behind events.

This sensitivity arises because farming communities are generally successful in fitting in their activities to the climatic constraints. If this were not so, farming would not have survived as an industry over the centuries. Difficulties arise when new crops are introduced or when new methods become available. The old system of trial and error is too slow and has to be replaced by a more scientific appraisal.

The introduction of new materials and new techniques does not mean that the climatic factor becomes less important. Examination of the farming pattern over England and Wales and the changes that have taken place since the middle of the century show that the rate of change of crop distribution along a climatic gradient has increased over the years. At the same time, yields and stocking rates have increased, indicating that the improved efficiency of the industry is at least in part due to a better realisation of the climatic potential.

Many systems of climate classification can be found in the textbooks, but it is doubtful if any of them can serve better than as a general guide to the solution of problems of agroclimatology. The reason for this is that each crop has its own set of climatic criteria, so that no general system based on the most easily available climatic parameters will serve in all cases. There are limits to the virtues of taxonomy.

Once a decision has been made in respect of the type of farming most suitable to the site, then everything that follows on the shorter timescale depends on the ability of the farmer to take every advantage of favourable weather and to minimise the effect of adverse environmental conditions and their biological consequences. To do this he needs to know the effects of weather on his soil, his crops, his farm stock, and on the unwanted organisms which compete with him for a living. His reactions to the current weather must be logical and timely, and to help him in this difficult task he should be able to call on the advice of specialists in the numerous problems.

A man may be a born farmer, but it is difficult for him to be a successful farmer without outside help in a difficult situation. The better the quality of the help given to the producers of food, then the more food will be available for all.

The use of weather forecasts

If the weather has such a potent effect on food production, and if these effects are known (in principle if not in exact detail), it would seem self-evident that knowledge of the future weather would be of the greatest value. Many claims, and even more promises, have been made over the years regarding the value of weather forecasts to the farmer. A careful examination of the present situation might suggest a less optimistic point of view.

Ideally, such forecasts must satisfy at least three stringent requirements.

(a) They must be accurate in detail, especially in regard to site, timing and intensity.
(b) They must be readily available to a farmer in a form and style which are specially designed for his particular purposes. The nature of the critical weather varies with the type of farming and with other local and individual factors such as labour force, available machinery and degree of operational urgency. No two farmers want exactly the same kind of details in their forecast, which has to be 'tailor made' or 'custom built' to be of the most use.
(c) The forecasts must be more than merely informative; a useful forecast is one which can be acted upon. To tell a fruit grower that a heavy shower of hail will fall on his orchard at 2:30 tomorrow afternoon may be a forecasting triumph, but the recipient can do exactly nothing about it, except hope that the forecaster is wrong. If a forecast is to justify the claim of 'value', somebody has to be able to take action to make the most of favourable weather or reduce the impact of future adverse conditions.

These very demanding requirements are extremely difficult to satisfy, and even if the standard of accuracy continues to improve, such improvements may still fall short of the ideal. Agriculture may have to accept its frustrating dependence on the relative uncertainty of future weather and plan accordingly.

The reason why an optimistic view is taken of the potential value of accurate forecasts to agriculture is partly historical. The first official weather forecasts were successfully applied to problems of sea and air transport, firstly with the aim of saving life and subsequently with the additional aim of improving operational efficiency. The reason for their success was that with ships and aircraft there are ways and means to alter planned operations to fit the future weather conditions, even to the extent of cancelling voyages or flights at times when dangerous weather was expected; ships can return to port and aircraft can return to base or make an emergency landing. A farmer has far less scope for manoeuvre; he is often committed to a course of action which he cannot change. Generally his only choice is one of timing: he may have to abandon the sowing of seed, but he cannot abandon an attempt at harvest.

Forecast accuracy

The accuracy of weather forecasts varies not only with the competence of the forecaster and the reliability of the forecasting methods, but also with the period covered by the forecast and with the degree by which the weather is liable to vary.

In the extreme case of a climate with only two seasons (one wet and one dry), it is almost impossible to get the forecast wrong in the dry season. The only two occasions in the year when a forecast is liable to a major error are when the wet season starts and when it ends. In such a climate the really important weather advice concerns the amount of rain likely to fall during the wet season, which is a far more difficult problem. In a climate when the weather can change every day, there are far more opportunities for the forecast to be in error.

It is not easy to assess the accuracy of a set of forecasts, because so much depends on the purpose for which they are used. Much also depends on the sensitivity of the project for which the forecast is required. Small errors in timing or intensity in the meteorological forecast may have major effects on the particular activity.

Short-term forecasts

Accurate short-term forecasts, covering periods of up to 48 hours, can sometimes be of great tactical help to the farmer, but there are difficulties arising from their mode of distribution. A newspaper forecast may be out of date before it is read; a radio forecast, unless given by the forecaster himself, can be so abbreviated or so garbled that it can be beyond effective comprehension; and a general statement covering large areas is relatively useless except in fine settled weather.

The most helpful forecast service is provided when a farmer can speak by telephone directly to the forecast office and can discuss his own individual weather problem or request advice on one particular aspect. A published public forecast must concentrate on the most probable future weather, but a discussion can reveal the possible alternatives and the chances of their occurrence, information which is far more valuable to the farmer or any other specialist user.

Extended-range forecasts, for periods of up to a week ahead, can also be of considerable help, especially in regard to the general timing of farming operations. The farmer wants to know if the weather is likely to improve or deteriorate over the next few days in specific relation to his planned work. He uses the information to decide whether it is better to hurry up and try to complete the work in hand, or have patience and delay action with the chance of better weather to follow.

Long-range forecasts

Forecasts of the weather for the following month are of much less agricultural value, even in the unlikely event of them being correct. A farmer is committed to certain operations during this future period which are determined by the needs of his crops or stock, and there is little that he can do about it in advance. Such work has to be done and can only be dealt with as and when conditions permit.

Forecasts of extreme weather, such as heavy rainfall or long dry periods, might be of some use in medium-term planning, but the science of weather prediction seems to be at its least promising stage in regard to such abnormalities. It can be correct in suggesting that the following weeks will bring more rainfall than usual (i.e. above average), but it cannot attempt the long-range forecast of severe flooding.

A foreknowledge of the general type of weather to be expected over the following season would be of more use to the farmer: what he really wishes to know is not the weather of the next season but of the next season but one. He would like to know in early summer the probable extent and severity of the next winter, so that he can decide how much fodder he should conserve for his livestock. At sowing time in early spring, it would be a great help to know the probable harvest conditions in late summer and early autumn. He would be more than satisfied if he could be told with a fair degree of certainty if the following summer was going to be wet or dry, but to make any difference to his cropping plans or stocking densities he would need this information long before there is any chance of a professional forecaster being able to supply it. He can thus only plan ahead in accordance with the climatic odds, modified by his personal inclination to optimism or pessimism.

Amateur forecasters seem to love to paddle in the muddy waters of seasonal forecasting. Their attempts often receive considerable publicity in the press, ever hungry for what they regard as 'news', and they are quick to claim their list of past successes, but slightly more reticent about their failures. Nature lovers believe that animals, birds and plants can foretell the coming seasons, but it would be a brave farmer who put much money at risk on the strength of their predictions. A cynic would suggest that the best time to quote an old adage on long-range forecasting is when the events have taken place.

Climate forecasts

The forecasting of changes of climate lies within the most difficult realms of meteorology and climatology, and yet from the view of forward agricultural planning, such changes can be of the greatest significance in regard to world food production. Personal opinions on the possibilities of such changes, sometimes expressed as near certainties, receive considerable publicity, but those scientists who know most about this difficult subject tend to say least, as they are aware of its complex nature and the limited understanding of the underlying physical dynamics.

The individual farmer is more concerned with what is going to happen within his own lifetime. In most areas of the world (and especially in the temperate latitudes), the climate is always changing slightly as far as farming is concerned. One farming generation faces a different set of weather problems to the preceding or following generation. Even during one farmer's tenure there may be a succession of years with weather favourable to one aspect of his plans, followed by another spell of less helpful conditions.

As pointed out earlier, these changes are most significant on the fringes of a climatic area where a small climate change can have large agricultural consequences. There are many who believe in weather cycles or the influence of sun spots, but extrapolation on the basis of such theories is not recommended by many scientists.

In olden times, the farmer took few risks because the penalty for failure was starvation. Possibly in modern times he is tempted to take too many. One thing is certain, major changes in land use should not be undertaken lightly.

Part II

The land factor

3

The field and the soil

It is said that history is written in the ink of prejudice, implying that historians tend to find what they are looking for. Scientists are, at least in theory, impartial. Nevertheless, they are subject at times to a somewhat similar bias generated by their own field of special knowledge, and they tend to deal with a complex subject in terms of that aspect with which they are most familiar.

If a number of scientists of different disciplines considered the problem of the potential productivity of a region, each would first analyse the available evidence in the light of his own specialised experience and in terms of his own particular subject. Such an analysis, however accurate, could never provide the full answer, being only one of the many aspects of a multivariate problem. The day of the polymath (a man with a good working knowledge of several sciences) is now virtually over. He has been replaced by a series of specialists, each with a more extensive knowledge of his own branch of science, but who has to turn to a fellow scientist when another discipline is involved. It is not a crime to be ignorant of the details of an unfamiliar science, but it is unforgivable not to be aware of such ignorance and not to know when additional guidance is required.

It is not possible for all agronomists to be specialists in soil science, but it is important that such specialists are consulted when the necessity arises, and there are few occasions when the soil factor can be ignored. The whole answer may not lie in the soil, but it is the major semi-permanent feature of the farm, and because there are serious limits to any possible change in its nature, its effects on food production must be given full and careful consideration.

Soil classification

Most sciences in their early stages of development go through a period of intense effort in classification, a process of identification and labelling, by means of which those concerned can hope to understand the magnitude of the problem and can communicate with each other in terms and nomenclatures that are understood. This is an essential first step, but it is by no means the only one. The fact that a soil has been named, that soil maps have been drawn up and published, does not mean that all the important soil properties are fully understood, still less that the problems facing the farmer have been solved. Recording is simpler than comment, and interpretation is more difficult still.

The major differences between soil types can be fitted into systems of classification, but there are endless small variations within classes, and the lines separating the classes are by no means clear cut. In fact, there may be greater differences throughout a class than on the boundary between one class and another. A similar difficulty arises in giving names to the colours of the rainbow, from red and orange to indigo and violet, but in that case it is possible to allocate to each shade of colour an individual wave length. Such precise specification is as yet impossible in all aspects of soil science, although certain soil properties can be accurately measured.

Years of patient fieldwork have resulted in the production of soil maps with varying degrees of complexity and scale. These form an excellent starting point for the consideration of the problem of the effect of the nature of the soil on potential production. Modern chemical and physical analyses can provide detailed reports on the soil properties which are of importance to the land user. The real difficulty is to understand what such properties mean, how they change in different weather conditions or under different management, how they hinder or help crop growth or the use of machinery, and, most of all, how they impose insuperable limits on farming activity and food production.

Soil depth

The extent of a field is measured by its horizontal area, a question of length and breadth. The extent of the soil must include the third dimension of depth. It is the vertical profile of the soil which is so important in determining the growth of crop roots and the availability of moisture and nutrients.

Soil depth may be terminated abruptly by a rock surface which places a permanent obstruction to the downward-growing roots. There is another form of horizontal barrier at some depth below the soil surface which, although less obvious, can be equally obstructive to root range. This is a layer of a type of soil which is different in form and texture from that in the surface layers, a type which, because of hard compression or lack of suitable available nutrients, prevents any further root penetration. As far as a plant is concerned, it might just as well be rock. This lower soil 'horizon' can also present serious problems in the drainage of water.

It is sometimes possible to overcome this subsoil problem, changing its properties by various techniques, but the process can be long
and costly in men, machines and material. The problems then
become: can it be done, is the cost worth the possible improvement,
and is the capital available?

Two other forms of limitation to the depth of soil available to plants
are the height of the water table (or, in arid regions, the depth of the
dry soil layers) and, in cold regions, the depth of the permafrost layer.
The latter restriction is self-explanatory, being the depth at which the
soil temperature never rises above freezing point throughout the year.
Below this level, all soil moisture is in the form of ice, and all root
growth is restricted to the surface layers where temperatures permit
root activity in a brief summer.

The questions raised by a high water table are more complicated.
All moist soil contains both water and air, but below the water table
(roughly equivalent to the level of water in a well) no air is present.
This level may be very close to the surface in the immediate vicinity of
a lake or river, but elsewhere it may be very deep indeed. The level
tends to vary with the seasons, generally being closest to the surface in
spring and lowest in early autumn, but much can depend on the time
lag of excess winter rainfall distribution by underground water
movement and by hidden springs.

Circumstances can arise when there is a temporary high water
table in the soil in local areas, where a subsoil layer of an impermeable
nature prevents the rapid deep seepage of water after a period of
heavy rainfall. In such circumstances, the soil will become waterlogged and crop roots may be damaged.

Temporary waterlogging can usually be eliminated by improved
drainage, and in regions where drainage is skilfully designed and
operated, as in the Dutch polders, the water-table height can be
controlled throughout the growing season, with great beneficial effect
on the growth and production of the crops above. Under these
conditions the water table can be adjusted to act as a form of
subirrigation, but accuracy to the order of centimetres is necessary.

A permanent lack of soil depth severely restricts the type of crop
that can be grown and the extent to which it can be relied on to thrive,
especially in a dry season. The reasons for this limitation are simple:
an insufficient volume of soil restricts the root range, with a consequent inadequate supply of plant nutrients and soil moisture. The
plant growth will slow down, and drought comes early in a dry period
on a thin soil. Labour-intensive attempts to counteract the limitations
of shallow soil depth are common in agricultural communities all over
the world, examples being the placing of seaweed over the almost bare
rocks of Connemara and the Aran Islands of west Ireland, and the
manual movement of soil from the bottom to the tops of sloping

vineyards in Europe. In areas where the population density is such that land is not at a premium (such as the United States of America and Australia), no such desperate measures are necessary because, up till now, there has been land to spare, and, in some cases, to waste.

The physical nature of the soil

The physical nature of the soil affects the variations of temperature with depth and time of day and season known as the thermal regime. It also affects the moisture regime, determining the amount of water that the soil can hold against the pull of gravity, and the suction that is needed to extract such moisture, the speed of drainage and infiltration, and possibilities of lateral water movement. A favourable soil-moisture regime is essential for the maximum growth of crops and if moisture supplies become limiting, transpiration will slow down and ultimately cease when all available moisture has been extracted and wilting point is reached.

A less obvious effect of soil texture, but one which all farmers know to be of the greatest practical importance, is the control it imposes on the timing and extent of the necessary farming operations such as ploughing, harrowing, seed sowing, planting, spraying, and, finally, harvest. The delays that can occur in such farm work can have a great effect on the final yield of any crop.

The grassland farmer is also concerned with soil texture, and not only at times of the reseeding of grass leys or at haymaking. The texture affects the extent to which fields can be grazed, especially in regard to stocking rates and to the timing of the opening up or closing down of a pasture or summer range. If stock are turned out into a field or paddock which is not in a physical condition to bear the heavy tread of animal hooves, not only is more grass damaged than eaten, but also there is a risk of reducing subsequent regrowth. The importance of the state of ground in relation to the length of the grazing season was discussed in a previous chapter.

The workability of the soil (summing up the conditions suitable for the operation of farm machinery) is a problem which differs in nature and extent according to whether animals or machine power are used to draw the implements across the soil. Animals, be they horses, oxen, mules, asses, camels or even humans can work a field in far less favourable soil conditions than heavy tractors, but they cover the ground very much more slowly and more time is needed. On the other hand, they do far less structural damage to wet soil than the much heavier machinery. Such energy-consuming machines save essential time and obviate the need for large numbers of farm staff, who have to be paid, and draught animals, which have to be fed, but they may bring about serious long-term adverse effects on soils with difficult textures. The term 'workability' tends to be replaced by the word 'trafficability' in modern farming.

Soil texture also tends to determine the type of crop that can be grown, for certain crops can thrive on the 'lighter' soils and others do well on the heavier or stiffer clays. For example, crops such as oats, rye, lupins, early potatoes and some vegetables can be grown on sandy soils with some hope of success. Wheat, barley, beans, turnips and mangolds can do well on the heavier types of soil.

Grass is often grown in an area where the climate might be thought to be more suitable for cereals if the soil is so difficult to work that the annual cultivations are almost impossible to carry out at the required time. Such fields are often regarded as 'permanent pasture', and are rarely broken up by the plough for the sowing of any other crop.

Soil texture is also a factor to be taken into account in the planning of crop rotations, often thought to be only a question of soil fertility. Before any seeds of a new crop can be sown, the previous crop has to be harvested, the ground has to be cleared, and the seed bed has to be prepared. All such operations need good trafficability conditions. In some years there can be serious weather restrictions on the time available for this work to be done, and these restrictions are strongly influenced by the nature of the soil texture.

On an arable farm there are effectively two annual races against time, one in the autumn and the other in spring. In autumn the soil trafficability problems tend to get worse on all soils as the days get shorter. The probability of rain increases and the rate of drying out of the surface soil decreases with the weakening sunshine, and this tendency to more difficult conditions is worst on the heavier soils. When conditions are very wet indeed, the autumn sowing may not be completed, and may have to be held over until spring, with a possible consequent change in crop variety or even type of crop.

If autumn ploughing for winter fallow can be completed before the heavy frosts occur, better seed beds for spring sowing can be prepared. As mentioned previously, very dry weather in autumn can also be a disadvantage because the soil is too hard and dry to cultivate or even to allow lifting of the previous crop, especially on the heavy, bad textured soils. Any seed that is sown in a dry autumn may germinate unevenly because of the absence of soil moisture.

The autumn race is one against deteriorating weather and soil conditions. In spring the reverse is true, as it can be expected that the weather will be improving. Even so, the race is still on, because late sowing means lower final yields in many annual crops, and a crop sown very late may not reach full maturity in some areas.

The soil texture is again a major controlling factor, As a farmer can start work on a well-drained light soil with a shorter period of delay after a spell of unsuitable weather. On a heavy, slow-draining soil the waiting period is longer, by which time the weather may again have turned unfavourable. On such soils a period of moderate or heavy rain every three or four days may cause a delay of virtually a month. It is not always realised that the effects of soil and weather on a crop yield often include events that take place before the seed is even sown.

A similar struggle against time takes place in those climates where the growing season is controlled, not by the seasonal temperature rhythm of the temperate latitudes, but by the onset of the dry and rainy seasons, such as occur in some tropical and equatorial regions. Correct timing of the farming operations in harmony with the weather of the year is still essential, and the difficulties arising are greatly compounded by the type of soil, especially in countries where machine power is limited and reliance has to be placed on the slower rate of human labour.

Although the problems of cultivation of difficult soil in unfavourable weather can to some extent be overcome by the use of increased power, other problems are less easily solved, especially those regarding the preparation of a good seed bed. A fine tilth is very beneficial to good germination, but it may be very difficult to produce if conditions are unsuitable, and again the soil texture is a critical factor.

It is not easy to specify simple accurate descriptions of soil texture, and even though several versions of soil classifications exist in various countries, and no doubt new ones will be put forward in the future, it must be said that the variations of quality, even within a single field or farm, present more puzzling problems than any generalised picture would suggest. Detailed specifications of soil types must be sought for in the appropriate textbooks, but for present purposes soil texture can be regarded as the important property which involves consideration of soil particle size, aeration and pore structure, organic or humus content, presence or absence of stones, and even soil colour.

The way in which a farmer describes his soil is often very different from that of the soil scientist, because he tends to refer to its behaviour rather than its contents. The words 'early' or 'late', 'sad' or 'thin' come more easily to the farmer than do more specific scientific terms. Almost everyone would know what was meant by reference to a sandy soil or a clay soil, but the word 'loam' seems to cover a multitude of possibilities. Whatever name is given to a soil, scientific or vernacular, the important critical properties are concerned with its physical nature and its chemical content and the consequent agricultural effects. The main physical properties are the temperature regime and the moisture regime.

Soil temperature

The temperature of the soil is not constant, either in depth or with time, even though it is often referred to in speech or writing as though it were a fixed quantity. It is continually changing, like the temperature of the air above but at a slower rate. It has two major cycles of change, a 24-hour daily cycle and an annual rhythm. Such changes are always greatest at the soil surface and decrease in amplitude fairly quickly with increase in depth. The lowest soil temperatures near the surface occur a little after dawn and the highest in early afternoon; the lowest annual values occur at the end of winter and the highest towards the end of summer.

Soil temperatures at seed level or around the main plant roots are very important environmental factors in plant growth, especially in the initial stages. They affect the speed and success of germination, the rate of root growth and extension, and microbial and bacterial activity. They are a better standard of reference than air temperature for assessment of the warmth of a season, and they can be affected by soil type and by soil-moisture conditions. The expressions 'an early soil' and 'a late soil' are reflections of this temperature control.

More heat energy is needed to heat up soil than to heat the air, and more heat still is needed to heat up water, to raise their temperatures by the same amount. Therefore, a soil which is dry and with plenty of air spaces between the earth particles will, with a given supply of heat from the Sun, warm up more rapidly than a compact wet soil. The reverse is also true: a dry, light soil cools down more rapidly than a wet, heavy soil, both during the night hours and in the annual cycle.

This is not the only important effect; heat and the consequent change of temperature are transmitted vertically within the soil by conduction. Water is a good heat conductor; air is not and tends to act as an insulator. The result is that a dry soil can be warm in the uppermost layers and yet relatively cool beneath. Under the same external circumstances the wet soil may be cooler in the surface layer but more heat is conducted downwards. At night this effect is reversed, and as the surface cools because heat is lost by radiation, in a dry soil compensating heat is not easily transmitted upwards from below and the surface temperature can drop considerably. With wet soil, this heat from below can be transmitted upwards and so the effective cooling at the surface is less. Dry soils have more severe ground frosts than wet soils.

This means that the frost risk is greater over sandy soils than over clay soils, even though the latter are referred to as 'cold'. The lowest temperatures on a frosty night are often experienced over peaty soils when they are drying out. The worst night frost conditions of all are those over a loose vegetable mulch, simply because the mulch prevents the upward movement of heat at night.

As almost always in natural circumstances, there are few gains without an accompanying loss. A light soil will help early germination because it warms up quickly by day in spring, but it is more liable to a late frost because it cools down rapidly at night. A heavy, wet soil will be slower to respond to the spring increase in warmth, but will be far more hospitable to tender young growth on a cold clear night. Through years of experience, a good farmer or grower learns how best to cope with these contrasting properties, but his plan of action is dictated by the soil type, both in regard to choice of crop and operational timing.

Soil moisture

Only in a few limited areas with a high water table can moisture enter the main root zone of a crop by capillary rise from the water below. In the great majority of farm soils, the water can only enter at the soil surface as rain or melted snow or by irrigation. It then moves downward through the soil profile, but only when it has thoroughly moistened the upper layers (unless there are deep cracks in the soil to facilitate entry). This process is known as infiltration, and can be impeded if the top soil surface is dry and crusted. Heavy rain can sometimes fall at too rapid a rate for the soil to absorb the water by such infiltration, and surface runoff is the result, especially on a slope. Furthermore, heavy raindrops can compact the surfaces of some soils, and this 'capping' hinders the downward penetration of water.

The amount of water a soil can hold against the downward pull of gravity and still retain a degree of aeration is known as the 'moisture-retaining capacity' or, more simply, as 'field capacity'. If more water is added and cannot drain away, then the soil becomes waterlogged and harmful for good plant growth. This maximum amount of retainable water, sometimes referred to in drier countries as 'reserve irrigation', varies with the soil texture, and especially with its fibrous organic content. It can be as little as 10–15 mm per 30 cm depth in large-grained sandy soils, and as much as three or four times this amount in a rich organic soil.

Most of this water can be extracted by the suction of plant roots. The greater the amount of this water within the root range, then the better is the plant able to survive in a dry spell. When all the available water is extracted, the 'wilting point' is reached, but the rate of water extraction and consequent use of plant nutrients may well have slowed down before this end-point. The rate of plant growth, especially in regard to the production of green matter, is strongly related to the soil-moisture status. Some plants react quickly to any soil-moisture shortage, particularly at critical developmental stages; others have what is known as drought resistance and can withstand shortages, but all plants need a good moisture supply to grow well.

The choice of crop, or even the variety of crop, thus depends on the soil-moisture characteristics of the field and on the climatic risks of a rainfall deficiency. Any decision has to be one of calculated risk, and a very dry summer like the one experienced in 1976 over much of Western Europe cannot be allowed for in any farming plan because it happens too infrequently. In all areas where the weather varies from year to year, some climatic risks have to be accepted and attention has to be concentrated on the most probable range of moisture conditions in the soil.

During seasons when the transpiration exceeds the rainfall, the main problem is one of soil-moisture deficit; when the reverse is true, the problem changes to one of removing the excess water from the soil, either by natural drainage or by the planned introduction of mole or tile drains. A soil through which the excess water drains away quickly is likely to be thin in structure, short of nutrients and liable to leaching. Most good agricultural soils drain slowly in the natural process and need some form of assistance.

Drainage

It is easy to say 'good drainage is essential', but to imply that such a state of soil affairs is always attainable is an error, sometimes an expensive one. Man-made drainage systems are designed to remove any excess water from the soil as efficiently as possible and to transfer it to somewhere where it can be put to good use, or at least do little harm. This is not always as easy as it sounds, and there are occasions when improved rapid drainage can cause extra troubles elsewhere. The dangers of erosion and possible flooding may be increased; an environmental problem is not solved by merely transferring its location.

Over the centuries, the Dutch have been thought of as the leading European drainage experts, if only for the fact that they succeed in farming land which lies below sea level. Recent years have seen improvements in drainage design and an increased use of modern machinery and materials. More information is now available concerning the probable benefits to be gained by improved drainage in the shape of increased crop yields. Experiments designed to quantify these gains in production may not always confirm the full expectations of the optimists, but at least farmers can now make a theoretical comparison between the costs of a new drainage system and the potential increase in profits.

It is not easy to put a precise monetary value on the expected benefits because, apart from the unknown future crop-selling price, there can be other gains, such as the improved trafficability of the land, which are almost impossible to cost. If drainage leads to a quicker drying out of the soil after rains, this will increase the number of days available for the use of farm machinery, thus reducing the delays that can occur in cultivation, sowing or harvesting. A similar advantage might be expected on pasture land, where it would be hoped that the improved drainage would increase the number of days when stock could graze without damaging the grass by poaching. Better drained fields also reduce the dangers of certain parasitic animal diseases.

Farm work-days

The number of 'work-days', when machinery can be used without running the risk of damaging the soil structure, is determined by the weather and the nature of the soil. The frequency or regularity with which the rain occurs is more significant than the total rainfall, although small amounts of rain may have little effect on most soils.

Three factors determine the length of possible delays: namely, the rainfall distribution, the evaporation of water from the surface layers during the dry periods, and the speed of drainage. A light, well drained soil may be workable after rain in a matter of hours; similar work may not be possible on a heavy soil until two or three dry days have elapsed. Furthermore, the potential damage caused by compaction by traffic on soil in an unsuitable condition is likely to be greater in heavy clays, with their small particles and limited aeration, and much less on the more coarsely structured sandy soils.

Improved drainage can mitigate the adverse circumstances but cannot be expected to cure the problem completely; the nature of the soil composition will always be the ultimate limiting factor. If, for example, the types of soil were divided into four classes, good, above average, below average and bad, expressing their ability to bear heavy traffic in adverse conditions, then improved drainage might reasonably be expected to raise a soil by one class, rarely by two classes, and almost never by three classes. Drainage may work wonders; it cannot perform miracles.

A good, experienced farmer knows when one of his fields is fit to be cultivated, although in years with difficult weather he may have to go ahead with his work in less than ideal conditions. To convert his judgement into figures, using a soil factor, rainfall and evaporation data, is by no means easy. Even if such a computation is carried out and a formula obtained, its application in forward planning is difficult because of the uncertainty of future rainfall patterns. Nevertheless, this trafficability factor is of major importance when selecting the best cropping programme or sequence, and cannot be ignored as a possible limiting factor to production. As previously mentioned, in some soils it may make the change from grass to cereals inadvisable.

Chemical properties

Increasing knowledge of the chemical composition of the soil, of the elements which have been found to be necessary for good plant growth, the ways in which they are used and translocated by the crops, and the necessity for maintaining good fertility and the means of providing it, has led to an appreciable increase in the yields of all farm crops in modern agriculture. The extension of this knowledge into developing areas is taking place, but a good rate of improvement is not easy to attain. The first step is to realise that the soil needs treatment; the second is to find out how best this can be done; and the third step is to find the necessary money.

Although it would not be true to claim that all soil fertility problems have been solved (even in theory), it can be said that if sufficient money and materials are available, then of all the factors which restrict production the chemical status of the soil is the one which offers the best prospect of human control by appropriate and timely action. If mistakes are made, then it is man, and not nature, who is at fault.

The use of soil nutrients by a growing crop is not the only cause of change in fertility level. Excess rainfall can dissolve the chemicals, forming weak solutions which move downward in the soil beyond the reach of the plant roots, and ultimately into the drains as more and more water is taken in at the soil surface, a process known as leaching. The greater the excess rainfall, then the more the soil will be impoverished of the food which the plant needs for good growth. The need for careful attention to the level of soil fertility therefore increases in the higher rainfall areas, or in regions which have experienced a wetter than usual period of rains.

The elements most easily leached out of the soil by the throughput of excess water are the alkalis, leading to problems of soil acidity which can be measured scientifically and be expressed by a scale of values known as the 'pH'. This scale is familiar to the expert, potentially confusing to the layman, and incomprehensible to the innumerate. The letter 'p' implies that the scale is not linear but logarithmic, and the letter 'H' refers to the hydrogen ion. The least that the non-scientist needs to know is that the state $pH = 7$ is neutral (pure water, for example); if the value of pH is less than 7, the soil is acid; and if it is greater than 7, it is alkaline.

Most agricultural crops thrive best in soils which are slightly acidic, with pH values between 6 and 6.5. In climates such as those experienced over much of the British Isles, excess acidity (with pH values less than 5.5) is rarely a serious limiting factor. These apparently small changes in pH can be misleading to anyone thinking on a linear scale. A soil with a pH of 5 is in fact ten times more acid than a soil with a pH of 6, but this does not mean that the effect on plant growth is ten times greater than the change in pH. Very few crops (with the exception of some conifer trees) can be grown in a soil with a pH as low as 4.5; agricultural crops such as ryegrass, oats or potatoes will tolerate high acidity but cannot do well, and yields will be low and corrective treatment of the soil is advisable.

Excess acidity can be corrected by the addition to the soil of some form of alkali, such as lime. The need for liming to obtain the better soil quality varies from area to area and from year to year, and depends on the rainfall regime. A wet winter in a normally low rainfall area is especially important because it can create a need for a pH correction in areas which would normally be free from such worries. Often in agriculture (as in other walks of life), it is the occasional need for corrective or protective action which is so important and so easily overlooked. Where action is regularly needed, it is incorporated into standard practice. For example, a country which has a snowfall problem every year will suffer less disruption than one in which heavy falls only occur infrequently; one area is prepared, the other is not.

Alkaline soils are likely to be those which contain free chalk and which were formed originally from limestone rocks. Soils with a very high pH value are practically useless for agriculture. Treatment of these soils with materials such as sodium carbonate can improve their quality, but in general it is true to say that while the treatment of acidity is relatively easy and indeed common practice, the correction of alkalinity presents much more difficult and expensive problems.

Soil nutrients

Numerous field experiments have been carried out in many countries in the hope of quantifying the effects of the addition of nitrogen (N), phosphorus (P) and potassium (K) to the soil. The main difficulty is the interpretation of their results and the introduction of the lessons learnt into commercial practice. This is not easy if the experiment report merely tells us what happened in a given set of imperfectly recorded circumstances and omits any attempt to explain why certain responses were observed. Solving the problem of timing the fertilizer applications is more difficult than that of how much extra nutrients should be used, if only because the timing depends on a weather and soil factor which is not easy to identify. This problem is most difficult when the growing season coincides with the rainy season, creating leaching problems which do not occur in climates where summer is usually the drier period. The problem of correct fertilization in areas of cleared tropical forest is very difficult to solve, and may be the limiting factor to continuing production.

Although it may thus appear that soil nutrient status can be readily and usefully adjusted, the world supplies of 'artificial' fertilizers are not infinite (many of them being by-products of the petroleum industry), and future supplies in adequate quantity are by no means assured. In any case, the mounting costs of supply will present yet another limiting factor to food production.

It is also important to realise that chemical additives, however beneficial in themselves, are not the complete answer to the problem of providing the ideal soil conditions for growth. Organic material, humus, has to be added to many if not all soils to maintain their structure and increase the moisture-retaining properties.

The addition of chemical fertilizers to the soil sometimes invokes vociferous protests and the use of emotive words in arguments which seem to emerge more from the heart than the head. When emotion comes through the door, common sense jumps out of the window, and science climbs up the wall. Passionate beliefs are not always identical with perfection.

Once anyone is convinced that the answer is known, it is not difficult to find some evidence that will support it. Such evidence can at times fall far short of the absolute truth, as once an error has appeared in print it is almost impossible to correct it. The solution of agricultural problems demands the strictest impartiality.

4

Soil and weather interactions

The continual reference to the weather in the previous chapter on soil properties emphasises the point that these two factors cannot be treated separately. Each affects the other, and it is the combination of their effects which is a decisive factor in production. There are times when the weather can improve the condition of the soil, as when frosts break down the heavy clods of a ploughed soil, or when wind and sunshine help to dry out the surface layers; at other times the weather can accentuate the soil's deficiencies. In adverse weather, some soils will minimise the possible ill-effects, others will become much more difficult to handle, and at all times it is the combination of the two effects that has to be understood and allowed for. Surface weather conditions tend to alter fairly rapidly with situation, and so it is appropriate to consider questions of site and general topography.

Topography

Weather conditions, and hence the climate, change rapidly with increase in height above sea level, both in the air and in the soil. The altitude of any field is therefore an important factor in regard to the combined effects of soil and weather. Soil temperatures decrease with increase of height, and thus growing seasons are shorter on higher ground. This is most important in spring, and any delay in the start of grass growth on the upland grazing can be a serious problem.

It is the decrease of sunshine with height and the increase of wind which combine to retard the annual warming of the upland soils. Evaporation from the soil and transpiration from plants also decrease with height, but on the other hand the rainfall is greater at higher levels. This results in upland soils staying wetter for longer periods than soils in the valleys, making them more difficult to cultivate even if they were of adequate quality.

Despite the increased average annual rainfall, upland soils are still not free from liability to drought, mainly because they are often very shallow. In a dry spell, which usually affects both hills and valleys, the upland grass will turn yellow and appear 'burnt out' before the grass in the lowlands, where the soil provides larger soil-moisture reserves.

Upland rainfall may be far more than is necessary to maintain crop growth, especially in the winter or rainy period. The result is increased leaching, and most upland soils tend to be acidic in character. Drainage may be naturally impeded by rocky substrata or variable terrain. In general, an increase in height tends to emphasise the adverse soil conditions rather than ameliorate them. Exceptions to this general rule occur in the middle ranges of the hills, where sometimes the gains (chiefly in more plentiful rains) outweigh the losses. In semi-arid areas, fields on the low plains can suffer badly from annual drought, but the surrounding hills may have enough rain to maintain growth.

Aspect and exposure

Any field on rising ground must face towards some compass direction or other, thus determining its aspect. A surface tilted towards the Sun will receive more incoming radiation and warmth than one tilted away from it. As a result, land on a north-facing slope will have a shorter growing season and less favourable growing conditions than one at the same height but with a southern aspect. The eastern and western slopes fall between these two extremes, with a slight advantage to the eastern side because clouds are less likely in the early morning than in the late afternoon.

All unimpeded aspects have one potential serious disadvantage: namely, an increased exposure to wind which is the weather element usually unhelpful for plant growth. This exposure effect is greatest on the sites facing the strongest winds, especially if these happen to be also the coldest winds. It is very difficult in a natural situation to find a site which is sheltered from the adverse effects of wind and also exposed to the maximum intensity of sunshine.

The slope of any field also presents another problem to a farmer because if it becomes too steep, it greatly increases the difficulties in the use of farm machinery, and there can be a serious danger of accidents caused by the overturning of vehicles. Cultivations and harvesting may become impossible by machine methods, and this means a greater demand on limited manpower. The only parts of the world where man has tried to overcome this problem by the construction of terracing are those where ample cheap or forced labour was available at the time of construction, usually in the fairly distant past.

Yields per unit area can never be high in upland farms because the conditions of soil and climate are too adverse for good growth and there is very little that can be done to improve them. Careful examination of such areas has shown that cultivation has been extended into such zones at times in the past when the climate was particularly helpful or when there was an intense population pressure. When conditions changed, such fields were abandoned. If there is only a slight deterioration in climatic conditions, farming at the limit of cultivations can become impossible. At best, it is an area of hard work and poor returns, and it is not for nothing that these are known as 'marginal areas'.

Soil variability

One further soil factor cannot be ignored, namely, its variability. Variations occur not only from field to field within a farm, but also within a single field. This mesoscale variability leads to subtle changes in microclimate, and can give rise to difficult problems in the timing of cultivations, sowing and harvest, thus adding to the costs of production. Such difficulties increase in adverse weather conditions, especially in large fields.

In the old systems of strip cultivation, such problems did not arise. When fields began to be enclosed they were usually small in size, especially in grass and livestock areas and where wind was a problem. With the advent of modern machinery, fields were enlarged for ease of management, and hedges began to disappear. Large fields may, on paper, be easier to work, but the benefits of uniformity may be lost. If work on a large field has to be carried out in two stages, it might just as well have been two fields anyway, quite apart from the possible deterioration in microclimate in large unimpeded areas and loss of the benefits of shelter.

Erosion

One final very important subject must be considered when dealing with soil and weather, and that is the liability of the soil to erosion. Soils are indeed initially formed by a process of slow natural erosion over thousands of years, but they can be damaged by heavy rain or wind erosion almost in a matter of hours. This damage is often irrepairable, any possible attempts at reclamation being a long and costly process. Erosion can be halted and the risks reduced by sensible land management, but the important fact is that it should never have been allowed to occur.

The major extensive erosive losses of productive soil are almost always due to the stupidity of man. There are two main forms of erosion: one caused by wind, which occurs mainly (but not exclusively) in low rainfall areas, and the other caused by the effects of rain, especially on sloping land. In other words, the soil can either be blown away or washed away.

The natural defences against erosion are twofold. One defence is the root system of a perennial crop which helps to bind the soil together against the disruptive forces of wind or water. The other form of defence is a ground cover of vegetation which reduces the tendency of the wind to lift small soil particles into the air and also modifies the impact of heavy raindrops on the surface. Erosion processes still continue on land undisturbed by man, but at a much slower rate than when his activities have removed these natural defences.

The really serious conditions arise when man, in a search for more areas to cultivate and thus to produce more food for himself and his animals, disturbs an ecological balance. He has, over many centuries and in many continents, ploughed up areas of natural grassland to grow cereals in a climate which was too dry to suit them. The permanent grass-root structure which was holding the soil together in the dry periods was replaced by the temporary root structure of wheat or maize. The scene was thus set for wind erosion during the dry fallow periods, and dust-bowls were formed. The Romans brought this type of disaster on themselves near Carthage in North Africa, and in more recent years similar mistakes have been made in many parts of the world including America and Australia, China and Russia.

Soil losses of this type are not confined to major disaster areas. Similar losses on a reduced scale can occur in any arable area if the soil surface is dry and if strong winds blow when there is no crop covering the ground or it has just started to emerge. The most dangerous time lasts from after the seed bed has been prepared until the crop has become established. The process is accelerated and the risks increased if there are no windbreaks around the fields or if there are large areas of monoculture. Man makes the mistakes and climate takes the toll.

When man was still a hunter and gatherer and had not learnt to become a farmer, much of Europe and many other parts of the world were probably covered by trees and undergrowth. When clearances were made in this forest for crop cultivation and animal husbandry, the easiest land was used first. The process continued over the centuries until almost all the level ground was occupied, and clearances began to be made on the hills and hill slopes, and it was at this time that the dangers of rain erosion increased. If the tree cover on a hillside was replaced by grass, then there was insufficient ground cover and root density to withstand heavy rainfall; whole hillsides began to slide into the valleys.

Such are the conditions which lead to extreme cases of wind or water erosion, and the results are at times painfully obvious in a landscape. In the less extreme cases there can be an insidious form of slight erosion, none of which looks very serious, but which over the years continues an irreversible process of soil loss, limiting the potential future production.

The losses are due to a lack of understanding of the processes and a consequent misuse of land prompted by necessity or greed. Some of the worst erosion in the world today occurs in countries which have overpopulated the land at their disposal and/or exploited the production potential of the land itself. No population, either of plants or animals, can afford to expand beyond the limits dictated by its food supply; if it does, the result is disaster.

The erosion potential of any soil is a function of its structure, the land topography and the weather to which it is subjected. The probability of serious erosion is largely dependent on man's decisions regarding land use. Such decisions are generally made by the farmer concerned, but sometimes under political direction. The results, if the decision is a wrong one, are the same; the only difference is one of scale, one field or one province.

Erosion on a restricted scale cannot be entirely eliminated from any farm system, but it must be kept to a minimum by correct land use and sensible farming practice. Major erosion not only causes the loss of the current year's crop, but that of every other year that follows.

Land use capability

A detailed agroclimatological summary and a comprehensive soil survey are the basic data needed for a reliable assessment of land use capability. Provided that there is a full understanding of the effects of soil and weather on the growth and health of crops and animals and on all the farming activities needed for their husbandry, it should be theoretically possible to draw up a ranking list of the uses to which the land could be put. At the head of such a list would be the type of crop or farming which would be best suited to the soil-weather complex; at the bottom would be those for which it is useless.

Such a ranking system would not, however, tell the whole story. From a practical point of view, land capability has two components, one being the assurance of a high output for a few commodities, the other being a freedom of choice from a large number of possible enterprises. In the words of a university class list, a small number in the first class would be more than compensated for by a large number in the second class. A large number of viable alternatives in land use enables a farmer to adjust to changes in demand or profitability with a greater degree of confidence. The versatility of land use capability is thus a great asset.

In areas with bad climates and poor soils, the choice of land use can be very restricted indeed. In such 'marginal areas' only one type of farming is usually possible, and the only hope of increase in output or profit is in the improvement of techniques or better breeds of stock. The major planning danger is the over-optimistic introduction of unsuitable new ideas, especially on a grandiose scale.

The old sailing advice that it is futile to struggle against both wind and tide could be converted into similar agricultural advice not to try to combat both soil and weather. A facile remark, perhaps, but governments of more than one country of more than one political hue have in the past disregarded such advice to their cost, and to the despair of the farmers concerned.

Climate and soil are the fundamental ingredients for food production; the use that man makes of them depends on his experience, knowledge and intelligence.

Part III

The biological factor

5

The allies

The main biological factors, the plants and animals, are more than allies in man's fight against famine, because their presence and relative abundance are vital to his very existence; without them he would starve.

In his earliest days man, like all other animals, spent a great deal of his time searching for food, hunting for animals he could catch or trap and gathering the edible parts of wild plants. Fundamental changes took place when he started to domesticate some of the animals and cultivate a few promising plants. His whole life-style began to alter, and for the first time in his history he had something approaching a reliable source of food in his immediate vicinity. He thus had a little more time to spare and a chance to think about improving his food supplies, whereas previously he was merely struggling to exist.

Better, regular food also increased his fecundity and his life expectancy; there were fewer deaths among the newly born and very young, and, most importantly, among the most valuable mature adults. Children could be replaced, but a loss of an experienced leader of men before he could use his acquired wisdom to good effect and train his successors was a heavy handicap to progress. Settled agriculture had started mankind on its long trail of improvement.

Since those far-off days, the beginning of civilisation as we know it, a slow but reasonably steady progress has been made. Once man ceased merely to observe the growth of plants and animals and began to ask himself why and how they grew, the sciences of biology and zoology emerged, offering the promise of more rapid progress.

The better understanding of the biology of plants and animals has since been an essential ingredient in the improvement of productivity. Continuing success in agriculture depends on knowing as much as possible about the processes involved, and without this knowledge the farmer could still be engaged in a frustrating game of trial and error, with the odds always tilted in favour of failure.

This need to understand the way in which biological material reacts applies not only to its nutrition, but also to its demands for energy, moisture and space. By using knowledge of the reaction to all the environmental variables, the suitability of plants and animals to a given site can be sensibly assessed, and estimates can be made of the best standards of production that can be attained.

A farmer making his plans for the future has to decide what is the best style of farming which would make the most of the environment of his farm, that is to say, the identifiable qualities of his soils and the calculated risks of his climate. He has to select the type and variety of crop which is likely to give him the most profit, and the best type of animal or breed (if any) which will suit his conditions and will find a ready market. He has two forms of assistance in the making of such decisions: first, the past experience of neighbouring farms, and secondly, his or his advisor's knowledge of the available biological material and its environmental needs.

The quality and potential of such biological material are not constant over the ages, and perhaps the most spectacular illustration of the value of biological knowledge in improving food production is in the science of genetics and selective breeding. The concept of improving stocks of plants and animals by the selection of individuals with desirable characteristics and using them as parents for the next generation arose early in agricultural history. Man, in fact, was giving evolution a push in a required direction. Progress was slow until it was discovered which characters were transmissible to offspring and what were the factors controlling the method of inheritance. This new comprehension changed breeding from an unreliable art to something approaching an exact science.

The levels of production attainable by modern varieties, especially those of cereals, potatoes, cows, pigs and poultry, would have been regarded as impossible by previous generations of farmers. In some new strains, the breeders have done much more than raise the quantity of output; they have included genes which introduce other desirable attributes, such as better quality, hardiness, early maturity and resistance to pests and disease. It was the discovery of the gene that was the important step; earlier generations of all ages had called them gifts of fairy godmothers or witches' curses.

Long before the present upsurge in plant or animal breeding, the main cause of any change in biological material was the introduction of new varieties from other parts of the world. Armed forces, traders, settlers and adventurous travellers all played their part in this transference of new varieties from their native habitat to new locations. Many such moves brought considerable benefits, the classic example being that of the potato, which arrived in Europe from South America some 400 years ago, since when it has been changed almost beyond recognition by selective breeding. Other introductions have been less successful, and at times disastrous. Rabbits taken to Australia from Britain became a major pest, and so, on a minor scale, have the deer introduced into New Zealand.

After introduction or production, new varieties have to be tested or tried out in their new situation. More precise methods for evaluating their performance have now been evolved. There is still no infallible way of predicting the results that will be obtained in unknown future circumstances, but if detailed tests are carried out under a range of conditions at various sites, then the results can give some guidance on how much consistency can be expected. Nevertheless, a trial is only valid within the range of conditions under which it was carried out; extrapolation must always be an act of faith.

Concurrently with the improvements in breeding techniques, methods have been developed for the speedier multiplication and distribution of improved stocks. For example, the introduction of artificial insemination in cows makes it possible for bulls of proven performance and an ability to get high-yielding daughters to sire many more offspring over an unlimited geographical area. It is far easier to move semen than a live animal, and far cheaper.

With plants, new techniques such as tissue culture permit the rapid vegetative reproduction of some desirable new types. Even when multiplication can only take place through the seed, modern transport may make it possible to halve the time needed to raise sufficient stocks by producing a second generation in another hemisphere.

The rapid adoption and distribution of improved, scientifically tested new varieties of plants and animals has undoubtedly been a major factor in increasing the total agricultural output, but the process is not without its dangers. If, by mischance, a popular new introduction has a hidden defect which was not revealed during the testing period, such as susceptibility to a new race of pest or disease, or intolerance of certain extreme climatic conditions, a large number of producers may simultaneously suffer a drastic fall in yield.

The cautious attitude of older generations of farmers and their opposition to change were no doubt frustrating to enthusiastic innovators, but they did offer a safegurd against possible failures. Not every new idea is an unqualified success, but not every old idea is incapable of improvement. A slow change may be less hazardous than a rapid one, but there are areas and motives which demand rapid action.

The understandable tendency of modern farmers to use the most promising variety of the moment means that there are now fewer varieties and breeds in extensive production than there used to be. This has aroused the fear that some strains may disappear entirely, taking with them desirable qualities which may be needed in later stages of planned breeding. A strong case can be made out for the creation and maintenance of 'gene pools' or 'gene banks' which can preserve such plants or animals. Complete genetic engineering may be a feature of the next century, but it would be wise not to depend entirely on such a development.

One final word about trials: the testing of any new variety has to be carried out under the pressure of limited available time, and each plant trial takes a year to perform, and several trials may be necessary. The demand for improved strains is great and the competition from other seed producers even greater. Under such circumstances, occasional errors are almost inevitable, but the continuing rise in yields per unit area shows that such errors are few.

Much concern is now being expressed regarding the preservation of biological material which does not appear to be of immediate importance to food production. It remains to be seen if man will be the only animal species which will restrict the prompting of the selfish gene in his struggle for existence.

6

The opponents

In an ecosystem unaffected by human interference, the combined effect of the behaviour prompted by the selfish genes of all biological species in an area results in an uneasily balanced situation involving a mixture of dominance and interdependence. The complexities of this balance are a fascinating subject for research, and their understanding is a very necessary component of human knowledge.

When man decides to use an area to produce food for himself and his animals, he inevitably disturbs this balance, and he tends to regard any biological competitors for such land as his enemies. The term 'opponents' would be a more reasonable word to choose, although some non-edible biological material is in fact helping him to attain his objectives.

Weeds, pests and diseases are the three major opponents to successful agricultural output and productivity. All of them are types of living organisms, unwanted by the farmer because they either compete with, or directly injure, the commodities he is trying to produce.

Many attempts have been made to calculate the extent of the losses caused by these three competitors, and there is fairly general agreement that they can be of the order of 20–30 per cent per annum, and possibly more if losses in storage are taken into account. Such estimates, no matter how eminent the authorities which quote them, must be treated with caution. They cannot be applied with accuracy to individual commodities, individual farms or particular seasons.

Such estimates of loss are usually derived by summarising the results from trials and experiments in which individual or small groups of weeds, pests or diseases have been successfully controlled. These results may be very precise, and their degree of accuracy and significance can be calculated with mathematical certainty, but they are only true for the year and situation in which the trials were carried out. Extrapolating them to other sites and other seasons would be no more reliable than forecasting the performance of a football team for the next season using the result of a single match played the previous week on its home ground.

Weeds

The effects of weeds on crop yields tend to be more consistent than those of pests and diseases, but even so there is much variation in losses. The weed population changes in magnitude from site to site according to weather, soil conditions and the timing of cultivations. Acid soils have a different selection of weed species from those in alkaline soils. The weed pattern also changes in response to variations in soil moisture, soil fertility, altitude, temperature and exposure. The number and type of weeds also vary in accordance with the previous history and crop pattern of a site. For example, the weed flora of a permanent pasture will be vastly different from that of arable fields in the same area.

Weeds tend to persist once they have become established on any one site, and eradication is a very difficult process. Unless man intervenes, the weed species which are present in any quantity will change little in composition, although those which are dominant at any one time will depend on the seasonal conditions. The degree with which they will compete with crops is also determined by the current weather.

Weeds usually cause the greatest depression of final yields if they develop rapidly before the crop itself is fully established. If they develop before the crop is sown or planted out, there is an opportunity to destroy them without causing injury to the crop. If they develop at a late stage, after the crop is well established and is growing freely, then they compete less effectively and may cause little loss of final yield.

For any system of farming, whether it be grassland, permanent or semi-permanent arable crops or an arable rotation, sufficient is known of the ecology of weeds to be able to predict the types which are likely to cause problems on a particular site with some degree of accuracy. The intensity of the weed problems facing the farmer will vary according to the previous history of the site and with the variations of the weather of the current season, but there are unlikely to be many disastrous surprises.

Pests and diseases

Foreseeing the problems which will arise from the infection of plants or animals by pests and diseases is a much more difficult and complex matter, which can be discussed under five headings. First, before it can be damaged by a particular pest or disease, the plant or animal has to be in a susceptible state, and complications arise immediately because strains, and even individuals, of the same species frequently vary in their susceptibility. Moreoever, such liability to infection may often change in accordance to age or stage of development. Both plants and animals, generally but not invariably, tend to be most liable to attack when young, and maturity often brings with it a degree of resistance. With plants there is the further complication that they may continually be producing new organs, shoots, leaves, flowers or fruits, each of which is liable to pass through a phase of maximum susceptibility.

Secondly, there is the requirement that there must be in the vicinity of the crop a nucleus, a potential striking force, of the pest or disease in an active state and in a sufficient concentration to launch an effective attack. Many pests are mobile and can move to their target under their own power; others are more passive, and almost all disease organisms need transport assistance from wind, water or intermediate animal hosts (including man). For successful long-distance transport, the numbers making the trip have to be high enough to allow for casualties along the route, so that there will be enough survivors to reach the objective – the susceptible host. The distances travelled by airborne pathogens, although normally relatively short, can at times be very long indeed. Pest and disease traffic is international and even trans-oceanic, and takes no notice of political boundaries.

Thirdly, having arrived at the potential host, the surrounding environmental conditions have to be favourable within quite precise limits if any attack is to succeed. In many cases there is only a very limited range of temperature, humidity and free surface moisture within which the disease or parasite can infect the plant or animal.

Fourthly, after the initial bridgehead has been secured, the pathogen can only multiply and spread to other hosts and thus bring about the start of a possible epidemic if the environmental conditions are still favourable. This consolidation stage may require somewhat different conditions from those necessary for the initial assault. Any interruption of the favourable conditions is likely to slow down the progress of the invader, and if circumstances change drastically for an appreciable length of time, then the invasion may fail without any action on the part of the farmer. In such a case, the whole process has to start all over again, and may, indeed, have to wait for the next year.

Fifthly, apart from man, pests and diseases have their own natural enemies and competitors. Pests may be preyed upon by other organisms so that their numbers are reduced to innocuous levels. Pathogens compete with each other and also with harmless competitors for food and living space. Slight changes in the environmental conditions may be sufficient to alter this balance, sometimes favouring the damaging invaders and sometimes the reverse. In this way, each plant and animal species is a living battleground on which a range of other organisms, some harmful and some beneficial, compete for survival and possible dominance.

There is thus a continuously varying dynamic situation which makes precise calculation of losses caused by the unwanted organisms a matter of extreme difficulty, even without the intervention by man. In practice, man constantly intervenes to try to minimise the harmful effects and tries to achieve an equilibrium which will allow his crops and livestock to attain their full potential. He has a number of lines of action available, constituting his defences, which may be used singly or in various combinations. These will be considered in detail in the following chapter.

7

The defences

The types of defence which can be utilised in attempts to control the unwanted organisms may be conveniently grouped under four headings: dealing with statutory, husbandry, biological, physical and chemical strategies.

Statutory strategy

All countries have animal and plant health legislation designed to prevent the introduction of pests or diseases which are not indigenous in their territory. There is unfortunately a lack of uniformity in such regulations, and also in the efficiency of the efforts made to enforce them in different countries, even those with a Common Agricultural Policy. These differences are partly due to the fact that each country has already present within its boundaries a different range of weeds, pests and diseases, and also has different fears about which 'foreign' organisms offer a serious threat to its own commodities. There are also differences in the range of products which nations need to import, and whether the import sources are such that the risk of introducing harmful organisms with such imports is high.

The success of prohibitive legislation depends on the degree of cooperation between importing and exporting countries in its enforcement. Any quarantine scheme demands the employment of highly trained staff to inspect the produce in the country of origin, and similar personnel in the receiving country. This is costly, both directly in the training and salaries of the staff concerned, and also indirectly in the expense incurred by slowing down the handling and transport of the produce. The more perishable the commodities, the more points of exit and entry, then the more staff are required to monitor the legislation effectively without unacceptable delays. The continual increase in volume and speed of international traffic makes the successful operation of any quarantine laws more and more difficult.

Most countries also have internal legislation aimed at eliminating or limiting the spread of certain pests and diseases. In its most extreme form this can be a policy of eradication, carried out by the destruction of all infected plants or animals, with or without any legal compensation to the owners. Such a policy may be adopted to try to eliminate a pest or disease which has been introduced despite quarantine regulations and import inspections but has not yet become widespread or endemic.

An eradication policy has been successfully put into force in Great Britain for the foot-and-mouth disease of cattle, pigs and sheep, and also for the infestation of potatoes by the Colorado beetle and the disease of bacterial canker of tomatoes. Success depends on having adequate numbers of trained staff available to take rapid action once the threat has been identified.

Such a policy may fail if the eradication is incomplete, or if conditions are very favourable for the spread and multiplication of the organism, and particularly if it has a range of host species which it can attack so that the speed of spread exceeds the rate of detection. This, indeed, was the case in Britain for the 'fireblight' disease of pears and related species. Failure does not always imply inefficiency, because in many cases the infected host becomes a potent source of further infection before its own disease symptoms are recognisable.

The eradication of a long-established pest or disease is likely to be so prohibitively expensive that it is seldom attempted, exceptions being when there is a threat to the health of human beings. Such a threat makes the large costs involved acceptable to the community, such as in the campaigns to eradicate tuberculosis and brucellosis disease of cattle, and the extensive use of DDT to kill mosquitoes to reduce the incidence of malaria.

Legislation may also try to restrict the spread of soil-borne organisms by prohibiting the planting of susceptible crops on land known to be contaminated with certain pests or diseases, or the use of such land for the production of propagating material which would spread the danger to other sites. Regulations can also exist which demand the regular treatment of animals against pests, such as compulsory sheep dipping at stated times of the year. If such regulations are relaxed when thought to be no longer necessary, there is always the danger of a re-emergence of the pest or parasite.

There are also both voluntary and compulsory schemes for the certification of animals and plants used for breeding or propagation. These either guarantee that the breeding stocks are free from certain types of infection or, at very least, they satisfy definite health standards. It can also be an offence to offer for sale plants that are visibly unfit for planting because of the presence of disease. All these policies, if carried out effectively and honestly, can make a significant contribution to the control of pests or disease. A poorly drafted regulation, or one which is not carefully enforced, is not worth the paper it is written on.

Husbandry strategy

The previous section dealt with regulations which are imposed upon a farmer; the present one is concerned with patterns of behaviour he imposes on himself.

The familiar structure of agriculture is the concentration of the plants and animals needed by man into compact areas where they can be conveniently managed, and from which it is hoped that predators and competitors can be excluded. Thus the practice of removing weeds from areas of cultivation, either by hand or by the use of farming implements, is probably not much younger than agriculture itself. The rotational growing of crops and the nomad grazing of flocks or herds were certainly practised without any clear idea that they constituted a way to control some pests and diseases. The land was said to be 'sick', and it was left alone until it was cured.

Many soil-borne parasites fall in numbers in the absence of their main host, and if this absence is long enough, they may, at least temporarily, be at an innocuous level when the host is re-introduced after a long enough interval. In this way, if a rotation is of sufficient length, it may prevent the numbers of parasitic organisms building up to a dangerous level. For some soil-borne problems, this still remains the most effective and economical strategy.

Timely cultivations encouraging the decay of infected plant debris may assist in lowering the amount of inoculum available to attack succeeding crops. Alternatively, such debris may be burnt or buried deep enough in the soil that a subsequent crop will be strongly established before its roots penetrate the infective zone. Timing of operations may also be adjusted to give the maximum opportunity to the crops under protection and the minimum chances to the harmful organisms. The host may be introduced onto a site before the conditions are favourable for the rapid development of competitors or parasites. The host, plant or animal, may thus pass through its susceptible juvenile period before an attack can develop, or at least be so well advanced that it can survive with little or no loss of productive yield.

Alternatively, similar benefits may be obtained by delaying the introduction of the host. Weeds may germinate and then be destroyed before the crop is sown; pests, parasites and disease organisms may die from starvation, or at least be reduced in numbers before susceptible crops or animals appear for them to infect. Essential husbandry operations which may cause injury (such as cultivations, singling, or pruning) may be timed to take place when the risk of wound infection is least. Animals can be introduced to pastures well after their soil-borne parasites have hatched.

Husbandry techniques may also be used to modify the environmental conditions close to the soil surface to the disadvantage of the enemies of crops and stock. A number of pests and diseases are favoured by wet soil conditions, and in some cases need the presence of free water. Improvement of soil drainage and the removal of standing water by appropriate cultivation can lessen the risk from slugs, snails (some of which carry animal diseases such as liver fluke), club root of brassica plants, and many of the fungi which cause the damping-off of seedlings.

Adjustment of the acidity of the soil by liming also reduces the risk of club-root infection, although if carried out immediately before a potato crop, this same operation will increase the risk of tubers being infected by common scab. Other examples could be quoted, but there are serious limitations (particularly those of cost) to being able to produce sufficient environmental change as to make significant alterations in the balance between the commodities the farmer is trying to produce in open fields and the unwanted organisms.

Much more can be achieved when products are produced or stored inside a building. Environmental control of the interior climate then becomes economically possible, and even, in some cases, essential. The avoidance of extreme temperature variations and the intelligent use of effective ventilation to prevent excessive relative humidity and condensation are important in reducing the incidence of respiratory and other infectious diseases in intensive indoor livestock production. Similarly, climate control in glasshouses is a major factor not only in the setting up of conditions favourable to maximum growth, but also those leading to the reduction in incidence of many diseases, especially those encouraged by high relative humidities.

The damage caused by pests and diseases is not limited to the production phase, but may occur with even greater effect during the period of storage. Within food or fodder stores, the correct adjustment of the physical environment is an essential factor in reducing losses. In some cases, this can be done by sensible choice of site and construction, but if precise and sophisticated adjustments are needed to control the internal climate, then the process becomes expensive and can constitute a considerable addition to the costs of production, and thus reduce the final profits.

Biological strategy

It could be argued that all techniques which modify the environment so that the balance swings in favour of the wanted organisms and against the unwanted organisms are basically forms of biological control. The deliberate interference with natural biological populations, by selection and breeding to produce plants and animals with a genetic constitution making them less susceptible to attack by certain pests and diseases, may also be regarded as a form of biological control. The degree of such control obtained in this manner varies from the rare occasions of complete immunity, through varying levels of resistance, to a state of tolerance where the hosts are attacked but their economic performance is not seriously affected, bearing in mind that such properties may not always be persistent. Opponents often change quicker than allies.

Races of plants and animals resistant to any serious pest or disease are naturally much welcomed by farmers. Although the costs of research and development and of the production techniques may make them initially expensive, this extra expenditure is usually more than counterbalanced by not having to take other costly control measures. Farmers are also prepared to pay more for the peace of mind which comes from the removal of a serious hazard. Regrettably, experience has shown that this peace can be of all too short duration.

Although there have been some successes, such as the potato varieties immune to wart disease, which have stood the test of time, far more examples can be quoted where the welcomed property of resistance has broken down after only a few seasons. This is due to the natural selection of races from a mixed population of predators, or even to the emergence of an entirely new type.

A long protracted war is thus in progress in which the geneticist and the plant or animal breeder strive to keep one move ahead of the changing pathogenic conditions. With an increasing understanding of the factors governing resistance, and with the reliance on mechanisms controlled by several genes rather than by a single gene, a higher success rate can be hoped for in the future. For some pests and diseases, a reliance on host resistance may provide the ideal long-term solution, but progress is bound to be slow and it is unlikely to become a universal panacea.

The use of the term 'biological control' is sometimes limited to occasions when a new organism is introduced (directly or indirectly) with a view to eliminating or at least reducing the effect of the unwanted organism which is causing a decrease in production. This may be achieved in various ways: the unwanted organism may be deliberately infected with a lethal viral or bacterial disease, a predator may be introduced which feeds on the seed, pest or fungal pathogen, the organism may be replaced by a less harmful race of its own species, or another species may be introduced to compete with it for living space. Such actions have to be undertaken with great care and maximum foresight; there is always the danger of converting a minor problem into a major one.

Although it is not often referred to under this heading, the greatest triumph in biological control is undoubtedly in the prevention of some important animal diseases by the use of vaccines. As plants do not produce antibodies, this technique is limited to veterinary problems. However, some successful attempts have been made to infect plants with a mild strain of virus to avoid later infection by a more damaging strain.

However attractive methods of biological control may be in theory (or wishful thinking), it must be realised that apart from the vaccination or inoculation treatments for some animal diseases, methods available for biological control are difficult to devise and to apply. There are few viral or bacterial diseases which can be introduced successfully into unwanted organisms without there being a risk of them spreading to nearby related organisms which are either harmless or perhaps even beneficial. Even if the introduction can be achieved without doing more harm than good, the possibility of the emergence of a new resistant race nearly always exists. For example, although the myxomatosis virus caused a dramatic reduction in the crop-consuming rabbit population wherever it appeared or was introduced, there have now emerged races of rabbits which are immune to most forms of the virus in all such areas. Despite enormous casualties, the selfish gene has gained yet another victory.

As already explained, the balance between wanted and unwanted organisms in a given situation is usually very delicately poised, and is governed by a number of fluctuating environmental factors. The introduction of any new organisms into an ecological system may sometimes have spectacular results favourable to man, but this desired state of affairs is seldom permanent. The introduced pathogens or predators which are most successful in eliminating the unwanted organism become victims of their own efficiency, and are likely to disappear quickly afterwards as a result of death from starvation, and thus for continued protection they have to be replaced in subsequent years.

It is often difficult to build up the numbers of the introduced species quickly enough to prevent damage by the established, unwanted populations. In one pest problem, that of white fly in glasshouses and greenhouses, this difficulty was overcome by the uniform introduction throughout the crop of colonies of both white fly and its parasite, *Encarsia formaosa*, before a natural infestation by the pest had occurred.

In the open field it is even more difficult to control the distribution of introduced pathogenic organisms, and there is little or no control over the environmental factors which have the major determining influence on the final balance between new friends and old enemies. It therefore follows that this type of biological control is likely to be available in practice for only a limited number of problems, although for these it may be the cheapest and most effective solution. Nevertheless, it must not be forgotten that many attempts to introduce a predator to control a pest have only resulted in the predator becoming an even greater pest than the one it was supposed to control. Some of the fatal mistakes have been made with the best of intentions, an injustice of fate which is not confined to agriculture.

Physical and chemical strategies

If all other strategies fail, the farmer usually has to resort to physical control methods, unless he chooses to give up the struggle. Indeed, the farmer may in practice regard them as his first line of attack, partly because chemical remedies are widely advertised, readily available and easy to apply. There is also the physiological satisfaction in taking definitive action to combat an enemy rather than sitting back and relying on more passive means, even if the latter could be eventually more effective and economical.

As with other forms of defence, problems are usually more easily solved within buildings than in the open air, whether such structures are used for production or storage. If the buildings are reasonably airtight, fumigation is a possible and very effective technique for eliminating many unwanted organisms, although it may not be very selective. If highly toxic materials are used, it may be necessary to remove livestock or plants before carrying out the operation, but they then may be returned to a pest-free and disease-free environment.

In some plant problems, fumigants are available which are harmless to the commodity but can destroy the existing pests or pathogens, particularly when the plant is in its dormant stage as a seed or tuber. Within the confined space of glasshouses or growth chambers, it is possible to treat the soil by heating (although the rising energy costs may soon make this process uneconomic) or by the use of chemicals. Such treatment reduces the level of unwanted organisms in the soil before planting takes place.

Soil treatment in the open field, either by heat or by chemicals, in an attempt to control a wide range of problems simultaneously is seldom economic, except for small areas used to raise high-value products. An eradication policy is rarely feasible, but it may be successful if a newly introduced species can be destroyed before the individual unwanted weed plants produce seeds, or before pests develop a resistant stage. Chemicals can also be successfully employed to eradicate weed species which are confined to the upper layers of the soil. The total destruction of soil-borne pests is seldom an economic or practical possibility, and the process may easily harm beneficial species. It is very difficult indeed to eradicate soil-borne disease organisms.

There is much more scope for a prevention policy. Weeds may be allowed to grow and then be destroyed by chemicals before the crops are planted or before they emerge from the soil. Alternatively, the ground may be treated with chemicals which temporarily inhibit the germination or growth of weed species. Other chemicals may be applied to plants or animals so that the invading pests are killed when they come into contact with, or ingest, the protective matter. The disadvantage of preventive chemicals is that they tend to disappear with time or with exposure to rain, and as the host grows the dose is diluted so that newly produced tissues have little or no protection. One treatment a season is not always sufficient.

A curative chemical strategy is one which is most widely used in practice. There is now available a wide range of chemicals which are almost entirely harmless to hosts but lethal to one or more of the pests attacking farm animals. The pharmacopoeia of curative drugs available to the veterinarian is almost as large as that at the command of doctors dealing with human diseases, very rapid advances having taken place in this branch of medicine over the last half-century.

There are a number of selective weed killers which can kill certain weeds without injury to the surrounding crop. The choice of chemical materials for this type of application becomes very restricted if the crop and weeds are closely related botanically, or if they have similar physiological characteristics. An increasing number of spray materials are available to help halt the progress of disease on the leaves of a crop, but at the present stage there are but few systemic chemicals which can pass into plants and destroy a pathogen present within the host. The weakness of a curative treatment is that it may be applied too late; the dangers are those of over-application. When all else fails, read the instructions.

The use of any chemical therapy poses difficult questions. Races highly resistant to specific chemical remedies have emerged within the populations of certain unwanted organisms. Other effective chemicals may cause undesirable side-effects, either in the host to which they are applied or in other species of desirable plants or animals, including man, with which they come in contact. The choice of any chemical must depend on the answers to the following questions.

- Does it work for the purpose intended?
- If so, is it likely to induce resistance?
- If so, how quickly and what alternatives are available?
- Is it likely to cause damage to anything other than the target at which it is aimed?
- Is it cost-effective?

Assessment of losses

It is very difficult to give any form of precise figure for the losses caused by unwanted organisms, because it requires the solution of some very complex equations. The range and intensity of such organisms present each year and the potential damage each may cause are determined by a number of factors largely outside human control. The farmer may reduce the losses by the successful use of one or more of the control strategies outlined in the previous paragraphs.

Each cultivated plant and animal species is threatened every year by not one but a varying number of unwanted species. It is unlikely that all farmers or growers in an area, many of whom produce more than one commodity, will choose the same crop protection or curative programmes, or even if they do, they will not carry them out with equal efficiency. Thus losses will vary according to the spectrum and intensity of unwanted organisms present, to the cleverness with which the farmer selects his strategies to oppose them, and to the tactical skill with which he and his neighbours carry them out.

The final cost is the amount of crop loss occurring despite the efforts of man, plus the total bill for all the control measures employed, effective or not. The extent of the damage in terms of crop loss is often difficult or even impossible to measure exactly. Reasonable estimates can be made, using knowledge and experience of a particular commodity and the factors determining its yield, but such estimates are often nothing more than an intelligent guess. The conversion of such estimated losses into monetary value introduces further errors in any attempt at detailed costing.

The high level of success achieved by modern control measures poses a new problem of hidden losses caused by unnecessary actions. It is important to decide how long after the level of a particular weed, pest or disease has been depressed to insignificant levels should routine control measures continue to be applied. In some cases, skill in control is not matched by ability in assessing the need for continued treatment. There is a danger that what was once an urgent necessity may become, by virtue of its evident success, an expensive and relatively unnecessary habit.

The process of assessing the total cost of control measures is also complicated. In addition to the direct costs of labour and materials, there is also the expense of the research effort involved in discovering the means of treatment and in devising means and machinery to apply them. Some of this background effort is provided by commercial firms which sell the materials or equipment to the farmer, and so the cost is incorporated into the price of the products sold. Much of the research and development can have been carried out by scientists employed directly or indirectly by the central government at national research stations or universities. In addition, there is the cost of formulating, administering and putting into effect any national or international statutory crop or animal protection policy, so that part of the true cost is being borne by the tax payer.

It therefore follows that no exact figures are available to enable a precise statement to be made of all the costs incurred by measures aimed at defending the crop or animal against loss. The only reasonable certainty is that, as knowledge increases, the losses caused by unwanted organisms will continue to diminish if the correct actions are taken. It is equally certain that the costs of achieving this desirable state of affairs will continue to increase.

Part IV

The human factor

8

The interested parties

The climate and the soil set the scene for food production. The players are the biological organisms, both plant and animal, some of which are helpful and others harmful. The backers of the play and the hungry audience are human, and so is the man with the most difficult decision-making role of all, the producer in the person of the farmer or grower.

Although in the theatre an audience can make or mar a play with little or no concern for those involved in the production, the same is not true in the drama of food production. None of the interested parties can afford a succession of failures.

In fact, the consumer may be thought to have the final say through his demand for food and his choice of what he wants to eat and drink. With adequate food supplies this choice may be a free selection. If food is scarce, there may be no choice at all, but merely a demand for food to sustain life. The history of man is a constant struggle to meet this demand.

In recent decades some sections of the non-agricultural public have sought to play a more active role than that of a mere consumer, seeking a right to say what a farmer can or cannot do in this fight for food. Although some of the more vociferous among them handicap their cause with excess emotion and limited logic, their aims and intentions are basically commendable. The two most important facts are that any civilisation, unless on the verge of starvation, needs land for purposes other than food production, and also that as land is limited in extent, it must never be ill used or destroyed. Sadly, some of the worst mistakes have been made with the best of intentions, a combination not unknown in other walks of life.

World agriculture tends to be discussed in terms of high technology and low technology, but this is a simplistic classification. An inefficient high technology might be less productive in the long run than a skilled low technology. Even inefficient low technology might survive, if only because it has to, while a highly organised modern system of farming might slide into bankruptcy, possibly damaging the land potential in the process. It is possible to argue that greed has led to more soil erosion than need.

The change from subsistence agriculture (producing food only for the family or for the immediate neighbourhood) to agriculture for profit (designed to produce a surplus of food which could be sold at market and not merely bartered for other services) took place in most countries many centuries ago. Without this change there would have been no towns or cities and little opportunity for change towards a richer style of life for all, whether in country or in town.

There are still regions of the world today where subsistence farming is still the norm, and while it is true to say that much could be done to raise their standards of nutrition by the application of suitable scientific knowledge, the future of the large-scale production of food for consumption outside the area of origin must lie in the adoption of an efficient high technological system.

It is clearly easier to raise standards and attain higher yields in areas with favourable conditions of soil and climate than to improve production where the environment is unsuitable.

Coming to terms with the difficulties of life often involves the tackling of the easier problems first in preference to the more difficult ones, no matter how important the latter may be. The best hope for solving the world food problems is to make the maximum use of the suitable food-growing areas. This does not imply that nothing should be done to improve production in less suitable environments, but merely that it is important to retain a sense of proportion. With the bulk of the world population tending to live more and more in gigantic cities, and with apparently only China of the major countries being able to enforce a policy of restricted population growth, production for local surplus and distant consumption is essential for survival.

Attempts may be made to allocate priorities to world food problems, but a farmer has often little or no choice. He has to face his own particular problem whether it is easy or difficult. Many of his problems are not of his own making, and the solutions of some can be outside his own control; nevertheless, face them he must. It is very important that everyone should realise the complexities of the questions he must answer.

If a food-production problem is looked at from only one point of view, it is deceptively easy to propose a solution. If a theory, political or scientific, has deteriorated into the status of a dogma, then its believers are never at a loss to explain any event or to propose a remedy for any defect. They argue that if it fits the theory, then it must be true; the possibility that the theory may be in error or in urgent need of modification does not occur to them. If they have any doubts, they may find it wise not to voice them; men have been burnt at the stake for less.

In truth, there is as yet no theory which fits all the facts and provides all the answers; if there were, it would no longer be a theory but a complete explanation. It is difficult enough to explain the principles of physics, chemistry and biology which govern events in any ecosystem; it is far more difficult to understand human reactions to a series of events. It thus follows that the human factor is the most difficult to explain, and yet in theory it is the most controllable aspect of food production. Everything depends on who is at the controls, his powers, his motives and his ability, and, perhaps most of all, his awareness of the complexities of the situation and his willingness to admit an error and to apply any necessary adjustments.

In an attempt to throw some light on these complexities, the following chapters will deal first with the help that can be expected from science and technology, including an attempt to outline their limitations. Attention will then be drawn to human problems on the farm itself and a discussion of the many important political, social and economic problems which affect food production, and the possibilities of improvement.

Dean Swift, author of *Gulliver's Travels*, has often been quoted in this context, but his words will bear repetition.

He gave it for his opinion, that whoever could make two ears of corn or two blades of grass grow upon a spot where only one grew before, would deserve better of mankind, and do more essential service to his country than the whole race of politicians put together.

9

Technological progress

An example of technological progress is the amazing success story of
the transformation of British agriculture from a depressed industry to
one of the most efficient in the country in the space of less than 50
years. By any method of calculation, the total output and productivity
have continually improved in spite of a diminishing labour force.
Furthermore, this technological evolution has been achieved without
strikes or industrial unrest.

Similar far-reaching changes have taken place in many other parts
of the world, such as north-west Europe, North America, Australia
and New Zealand. A complete history of such changes and details of
all the innovations which have been introduced would fill several
large volumes. It is sufficient in this context to summarise the broad
influences of the main factors involved. They can be conveniently
grouped under three headings: mechanical, chemical, and biological.
The biological progress, providing the food producer with better
genetic material, has already been discussed in Chapter 5.

Mechanical factors

On arable farms, the most important single factor was undoubtedly
the introduction of the powered tractor. This machine provided a
compact, efficient, mobile power unit, the smallest example of which
could be afforded by even the poorer farmers. Use of this machine
enabled a wide range of essential farm operations to be carried out
more quickly than they could have been using horses or other draught
animals.

This increased speed of operations reduced the number of men
required to carry them out, and the increased power enabled arable
farming to be extended to land previously regarded as unsuitable for
such crops, or in climates that imposed restrictions on the time
available for cultivations. Land had no longer to be set aside to
provide fodder and grazing for draught animals, so that effectively the
farm grew in productive area.

Probably the next most important innovation was the development
of harvesting equipment. The bringing in of the final agricultural

product was often the critical point in almost all farming systems. Even on a dairy farm, the size of the herd was largely determined by the number of skilled hands available twice daily to carry out the hand milking. The harvesting of cereals, grass, potatoes and root crops involved slow, wearisome operations which, on most farms, could only be carried out by employing extra casual labour, if and when available.

The introduction of the mechanical cutter and binder for cereals (so that the sickle and scythe virtually became museum pieces) was a great step forward in reducing the number of additional hands urgently needed at harvest, but the real major improvement was the development of the combine harvester. This machine has transformed the agricultural picture in all the major grain-producing areas of the world. A modern fleet of giant combines on their yearly northward progress through the American states would have astonished previous generations.

The disappearance from the late summer fields of stooked corn, ricks and itinerant threshing machines may be regretted by the 'country lover' or landscape artist, but not by the men and women who had to endure the long hours of tiring work. Nowadays, the use of machines can complete in days a process which used to occupy a team of men and horses for up to several weeks – weeks which might extend into months if the weather were unkind.

Harvesting methods have improved for many other crops. Hop-picking machines have brought to an end the large-scale traditional migrations of pickers to the hop gardens in the autumn. Similarly, the pea-viner has ended the need for gangs of pea pickers. Almost all the sugar beet crop and much of the potatoes are now lifted by machine, although in the latter case soil and weather conditions still impose limitations. Machines have not as yet been perfected for the full mechanical harvesting of fruits and most brassica crops, though some are in commercial operation to remove brussel sprouts from their stems and grade them for market. Grapes for wine are still harvested by hand. Mechanical harvesting has not in all cases reduced the cost of harvest, but the important contribution to progress is that it has greatly increased the chances of successful food production.

Many modern farmers thus no longer need additional casual labour to help them with the annual harvesting crisis, but the introduction of machines to the farm has brought other important consequences. The development of more efficient, specialised machinery for cultivating the soil, subsoiling, laying of drains, sowing of seeds, protecting the crop against weeds, pests and diseases and other necessary farming operations has led to production systems for some commodities in which extensive hand labour is no longer required. The modern arable farmer is less dependent on casual labour, but he needs a small permanent, highly skilled workforce. This has resulted in fewer chances of employment in rural areas, but has increased employment in factories producing the machines.

It is more difficult to achieve the successful complete mechanisation of a livestock farm. The major change has been the development of milking machines enabling the herdsman to tend a greater number of cows. The harvesting of fodder crops has also been improved, mechanised systems for the feeding of stock have reduced the labour requirements for pig, poultry and dairy producers, especially when the stock are housed in specially designed buildings.

Possibly the greatest problem in animal production systems is the disposal of excreta, and the more intensive the system, the more difficult does the problem become. For many livestock farmers there is no completely satisfactory solution, although improved mechanical methods for handling, distributing and even recycling this unwanted by-product have helped to alleviate the problem, which can involve hygiene hazards which are potentially serious to both animals and human beings. Future years may see considerable improvement in this state of affairs, and yesterday's waste may become tomorrow's asset.

The mechanical revolution in farming has produced two other less obvious but nevertheless important benefits. The easier and quicker transport of men to and from their work and within the farm boundaries has greatly reduced the total of unproductive time. The ploughman does less plodding and the shepherd less upland tramping; both expect to be able to use a powered vehicle on two or four wheels to take them to their scene of operation. A less desirable side-effect of the easy transport of materials is that farms no longer carry a large stock of consumable goods to last through the winter season; this can be a mistake if the transport facilities on which they rely are interrupted for any reason.

The other time-saving innovation has been the introduction of efficient equipment for the handling and moving of heavy and awkward loads. Conveyors and fork-lifts have not removed all the back-breaking toil from farming, but they have helped the worker to cope more quickly, safely and efficiently with many hard tasks which previously relied on muscle power.

Mechanisation has helped to bring about a remarkable increase in the output of food per unit area of farmland and of food per worker, but progress such as this is not achieved without paying a price. Machines require fuel, usually in the form of oil or electricity. The more that a farmer relies on machines, then the more is he at the mercy of these supplies and the suppliers of such forms of energy. He has to pay the price demanded, and even a short disruption of supply can be catastrophic. No wonder then that older farmers, at times of a fuel crisis, sigh for the days when horses were fed on the farm and when mills and pumps were driven by on-site wind or water power which made them relatively independent of the failings of others.

The reduction in the number of farm employees may, and usually does, make the problem of man management more difficult rather than more simple. When the farmer had a large labour force, he could allocate men to tasks for which they had a particular skill or aptitude. Nowadays, the few men still employed on a farm have to possess the skills to operate all the machines needed to complete the work programme. When a farmer employed ten men, if one was temporarily absent, the remaining nine could and did carry out the essential tasks, even if overtime was involved. Where the labour force has now been reduced to one or two, accident or illness can precipitate an immediate crisis which is not easily resolved. The eight or nine men previously working on the farm are no longer living in the vicinity waiting for such an emergency. They have probably left for the towns to make the machines which now lie idle for the want of the absent operator.

Machines do not last for ever, nor do they (unlike horses) reproduce their own replacements. They have to be constantly maintained, and sooner or later have to be replaced at an ever-increasing cost. A farmer of today is likely to have to pay more for a single combine harvester than his father did for the whole of his farm, and that for a machine which is only in use for part of the year. Thus the profits which the introduction of the new mechanised methods make possible have to be large enough to provide for the upkeep, repair and replacement of the machines which are now indispensable.

As machines take over more and more complex operations and are required to carry them out with increasing precision, they inevitably become more intricate. Consequently, the costs of developing and maintaining them also escalate. The old idea of 'If it does not work, kick it' is no longer a practical solution, even if it does relieve frustration. The increasing background fear is that of diminishing supplies of hydrocarbon fuels to power the machines or generate the electricity. It was relatively easy, given the money and the will to do so, to change from animal power to machine power; the reverse process, if it ever becomes necessary, could be a far more difficult process.

In previous discussions of the influence of unwanted biological organisms in agriculture, the increasing importance of chemical control has already been mentioned. The introduction of such controls over large areas demanded the invention of special equipment and machines, including aircraft, to ensure correct applications. A gardener can spray his plants by hand; a farmer has a somewhat larger problem to face.

Chemical factors

The chemical control of pests, diseases and weeds has had a significant effect in raising productivity, but it is not the only role that
chemicals play in enhancing farm output. All plants and animals are
composed of complex chemicals, and one of the great advances in
modern agriculture is due to our increasing knowledge of how to
supply the ingredients which make up these compounds, in other
words, how to promote rapid healthy growth.

All green plants have the unique ability of synthesising their own
carbohydrates from atmospheric carbon dioxide, but they also need
to be supplied with sufficient quantities of nitrogen, phosphorus and
potassium, as well as minor amounts of elements such as calcium,
iron, magnesium, manganese, copper and boron. With the exception
of the few plant species capable of utilising nitrogen from the air, all
these chemicals have to be taken up through the soil.

Thanks to the advances made in agricultural chemistry during the
last century, this uptake is no longer a matter of chance or reliance on
a system of crop rotation. The necessary quantity and quality of the
kind of nutrients required are known for almost all crop plants.
Modern methods of soil and plant analysis provide the information
needed to be able to supply these nutrients in near-optimal amounts.
It is also possible to detect any dangerous imbalance of soil chemicals
and to identify the presence of toxic materials, so that it is possible to
take remedial action, or at least avoid growing the species most
susceptible to injury. Crop nutrition and soil fertilisation are now
based on knowledge and measurement rather than informed guess-
work, with a marked benefit to the size and consistency of yields.

Although many such plant problems have been solved, the problems of animal nutrition are more complex and more difficult to solve
with the same degree of precision. Animals eat a complicated mixture
of chemicals, carbohydrates, fats and proteins, as well as vitamins
and other minor components. The conversion of these substances into
consumable products such as meat or milk is much more involved
than the relatively simple process of synthesis in plants. Consequently, the analysis of animal feedstuffs and the relation of the
results to the production of diets suitable for maximum output are
more difficult than prescribing plant fertiliser requirements. The
planning of the quality of animal food is even more complicated if the
stock are free grazing.

Nevertheless, considerable progress has been made in devising
balanced rations for livestock, and this has led to improved performance and avoidance of serious losses due to deficiencies or excesses in
their diet. On most modern livestock farms the diet of the farm
animals receives more thought and attention, and is probably nearer

the optimum, than does the food consumed by an ordinary human household.

A minor use of chemicals, which is important in the production of some commodities, is for the regulation of growth processes. Examples of this type of usage include the stimulation of rooting by the application of hormones to vegetatively propagated plants, the prevention of the premature fall of fruits, the shortening and strengthening of the stems of cereals to prevent lodging, the treatment of animal and plant products to increase their storage life, and the enhancing of the food-conversion efficiency of livestock. As knowledge of the biochemical process which take place in plants and animals increases, so will the opportunities to influence such processes to man's advantage. It may, however, always be easier to increase the quantity of production rather than the quality.

Coordination of improvements

Although for convenience the several technological factors have been grouped under separate headings, no such distinction exists in practice. Developments under two, or even three, headings may occur simultaneously, and interactions between them are common. The introduction of new strains of plants or animals with a potential for greater output may demand a reappraisal of their nutritional needs if that potential is to be fully realised. The much-praised 'green revolution' is a case in point. Improved knowledge of the precise chemical requirements for either nutritional or prophylactic purposes is of little value without the means to deliver the right amounts to the right place at the right time. For example, the ability of spraying equipment to apply low volumes under field conditions at present lags behind the requirements of the producers of new chemicals, principally because the sprays are not accurate enough in their distribution of the materials on the crop.

It is important that all advances are kept in step. Frequently there is a type of 'Which came first, the chicken or the egg?' situation. It might be thought that the development of new machines and techniques for bringing upland soils into cultivation provides the plant breeder with an opportunity to fill a new environmental gap, but it is equally possible that the breeding of a new hardier species suitable for upland growth spurs the engineer into developing methods of tilling the hitherto unploughed hill lands.

Technological progress in agriculture does not follow any deliberate logical pattern. The concept of clever scientists and engineers doggedly identifying successive limiting factors and then modifying each in turn would make an interesting film script, but it would be largely fictional. A deliberate plan of research or development resulting in the total or partial solution of specific practical problems has certainly played a part, but so have lessons learnt by experience in the slow process of trial and error, or even the exploitation of chance discoveries. The old joke 'I've just invented this, can you think of something to do with it?' is at times not far from the truth. At the other end of the spectrum, every farm, every year produces fresh evidence of what or what not to do, and all that may be missing is an intelligent person who can interpret such evidence for the benefit of others.

In the past, much of agricultural science has been concerned in the explanation of why what the farmer is doing is right or why certain methods failed to produce good results, rather than in trying to tell farmers how they should farm. This is in no way a denigration of the achievements of the scientists. An understanding of how and why farming processes do or do not work is often the initial step towards finding the means of making them better. It is all part of a process of sifting the evidence. An agricultural fact which does not fit in with previous ideas is often the one which is most important.

Every science progresses by a mixture of theory and experiment. Agricultural science has one great advantage in that experiments are taking place all the time in all parts of the world. These are not just the planned experiments of a research station which are carefully arranged to obtain the maximum information in the minimum time. They are the production records of every producer of food. Every farm in every country is, in effect, running its own experiments. The difficulties arise when attempts are made to learn from such experience. The first difficulty lies in obtaining adequate details of what has been done and what has been the result; the second difficulty is explaining why.

Advisory scientists are often only called in to collect such important details when major troubles occur; they have fewer opportunities to analyse the success stories of production. Despite this lack of balance in the evidence available to them, they still have an advantage over their colleagues who never leave the laboratory. If they are sufficiently curious and alert, they can at times, with a little bit of luck, pick up a valuable clue which could lead to the solution of another mystery. This in turn should lead to a series of controlled experiments to make sure that no false conclusions have been reached.

Future progress

Although the application of science and technology has led to a major upsurge in agricultural output in many countries, there is still no simple explanation of why there have been steady rates of improved production of almost all food commodities over the last 40 or 50 years. It is even more difficult to forecast with any degree of confidence whether this happy state of affairs will continue.

Basically, technological progress depends on the flow of new ideas and their successful utilisation on a wide scale. Providing that the new ideas continue to emerge with practical qualities and in sufficient quantity, and if farmers continue to be willing to adopt and exploit such ideas, there seems to be no obvious reason why this progress should not continue. There may be other reasons than the scientific ingenuity of man which will slow down this speed of progress, and these will be considered in a later chapter.

In the meantime, it would be well to try to retain a sense of proportion, and appreciate the opinions of two men who were wiser than most. The first should be a lesson to those who either place too much hope in new ideas or who have too much reverence for the old:

> Science is the great antidote to the poison of enthusiasm and superstition.

which was the view of Adam Smith, the Scottish economist. The second is the encouraging advice of Albert Einstein:

> The important thing is not to stop questioning; curiosity has its own reason for existing.

10

The farmer and the farm

Reading books or articles on agriculture, especially those written by pundits whose sense of self-importance outweighs other more desirable qualities, it might be thought that the reactions of farmers to changing circumstances are as uniform and predictable as the responses of a file of soldiers to the orders of a drill sergeant. However, in this, as in other complicated situations, the presumptive printed word bears but little relationship to the actual happenings in real life.

A typical farmer is just as much a mythical figure as the average man. The manifold variability of farmers' reactions to any given set of circumstances and the causes thereof would fill the pages of several volumes and would still leave many questions unanswered. No attempt will be made here to explore all the permutations possible, but only to indicate some of the main reasons for the divergent attitudes and consequent actions. These will be dealt with under five convenient headings:

- type of land tenure
- type of farming system
- size of farming business
- motivation
- training and education.

Type of land tenure

There can be a vast difference in outlook between the farmer who is an owner–occupier of his land and the tenant farmer. Apart from the obvious difference that the latter has to pay rent and the former does not, there are other important distinctions which affect policy decisions.

A rise in land prices provides the owner–occupier with an increment in the value of what is probably his most valuable asset. He may not be able to turn this into ready money unless he wishes to retire from farming, but it does provide an acceptable security on which additional capital can be raised to invest in his farm business or elsewhere.

To a tenant farmer, the rise in land prices poses a threat of increased rent, and the problem of having to raise even more money if he wishes to join the owner–occupier group. If land prices fall, the position is reversed; but in a world where inflation seems to be the norm and with good farmland an ever-diminishing commodity, this does not seem to be either a short- or long-term probability.

The ownership of land confers other benefits to the farmer. With security of occupation for himself, and (it is hoped) for his descendants, long-term planning is more attractive and potentially more remunerative than it is to a tenant. An owner is subject to very few restrictions on any changes he wishes to make in his farming activities. On the other side of the picture, a tenancy may impose very definite limitations as to what changes are allowed. Even if a landlord is agreeable to the introduction of drastic alterations in farming policy, a tenant may have far more difficulty than an owner–occupier in borrowing the necessary capital to put them into effect. A tenant also has to calculate the chances of recouping the value of any such investment made on someone else's property very carefully indeed. Thus the owner–occupier tends not only to have advantages from the capital value of his land, but also has greater freedom in the making of innovations.

This being said, it must be realised that it is not always a clear-cut, black-and-white situation; there can be various shades of intervening grey. Owners may have to, or may wish to, mortgage their land and so incur interest charges equivalent to a rent. Interest charges can change more rapidly than an agreed rental, and not always for the better. In mortgaging their land, they may have to accept as a condition of the loan certain limitations on their freedom of action. Not all tenancy agreements are unduly restrictive, and they can vary considerably in the degree of freedom allowed to the tenant. For example, some landlords in Worcestershire, England, have comparatively little control over market-garden land under customs prevailing in the Vale of Evesham. There, the tenants have the right to nominate their successors when they give up a tenancy, and they may negotiate with the new tenant a payment of 'in-going' to compensate them for the improvements they have made to the land. If the landlord wishes to take over the land himself, then he also has to pay the same 'in-going' to the previous tenant. At possibly the other extreme, tenants on the newly reclaimed polders in the Netherlands are both carefully selected in regard to their farming ability and also have to conform to very strict conditions concerning their use of the rented land.

There are also farmers who have a foot in both camps, and who own some of their land and rent the remainder. They have the opportunity of installing permanent buildings and other fixed equipment on their own land which are sufficient to serve their total acreage. In this way they have greater freedom and flexibility than the purely tenant farmer, but they have proportionately less capital locked up in land than the farmer who is entirely an owner–occupier.

The type and conditions of land tenure can exert a considerable influence on productivity. The tenant farmer may be under pressure to enhance his productivity in order to pay his ever-increasing rent. Paradoxically, the owner–occupier who is not driven by this incentive may have greater freedom in adopting innovations which will raise his efficiency. As indicated previously, this factor varies in intensity from farmer to farmer, and it is subject to further modifications by other factors which will be discussed later in this chapter.

Type of farming system

Farming should not be envisaged as a single industry; it is a conglomeration of different spheres of activity with a wide diversity of end-products, ranging from essential basic foods to expensive luxuries such as orchids or fruits grown under heated glass. Some of the products are highly perishable and have to be sold within one or two days, but others may be stored almost indefinitely.

The type of farming system is often largely determined by the climate, and in the temperate middle-latitude zones, there is a range of possible systems. They can be divided into: arable systems, in which the end-products are plants or the materials extracted from them; livestock systems, in which little plant material is sold off the farm and the main commodities providing income are animals and animal products; and, finally, mixed systems, with products from both the first two types.

A wide range of commercially viable plants can be grown in a temperate climate, but there is a vast difference between those which merely survive until harvest and those that attain the peak development which site and season permit. This difference is largely conditioned by the knowledge and experience of the farmer. The cultivation of each plant species requires its own special skill, which differs in many ways from that needed to cultivate other species. The same species may need different treatment to obtain the best results in different climates.

Farmers, like sportsmen, differ in their abilities. Some are extreme specialists, but others are all-rounders, and even the latter may be more adept at dealing with some crops than others. Generally speaking, plants which are closely related botanically require similar types of skill. The competent grower of winter wheat has little difficulty in dealing with the requirements of other cereal crops, and the expert apple grower can easily acquire the additional knowledge needed to grow pears, cherries or plums. Even so, any change, however small, implies a different set of problems and subtle changes in timing. Not everyone is capable of making a cropping change successfully, especially if it involves a major alteration in an annual programme.

A further complication to the problem is that the skill required varies both with the crop and also with the system within which it is produced. The farmer who changes from growing winter wheat alternating with grass breaks to the production of wheat in an arable rotation, or even to growing it continuously year after year on the same site, has to reconsider all his requirements and make considerable changes in his annual campaign. He has to think afresh about his choice of varieties, about the methods and especially the timing of cultivations, about fertilizer needs, and about the programme of control of pests, diseases and weeds.

Any system of crop rotation presents its own particular problems, varying in complexity from having only a single species to tend and harvest to the difficulties arising in having five, six, or even seven crop species in the system. A farmer's success thus depends not only on his knowledge of how to grow the crops of his choice, but also his ability to plan and manage his production system.

These difficulties are to some extent diminished in the cultivation of semi-permanent crops such as fruit orchards or hop gardens, but they tend to be replaced by another set of problems. Because the land is committed to the production of only one crop for many years in succession, it is all the more important that the fewest mistakes possible are made in its cultivation. There may be no alternative income.

The type of expertise neded for the successful growing of crops in the open field is totally different from that required for the cultivation of crops under temporary protective cover or in permanent structures such as glasshouses. It might be thought that the possibility of controlling the growing conditions makes the work easier, but in practice it demands the greatest accuracy and avoidance of error.

There is a belief, shared even by some farmers, that modern technology, and in particular the development of the so-called 'blue-print' systems of crop production, has taken away the need for the exercise of skill in the growing of plants and managing a cropping system. Surely, it is argued, all that is necessary is to follow the instructions. The falsity of this hypothesis is proved by the wide variation in results achieved by different growers using the same system and following the same recommendations. The 'blue-print' plans indeed give precise guidance on factors which must be studied and which direct the grower towards the correct procedures for improving yields but, like textbooks on the art of painting or playing a musical instrument, they cannot transform novices in masters in one easy lesson.

An example from a large glasshouse nursery will illustrate the truth of this. During the cropping season, the glasshouse was divided into bays of equal size, each under the charge of one particular man who was to be paid a bonus depending on the output of his bay. All the bays were subject to the same procedures for cleaning, soil sterilisation, and flooding with water, and they all received the same dressing of fertilizers. Plants, all of one variety, were raised in a central propagating department; heating and ventilating were automatically controlled. Yet, in spite of this uniformity, over a period of five years the same workman always achieved the highest output, even though he looked after a different bay each year. Moreover, his yield was almost double that from the bay with the poorest production which was under the charge of the latest recruit.

The livestock farm

There are fewer major options open to the livestock farmer because there are fewer species of economic importance. The choice is generally restricted to poultry, cattle, pigs and sheep, although in the harsher marginal climates goats, camels and reindeer are also tended on a farm scale. The farming system will depend a great deal on the nature of the chosen end-product.

For example, egg production is essentially a different industry from that designed to produce poultry meat for the table; the problems of milk production are not the same as those met with in the production of beef, although both are concerned with the same animal species. Whatever type of food production is chosen, it probably requires an even greater expertise than plant production, although the arable farmer might not agree. The grass always seems to be greener in the next meadow.

There seem to be two main reasons why the difficulties can be greater. First, the metabolism of animals is more complex than that of plants, and secondly, there is a greater variation in the performance of individual animals than in individual plants, even within a given species. Therefore, the design of a system to provide the best conditions for all stock is a matter of extreme difficulty, and the managing of such a system even more so. At the other end of the scale, it is possibly easier to run a livestock farm badly.

There is a wide distinction between intensive and extensive systems. In the former, the stock are under constant supervision and the food intake of individuals can be controlled; this is especially true where the animals are kept in buildings where there is an opportunity to control some environmental factors. In the extensive free-grazing systems, there is little opportunity to keep animals under constant observation, and each beast tries to satisfy its appetite from the available pasture or rough grazing.

The rates of reproduction of animals are slower than those of most plants, which can be multiplied rapidly either vegetatively or from seed, and thus it is usually more expensive to start or to expand a livestock enterprise. It also follows that it takes longer and is more costly to change from one animal variety to another. The on-site upgrading of stock quality can take a lifetime of dedicated effort.

There are three main types of livestock producer. First, there is the intensive producer who keeps his stock almost entirely within buildings; secondly, there is the system of extensive grazing of cattle or sheep, with meat or wool as the main end-product; thirdly, there is the dairy farmer who concentrates chiefly on milk production. Each type has its own special characteristics, requirements, climatic suitabilities and degrees of risk. Every system has its own set of problems, each with its own solution specific to the circumstances. There is no simple universal panacea.

Although there are some intensive beef producers who run systems based on the housing of stock, the major developments in buildings for animals have been concerned with pigs and poultry. Within specially designed buildings, it is possible to control environmental conditions to a large extent and in this way help to eliminate one of the major causes of variability in production.

With pigs and poultry, the reproductive cycle is comparatively short, so that a constant replacement of stock is possible at reasonable cost. The system also permits of the orderly marketing of a reliable output and a consequent steady flow of income. With a high degree of mechanisation, it is possible to keep down labour costs. However, like all highly mechanised systems of production, the capital costs are high and the running costs are liable to increase well beyond those originally estimated because of factors beyond the control of the farmer.

All intensive animal production systems have a special problem to which, as yet, there is no completely satisfactory solution. What is required is an easy and cheap method of disposing of the very large quantities of excreta produced by the housed stock. There is no simple way of getting rid of either the total amount or the odour that it emits. Attempts to convert it into energy in the form of gas, into fertilizer or even into animal food have so far promised more than they have accomplished. A further problem of these intensive systems is that they require regular large quantities of purchased feeding stuffs, unless they can be carefully integrated with a parallel arable system.

Extensive grazing systems have several operational advantages, although it must always be remembered that they are very much more at the mercy of the weather. They have a comparatively low capital requirement, apart from the initial purchase of breeding stock. There is little need for expensive buildings, with the possible exception of the provision of permanent or semi-permanent shelter during the lambing season, a practice which is gaining in favour as an insurance against weather losses. Less expensive land, often termed rough grazing, can be used for summer feed, but this practice is often a matter for careful consideration.

Although grass may survive and grow to a limited extent in an unfavourable environment, it responds quickly to more favourable conditions, and especially to the installation of efficient drainage and the application of suitable fertilizers. Under more extreme climatic and soil conditions, arable farming may well be impossible, and yet the extensive grazing of either cattle or sheep may provide the farmer with a living. Under better growing conditions and with better husbandry, the productivity of grazing systems increases, and then the problem arises as to whether it is possible to compete economically in milk production or a semi-arable system. A change to milk production might provide a regular income and increased profit, but will require more staff and more continuous attention, especially in regard to the necessity of complying with the stringent hygiene regulations.

The appreciable advantage of extensive grazing systems for meat production is the low labour requirements except for limited periods of the year such as lambing, dipping or shearing of sheep. As in all methods of farming, there are always both advantages and disadvantages, the problem being to strike a favourable balance in relation to the unavoidable constraints. In many upland areas or areas of low, unreliable rainfall, there is no alternative to an extensive, almost nomad grazing system.

Meat-producing animals, especially beef cattle, are slow to reach maturity so that the farmer has to wait a considerable time before he gets any financial return for his efforts. Moreover, once his stock are at the optimum state for marketing there is little alternative to selling them, whatever the state of the market. Dealers may make their living by buying cheap and selling dear, but this is no consolation to the producer. If such stock are not sold but retained on the farm, they continue to consume fodder and may lose quality, with a consequent drop in value.

To provide a supply of animals for slaughter to match the needs of the market both in timing and in quality demands considerable husbandry skill, and not a little luck. It is true that meat can be frozen and held in cold store if there is a surplus on the market, but this adds to the expense, and if it happens after the farmer has sold the produce, he does not share in any possible benefit. It is well nigh impossible to control the exact supply of animals for market when they come from a large number of separate farms. There are thus bound to be periods of temporary glut and temporary shortage; the pig industry in particular seems to suffer from this kind of variability.

Milk production

The range of problems associated with milk production is entirely different from that of beef production in many ways. Some producers depend largely, or even entirely, on bought-in feeding stuffs to provide their cows with energy to produce milk. At the other extreme is the farmer who relies on the grass grown on his own farm (either as grazing or as conserved hay or silage) to provide as much as possible of the fodder required by his stock. In between these two extremes there are others using every possible combination of grass and supplementary foodstuffs. Each farmer, whatever his system, has his problems, which vary in incidence and intensity according to his situation and the prevailing circumstances. There is no common answer.

There may not be a common answer, but each dairy farmer has a common objective, namely that the value of the milk per cow should exceed by the greatest possible margin the cost of the food consumed plus the cost of skilled attention. To achieve this needs a subtle blending of scientific knowledge and an understanding of the individual peculiarities of each of the animals involved or, in other words, a marriage of reason and experience. No matter how carefully bred, each cow, like its handler or its owner, has its own potential level of achievement which may or may not be attained. Much can depend on the skill and handling care of the milking staff. Machines may have speeded up the milking process but they have not replaced the need for individual care and attention, and in fact they may have made it more important.

Milk production also requires special buildings and equipment to ensure that the milk is produced and stored in suitably hygienic conditions until it leaves the farm. The standards of hygiene required are legally enforceable in most countries, and a failure to comply with them may result in the withdrawal of the farmer's licence to produce, or at very least deny him a marketing outlet. Very little milk is now sold at the farm gate or delivered daily by the farmer to local customers. The dairy farmer is thus very dependent on the efficiency of the organisation collecting his daily production.

For some, the main attraction of dairy farming is the regular and largely predictable amount of income, often paid monthly, which is something of a rarity in the farming industry. The main disadvantage is that the cows have to be milked twice every single day of the lactation period. Machines have made the process easier in terms of manpower, but someone always has to be present to operate them.

It is customary to regard the beef industry and the dairy industry as separate entities, but in recent years in Britain there has been a large increase in the production of beef on the dairy farms. This is partly due to the increasing economic pressure on small dairy farmers, forcing them to turn to another source of income, and has been made a practical proposition by the introduction of new cattle breeds from France. The Charollais and Simmental bulls have been found suitable for the siring of calves with a capability of high live-weight gains and lean carcases which are acceptable to the butchers and the public.

MIXED FARMING

If it is accepted that man is not normally a herbivore and is likely in the foreseeable future to demand his meat, milk and eggs, then a mixed farming system combining arable and livestock farming would appear to be the best response to his needs. Those that would maintain that all human food should be grown in the form of crops, and not be processed inefficiently through the animal to produce milk and meat, tend to forget the important fact that certain environments are only suitable for the growth of grass, and humans, as yet, have not learnt to appreciate grass as an unprocessed food.

Mixed farming has certain advantages from the point of view of the farmer. The animal excreta which are such a serious embarrassment to the intensive livestock specialist can be distributed over the arable area, improving the soil and causing little offence to the community. This addition of animal manure to the soil provides some of the plant nutrients which the wholly arable farmer has to purchase in other forms. Its incorporation with straw previously used as bedding or floor litter, and subsequent ploughing into the soil still remains the most effective and economic means of maintaining or improving the essential fibrous structure of many soils, giving an example of recycling at its best.

Depending on which types of crop are grown, the mixed farmer often has the choice of selling some of his arable products for cash or converting them into animal products. He can thus take advantage of the prevailing circumstances in a manner denied to the purely arable farmer. The mixed farmer is also less dependent on the selling price of any one particular commodity because he is able to sell a diversity of products. Furthermore, he is less dependent on the nature of the seasons. Whatever the weather, one section of his enterprise is likely to find it favourable.

To be successful, any mixed farming enterprise requires that there should be available on the one farm all the diverse skills needed for each of the arable and livestock projects involved. Even if all such expertise is available, problems can arise in its application. There can be unavoidable conflicts in the demands of the animals or the crops for the available time and labour. Priority has to be given to the needs of livestock at such critical times as birth, sickness, feeding and milking, even if this causes the postponement of arable operations beyond the optimum time for the best results. Mixed farming thus requires an extra level of management skill above that demanded by either wholly livestock or wholly arable systems.

The size of a farm business

The size of a farm business may not be directly related to the area of the farm; a small area of heated glasshouses may be the working site of a bigger business project than a relatively unproductive upland farm covering many times the area of the glass. A better measure of business size is the amount of capital invested and the annual turnover. Even on this basis, the size of the business is not synonymous with either efficiency or productivity.

Although some economists may point out the advantages of economy of scale, the figures others publish do little to prove the invariable truth of such a hypothesis. Comparisons of production per unit of land, or per unit of stock, for the same commodities show surprisingly little difference between the large and small farms.

Such comparisons may not always be completely valid. Most of the data are obtained from surveys carried out by the agricultural economics departments of universities. The staff involved are highly competent in the making of such surveys, knowing exactly what questions to ask, but it is often not possible for them to obtain figures from a completely random selection of farms, so that it is difficult to compare like with like. The farmer who is approached has to be willing to cooperate and also be able to provide the necessary, properly recorded, data. The least able farmers with few or no staff may not have the time or the ability to provide the necessary accurate information. On the other hand, almost all large farm businesses keep comprehensive records compiled by trained staff. Thus the surveys of the relation of efficiency to size may tend to compare the best of the small establishments with a more random sample of the larger ones, likely to provide an answer nearer to the average for the 'large' class.

Another difficulty in any analysis of performances of farms with large differences in size is that comparisons are being attempted amongst farmers who are doing fundamentally different types of work. The success of the one-man business, employing no staff, depends on the skill of the individual. Once the business is large enough to employ additional labour, then the farmer needs not only skill in husbandry, but also the ability to select and organise his other workers efficiently. Still further up in the scale of size there is the farmer who does little or no physical labour himself, but is entirely engaged in the direction of operations and in organising a paid workforce. Although obviously he must have a technical knowledge of the system he operates, his success is greatly dependent upon his skill in picking the right men for the work, organising the farm programme, controlling the financial aspects, and selecting the best farming strategy to match the needs and opportunities of the moment.

By means of what has been termed the 'farming ladder', it is theoretically possible for a farmer to progress from one end of the scale to the other, from a one-man farm to a large farming enterprise. In practice, as in other types of business, the transition from craftsman to manager represents a formidable barrier to expansion. The most skilful technician is not always capable of organising others to match his proficiency, and the best organiser cannot always induce his staff to reach the same level of output as an individual working for himself.

Indeed, one of the many difficulties in making financial comparisons between a one-man farm and larger organisations is that the former can involve a considerable amount of unrecorded and often unnoticed overtime, work that is done by the farmer or his unpaid family. Although it is thus not easy to quantify the effect of size, it must be realised that such factors do have an influence on the role of the farmer and the productivity of the farm. Perhaps the most important criterion of all is that the several abilities of the farmer and the size of farm must be compatible.

Motivation

The motives that prompt men to farm are undoubtedly important in the determination of levels of productivity, but it is difficult, if not impossible, to assess them accurately. The somewhat sentimental myth that farming is not a business but a way of life has long been exploded, only to be replaced by the more cynical but equally false generalisation that all farmers have the sole aim of achieving the greatest profit.

There are a fortunate few who derive their main income from sources outside farming. They are able to farm in a more relaxed manner, in the nature of a hobby, and in so doing can enjoy the capital appreciation of the land they own. Such farmers often put more into the land than they take out, so that there is a long-term gain in farm potential in the improvements in soil fertility and additional modern farm equipment and buildings. Other so-called 'hobby farmers' may prefer to make as much money as possible in their second profession, but in any case the total numbers involved are too few to have a significant effect on the industry as a whole.

There are other part-time farmers who opt for this style of living because their farm is too small or the land too poor to provide them with an adequate income. In some situations, this may well be a sensible solution to the problems of land use. It also may be an important part of the lower rungs of the 'farming ladder', enabling a man to start in farming with a relatively small amount of capital.

Most farmers, however, depend entirely on their farm income, so that the profit motive is often the dominant one. This is particularly true of the smaller farms where sheer survival may depend on achieving the maximum profitability. Higher up the farming scale, the quality of life may become more important than the highest possible income.

For those who wish to spend their life in something other than endless work, amenities such as pleasant surroundings or sporting facilities may be created, conserved or extended within the farm, even though this use of land may reduce the profit margin. The leisure time taken to enjoy these facilities may further erode the maximum productivity.

It is not unknown for a successful farmer to reject an expensive consultant's report showing how he could increase his profits, not because he distrusts the reasoning or finds the proposed plans impracticable, but because to carry them out he would have to curtail his leisure activities such as hunting, fishing or shooting, and have less time to spend with his family and friends. Every aim in life, major or minor, is worth so much time and trouble and no more. A large bank balance is a poor compensation for an early heart attack.

During a working lifetime the motivation of the farmer may change more than once. At different stages, the needs to build up his business, to bring up a family, to provide additional capital to expand his holding or acquire farms for his offspring, may each spur him to attain maximum profitability. When such pressures do not apply, he may be more concerned with improving amenities, increasing his leisure facilities, or adding to the capital value of his farm.

Two powerful factors which cannot be ignored are pride and ambition. These may manifest themselves in many ways, one of which is the desire to attain a high level of success for the pleasure of personal satisfaction. This may not always lead to large profits, because there are some farmers who so enjoy producing certain commodities that they will not abandon them for more lucrative enterprises.

Another motive is the love of competition and the desire to be seen to be better than other farmers. The goal is to produce the earliest, the largest, the most handsome or the most prestigious (in its modern sense) of their chosen commodity on a local, national or even international scale. This again may be highly profitable, but it is all too possible to achieve success at the expense of extravagantly high inputs with a consequent lower productivity.

A third type of ambition is to build up bigger and bigger 'farming empires', but this again is not always synonymous with seeking, or even attaining, maximum profit. Acquisitive skill is a different talent from that required to ensure the highest day-to-day efficiency in running the enlarged enterprise. Farming empires have much in common with political empires: few are endowed with the special talents and meet with the opportunities to build them, even fewer are blessed with the wisdom to maintain them, and very few indeed are fortunate enough to have equally gifted heirs to succeed them. The old adage 'Three generations, clogs to clogs' is often sadly true in agriculture, as in the cotton industry where the saying originated.

The influence of the farmer thus involves a number of different factors, all of which interact with the others in ways which are not easy to identify, define or explain, let alone quantify or put in numerical form. Such influences are worthy of more careful study than they usually receive, because it is the farmers who ultimately decide what commodities are produced, and productivity is closely related to the skill and determination with which they implement their decisions. This skill may be learnt by hard experience, often dearly bought, or it may also depend on their initial training; facts acquired in youth often last a lifetime.

Training and education

There is a very wide variation in the quantity and quality of training and education which farmers and farm workers receive, and this can be an important factor in determining the future performances of an industry which is becoming more and more technological and scientific in its methods. Stupidity and ignorance have no place in work where small mistakes can incur large penalties.

At one end of the scale are farmers with high honours degrees in science or agriculture awarded by the most ancient and revered universities. Others may have graduated from modern universities with a more practical bias and well equipped with experimental farms and other agricultural facilities. Some, after following whole or part-time courses, have diplomas from specialist agricultural schools or colleges.

In addition to this wide range of formal educational opportunities there are still lessons to be learnt from hard experience. Indeed, there are many farmers who have received little or no special training after they left school and possess only such degrees as are awarded by the university of life, and in some countries they are in an outstanding majority. Nevertheless, the outstanding alumni from this exacting school of harsh reality seem able to compete successfully on many occasions with the graduates from the most learned establishments.

This does not imply that a sound appreciation of the principles of agricultural sciences and the practices of modern farming is unnecessary. The source from which such knowledge is gained is perhaps less important than the opportunity for the learner to understand the necessity of three other qualities which can be of the greatest help in the struggle towards improvement.

First, whatever the mode of education or its academic level, it must not only provide reliable basic facts, but it must also inspire the student to think for himself and encourage him to continue to pursue the search for knowledge throughout the rest of his life. The mere teaching of facts may develop the memory, but it tends to close the mind. Secondly, the novice must learn how to exercise judgement in the selection of information and how to use it to his best advantage in any given set of circumstances. The third quality is the art of timing and knowing when to apply the knowledge. This can be difficult and could be thought of as more of an inherent ability than an acquired skill, although one might hope that at least some lessons could be learnt from experience.

Some people never seem to learn; others, with more imagination or less caution (or both), jump at every new idea as it comes along. It is very difficult to steer a sensible course between rigid practice canonised by tradition and volatile innovation. What appears to be dogged courage in adversity may only be pig-headed stupidity, but rapid acceptance of new ideas can indicate either sharp perception or sheer gullibility. Youth, they say, is the time for ideas, judgement comes with age, and there is little hope of progress in any walk of life without the help of both mental exercises.

A farmer should also be aware of the limited extent of his knowledge. No responsible scientist will stray beyond the boundaries of his own field of understanding; no sensible farmer will assume that he knows everything about all branches of agriculture. In other words, the realisation of what he does not know is just as important as the utilisation of what he does know.

There is a great deal of truth in the old saying that the difference between a good farmer and bad farmer is only a fortnight. With modern requirements for speed and accuracy, this could be updated by reducing the time differential to a few days or even hours. The instinct for precise timing is as essential to the first-class farmer as it is to the first-class exponent of any sport if he is to reap the full reward for his work, skill and techniques.

Much of modern applied agricultural research is devoted to establishing reliable scientific aids to help farmers in this critical question of the timing of operations. This factor is of particular importance in sowing and harvesting, and in the attempts to control the adverse effects of weeds, pests and diseases. With correct timing, less money is wasted and better yields are made possible.

The differences in the extents of skill and knowledge, and the variations in individual judgements as to how, when and where to apply them, will always lead to a wide range of performance among farmers, even among those experiencing similar growing conditions. These differences are likely to persist unless we arrive at a brave new world when, through the control of human genes, the breeding of farmers is a state-controlled monopoly – a consummation devoutly to be feared.

Finally, there are two serious limitations which must be kept firmly in mind: namely, the limitation of the extent of current knowledge, and the difficulties which are encountered in the application of such, as yet limited, knowledge to farming practice. Even if these limitations are to some extent removed, there still remain the problems of how to do the necessary work.

11

Knowledge

All is not yet known, and it is a wise man who is aware of the limitations of his own knowledge; it is only the ignorant and the arrogant who think they know everything. Unjustified over-confidence is often the passport to disaster, especially when facing an intricate problem in uncertain circumstances.

Admittedly, a great deal is at least partially known about the complex soil–plant–atmosphere ecosystem which helps the emergence of new methods to increase food production, but many details are still missing. Indeed, what we now think we know may in the future prove to be wrong, as the forward progress of science has always trembled on the brink of error. Those prone to dramatic phrases, prompted by ignorance or a desire to impress, are liable to speak or write of a 'breakthrough', or use some other similar exaggerated phrase. Events rarely justify such a hyperbole, or, even if they do, they are not often recognised as such until long after the time of occurrence. Major advances in science are few and infrequent, demanding from their progenitor immense personal integrity and more than the usual amount of talent equivalent to a touch of genius; lesser mortals are content with more modest contributions to our store of knowledge.

Advances in science are usually made at a slow pace, stumbling from point to point in a fog of ignorance and previous error, exploring all too many blind alleys in the process. The one sustaining hope of many research workers is that the light at the end of the tunnel is really a glimpse of the truth, and not merely a train coming in the opposite direction. All research work is an act of faith, and the least the rest of the world can do is to have faith in those who are attempting the most difficult of tasks.

If science is to be put to use for the good of the many, and not merely remain a mental exercise for the few, it must be applied to solve practical problems. This again is a slow process, holding on to what is good from the past and adding to it anything that proves to be better. In agriculture and food production, the natural cycle of plant and animal growth allows for one testing period per growing season, so that even the best of new ideas cannot take hold of an industry overnight.

The pace of past progress

Over the centuries, knowledge in agriculture was gained very slowly indeed, profiting only by a painful process of trial and error. In the earliest stages, the penalty of error was starvation or death, and the survival of the fittest was a ruthless fact, not an abstract thought or an evolutionary principle. A further limitation to any skill born of experience was that it had to be heavily biased on the side of safety, because none could afford the risk of failure. This inhibited progress, being a good recipe for the continued existence of a peasant community but offering little chance for any rapid improvement.

The small farmer is better off than the peasant: he has more land, his methods are generally sound and usually successful, but he still has little chance to make any major change with a view to improvement. It is only the emergence of social conditions which create the large landowner that brings about a significant increase in the pace of progress. For example, it was mainly because the abbeys and monasteries took control over large areas of land after the Norman Conquest that sheep farming prospered in areas such as the Yorkshire Dales in northern England; the emergence of quality wine production in France and Germany owes much to the influence of rich religious establishments. The great landowners of the 18th century in England were the ones who introduced new farming methods and improved the quality of their farm stock because they had the time, the ability, and above all the money to do so. They succeeded because they could afford to fail; a complete crop failure in one field means little to a rich man, but is a disaster to a poor one.

The advent of science

The 19th century saw the real beginnings of modern agricultural science, especially in Europe and North America. The professional often follows hard on the heels of the amateur, and finally surpasses him It was the heyday of the natural historians, intelligent people with no urgent need to make money, time on their hands and an awakening interest in the world of plants and animals. Although many of them came to be known as 'closet naturalists' because they devoted all their time, interest and energy to the discovery and classification of their beloved specimens, there were others who took the next steps along the rocky road to knowledge by trying to find out how and why biological events took place.

This period saw the emergence of many modern branches of science, even though it took a long time for some of them to become established. With the work of Mendel, the science of genetics was born, despite stern religious opposition; the true causes of many plant diseases began to be understood in the face of stubborn disbelief, and in many ways new avenues of approach were opened up on the road towards increased food production. The scientists of today owe a great deal to their predecessors, who, often self-taught, thought about the underlying biological processes, had the courage and ability to question existing theories, and who published their findings as the first shots in the long hard fight by scientific thought against the errors of the past and against customs that had long outlived their usefulness.

Progress in science is never easy because the subject is far too difficult. As Gilbert White pointed out some 200 years ago, 'It is much easier to compile than to make fresh remarks'. Leading 'authorities', in their old age, tend to become more sensitive to any implied criticism of their pet theories and may attempt to refute them by the weight of their reputation rather than by any logical reasoning. Interference by political or religious bodies, believing that to allow change will admit weakness, can often bring tragic results, or at very least retard the emergence of a new truth.

Moreover, progress in basic knowledge does not immediately lead to improvements in general husbandry and consequent increased food production. This is frustrating to the farmer, who often needs help concerning urgent problems. He cannot wait patiently for the results of another ten years of research, he has to do something quickly if he is faced with a difficult set of circumstances. In other words, he demands the least improbable answer based on the present inadequate knowledge, even though it may have to be based on limited and often conflicting evidence.

The application of science

The 'applied' scientist realises the urgency of the situation and the reasons for such demands. In a way, he too is an impatient man, following the Newtonian doctrine of dealing with small matters with a degree of certainty and leaving the remainder to others who come after. The 'pure' scientist in his laboratory or at his desk, searching for the elusive truth, has to have more patience, and if at first he does not succeed, he must keep on trying. His counterpart trying to solve field problems is more likely to adopt the attitude 'give up, there is no point in making a fool of yourself' because he probably has a host of other problems awaiting his attention, some of which might not be so stubborn. He also is able to accept a less than perfect solution provided that it is better than anything that has gone before. A conclusion is reached when thinking stops.

To emphasise still further the difficulty of practical scientific progress, it should be realised that any conclusion based on experiment alone can only be as good as the accuracy of the data and the range of experimental conditions permit. Moreover, small-scale trials cannot easily or accurately be translated into the larger scale of farm production. Pot trials with the dimensions of centimetres or plot trials with the dimensions of metres do not exactly represent field conditions, where kilometres are the unit of length. The scales are different, the climatic conditions are different, and results and methods which are successful on a small scale cannot instantly be applied to large-scale operations with complete confidence.

There seems to be no sensible alternative to beginning on a small scale and then extending the trials as experience and confidence grow. Farmers may be excused for doubting the value of new ideas and for preferring to retain their old and tried varieties and methods, but the most successful among them are those who adopt the new improvements when they are convinced that they have shown sufficient promise and reliability, a combination of caution and courage which is difficult to achieve. The farmer who never made a hot rick never made good hay.

Collaboration in science

It is often thought that the most useful progress is made in the centre of activity of one particular branch of science, but this is not always true in complex problems. The scientific investigation of farming activities involves a number of sciences, and some of the most helpful discoveries in regard to practical problems have arisen on the fringe of one science where it overlaps with another scientific discipline. Two heads are better than one; they can produce two sets of ideas which, when married together, can produce a useful answer.

It is no accident that the most useful applications of science often originate in countries where there is a tradition of communication between the various branches of science and a habit of collaboration, with or without administrative encouragement. It also helps if the country is small in extent, because then no great distances are involved when consultations are needed. Any demarcation disputes can only result in inefficiency and reflect the stupidity or false pride of those involved. It is always a pity when the selfish or over-ambitious do not understand that it really does not matter who gets the credit for an answer; the only important fact is that the answer should be correct.

Sympathetic liaison must also exist between science and technology. Rapid advances have been made in agricultural engineering during the last few decades, although they may have generated a new set of problems in a world facing a possible energy crisis. The ability to design an efficient piece of farm machinery is just as important as the solution of a scientific problem, but the two aspects must be dealt with together because new machines change the conditions influencing the problem. Both scientists and engineers must work in harmony, as the aim of both is to help the process of efficient farming. Neither can afford to be unaware of the progress and capabilities of the other, and, even more importantly, to be unaware of their limitations. It is no use to propose a solution to a problem which cannot be put into practice. It is equally useless to advance a solution which might create more problems than it solves.

The uses of knowledge

It is easy to say that every possible use should be made of existing knowledge, but less easy to put into practice. Knowledge is necessary at all stages and by all concerned in farming, because it is never quite certain when a small error can have serious consequences. Error, it is said, runs on oiled wheels and everyone gives it a push. Each farmer and farm worker can learn from his errors and from the mistakes of others. A mistake, unless fatal, can always be a source of enlightenment, but only to those willing to learn. Good instruction helps a pupil to learn from the success of others, but cautionary tales of failures are also useful.

The conditions under which farmers work are always changing. The principles of good husbandry are immutable, but there are no fixed rules of procedure, only a series of improvisations. It may take a brave or desperate man to improvise, but his prospects of success are increased if he really knows what he is doing and not merely guessing. He is much better prepared to take on such a difficult responsibility if he has had the opportunity to learn as much as possible about the many factors involved. Obedience to the laws of nature is the only safe way towards control.

Good teaching, whether by precept or instruction, is therefore essential, but it must be remembered that the mere teaching of answers tends to inhibit thinking. High operational standards can be maintained by the carrying out of instructions, but only thinking can improve them. A good farmer thinks in principles but acts in detail, and the more attention he gives to such details, then the better will be the final result. Knowledge and experience are good in themselves, but their correct application to the present conditions is essential.

It will thus be seen that two of the major limitations to improved productivity are the lack of knowledge and the inadequate use of such knowledge that exists. Ignorance can be remedied; but it is one thing to know what should be done and quite another to be able to do it. The use of knowledge to good effect can be hampered by other deficiencies: the lack of information, the lack of time, the lack of power, the lack of materials or the lack of money.

12

Information and advice

Knowledge cannot be put to good use unless reliable information and facts are available. In theory, there should be no shortage of facts; in practice, they can be in short supply everywhere to a greater or lesser degree, and even if they are available, they may not be used to good effect. A farmer may be unaware that the missing facts are important, or he may be over-confident, knowing that the fact is important but relying too much on his estimate and not troubling to check the details. To be certain, and be wrong, leads to greater troubles than to be uncertain and willing to take the time needed for clarification.

Ignorance can generally be cured if it is diagnosed, but over-confidence is a more insidious disease, because it is only when a major reversal occurs that its dangers are revealed. This may take time, because the immediate penalties for the inaccurate estimations of facts are often small. It is only on the infrequent occasions when they lead to serious consequences that their existence becomes obvious.

Although major losses may be few, there must be a constant succession of minor losses year after year on many farms. The cumulative total of such unnoticed losses could be as great as a major loss which is only incurred now and again.

Certain basic facts concerning the production potential of any farm should be available, and deserve consideration. A detailed appraisal of such information can save wasted effort, not to mention time and money, and can point the way towards a successful enterprise. Prime examples of such facts are those concerning soils and climate.

Soil facts

The nature of the soil, its physical and chemical properties, fertility, drainage, susceptibility to drought, waterlogging or erosion, are all examples of facts which can be ascertained to a fair degree of accuracy. There is really no reason why they should not be known in detail, and there is no excuse for waiting for any deficiency to show itself before corrective action is taken. Intelligent guesses can be made, but if these are incorrect, then decisions will be made which can lead to loss of productivity or financial loss.

In addition to the basic soil properties, the transient soil conditions, such as temperature and moisture status, are of importance to farming operations and growth conditions. Again, good estimates may be all that is necessary provided that they are based on knowledge and experience, but at critical times sample measurements may be the only reliable means of being sure of the facts.

Climate facts

The past climate of a farm area is a fact, even though it may not have been specifically recorded. A good working estimate, accurate enough for most practical planning purposes, can be made by interpolation from records made elsewhere. This should give sufficient information regarding the weather conditions, together with an assessment of the very significant risks of deviation from the average.

Such information should give details of the main weather factors of importance to farming operations (such as the air and soil temperatures, rainfall, transpiration and radiation), and also the derived functions of interest to the farmer (including the length of the growing season, the soil-moisture regime and the excess winter rain). If the needs of the crops or farming system are known, then these details provide the basis for the planning of a sensible cropping programme. Special attention has to be paid to the risks of abnormal weather, because it is the weather extremes and not the normal conditions which can cause crop failures and financial loss.

The permissible degree of risk varies with the extent and price of the crop. If the potential rewards are high, then greater risks can be taken; for staple crops, the risks should be minimal. No farm plan can be expected to allow for a climatic risk of the order of once in 100 years, but a risk of one in three of a late spring frost is surely the lower limits, and a risk of one in ten is a better operating margin.

When making his plans, it is for the farmer to decide what degree of risk he wishes to take, but he cannot do so unless he has obtained the best information about probable conditions. If he does not take these into account, he is accepting a severe limitation of missing facts.

Current information

The helmsman of an old sailing ship was often warned to 'Keep your weather eye lifted', the weather in this case meaning the direction from which the wind was blowing. A good farmer also knows which way the wind is blowing, and follows this precept in both senses of the word. He generally pays close attention to the daily weather over his own farm and also over the fields of his competitors, at home or abroad. He knows only too well that it influences his actions, can thwart his plans, and may determine his chances of success.

It is clearly not essential for a farmer or grower to run his own weather-recording station, although some may well choose to do so. He would certainly be well advised to measure and keep a record of his rainfall, especially if he is using any form of irrigation, when the use of the information so gained would repay the small cost of a rain gauge many times over. Soil and air thermometers, intelligently used, can provide a great number of helpful facts about conditions on the various parts of his farm or holding, and the physical conditions inside farm buildings can be of the greatest importance.

Careful monitoring of environmental conditions is essential if any form of climatic control is being attempted in regard to structures designed for plants or animals or for storage. Automatic controls are all very well in theory, but care taken to make sure that they are working correctly is well worth the extra time and effort.

Another traditional saying, 'the farmer's foot is the best fertilizer', or words to that effect, rightly implies that crops and stock do best when they are under constant vigilance. A good farmer keeps a close watch on his fields and, even if he cannot do everything himself, he relies upon his staff to speak to him if they see anything of possible importance. In some farming systems, especially in animal husbandry, this may involve the keeping of accurate records dealing with such measurements as the milk production of individual cows, egg production, or live-weight gains. It is also important to detect early signs of any pest or disease or an invasion of weeds. If the earliest possible evidence of such occurrence is noticed, then the chances of good control are greatly increased. It is often too late to take action when the danger is obvious to everyone and the harmful organisms are well on their way to victory and the farmer on the road to defeat.

In addition to information regarding the state of the weather and the condition of crops and animals, a farmer also needs to keep an eye on the state of the market. His attendance at weekly markets in the neighbourhood is not just a social occasion or an opportunity for a liquid lunch, it can also provide useful intelligence concerning current trends and prices.

Market reports, on the radio or in the farming press, are also valuable sources of information which the farmer has to consult. Although they deal with past events, he has to use such facts as a guide to future conditions and so get some idea of what and when to sell.

Good farming depends on the making of sound tactical decisions, and such decisions cannot easily be made without adequate facts. Once these are known, then knowledge and experience can lead to a correct decision. If the facts are false, then any deductions made from them are also likely to be false, and maybe expensively so.

Processed information

The information that a farmer acquires is fed into his own mental computer, and is then processed by his brain in accordance with his own personal program. This program is based on his previous experience, in accordance with his knowledge and skill or, in other words, he thinks. There are, however, specialists working for and with agriculture who can do some of the thinking for him, processing all the relevent data, making deductions and forecasting the probable consequences.

Under this heading would come the forecasters of weather, and the value and limitations of such forecasts have been discussed in detail in Chapter 2. A second category of specialists would include those who are concerned with the incidence and intensity of pests and diseases, pathologists, entomologists and veterinarians who, with information regarding the pathogens and the significant events of the past weather, make the best possible deductions concerning the biological hazards to production. It should also be remembered that the forecast of a non-event, implying that the intensity of an attack by a harmful organism is likely to be low or non-existent, can be just as important as advance notice of a serious attack. It can save hours of wasted effort, unnecessary expense and ulcer-producing worry.

A third category would include those who attempt to forecast future yields. The demand for this information does not appear to come principally from the farmer, but rather from the buyers and sellers of his products. Governments, quite rightly, want to know how much of any particular commodity is likely to be available in the foreseeable future. Their hopes can be slightly different from those of the farmer. They would prefer there to be a slight surplus, so that at least one item would be removed from their list of problems. The farmer would prefer there to be a slight deficiency, so that he is sure of selling his product, and he knows from bitter experience that even a small surplus can be made the excuse for a drop in prices.

Yield forecasting is a very difficult exercise, as no crop is safe until it reaches the market. It is possible to assess the effects of weather occurring in the early stages of production, but there must be an area of uncertainty right up to the very end. It can be very difficult to verify yield forecasts, especially in those parts of the world where production statistics seem to enter into the realms of fiction.

A fourth type of result which might be sought for by the processing of information is the forecasting of future prices, and this is certainly the most difficult task of all. To begin with, it depends to a great extent on the accuracy of the yield forecasts (a doubtful thing at best), and, secondly, the links between yields and prices are by no means crystal clear.

It is true that extremes offer the opportunity for apparently reliable conclusions. A severe shortage of one commodity in one region is likely to raise prices, unless the market is upset by large imports from elsewhere, if and when available. A world-wide shortage can only have one effect, and the only question is how big that effect will be. A crop surplus, whether real, reported or just anticipated, is expected to depress prices, which it may well do unless support mechanisms are brought into effect. In between the two extremes of far too little and far too much, almost anything can happen, and usually does.

Although any form of forecasting is a difficult and thankless mental process, there are certain types of forecast which can be more trustworthy than they are usually given credit for. These are the ones which make use of knowledge of past events, meteorological and agricultural, to quantify the extent to which the potential yield has already been depressed. They provide a kind of negative information, identifying the ground that has already been lost in the race for production and which cannot be regained by any future influence.

If adverse weather has delayed the sowing or planting of a crop, or has caused a reduction in the total area of production below the norm, then there must follow a depression in output below that theoretically possible. The exact amount of this depression will depend on the conditions over the rest of the production cycle, and may not be predictable; but whatever such conditions may be, they can never make up for the bad start.

The losses due to accurately recorded attacks of some pests and diseases may also be predicted as a percentage reduction of potential yield, although at the time it cannot be said what the full 100 per cent unaffected yield would be. Such estimates may provide useful guides to shortfalls in production, but as they are generally made at the time of an unfavourable event, they tend to be over-pessimistic.

Such estimates of lost production do not give much reliable indication of the possible financial outcome for the farmer. The mere threat of losses is likely to raise prices, and create a rush of forward buying at levels which may be inflated above those which are realised when final yields are known. This may benefit a producer who may receive more cash for a poor yield than he would from a higher yield sold under other market stresses, but this is little consolation to the consumer who ultimately pays the bill.

Food production and all those associated with it are hampered if they do not have access to the best possible forecasting advice, but they must not expect miracles.

Advice

'If you don't know, ask someone who does' is good advice, but a farmer seems to be bombarded with advice from all sides. Advertisements in the farming press are designed to attract his attention, and to persuade him to do this or buy that to his own possible advantage and to the certain profit of the advertiser and distributor. Agricultural shows and 'open days' at demonstration farms are full of posters trying to influence his future actions. Television commercials include pictures of ideal farms, with perfect stock and crops, in attempts to sell him materials he may or may not require.

The assault upon his ears is even worse, ranging from the exhortations or accusations of politicians, the smooth talking of salesmen or the outpourings of that regrettable modern innovation, the public relations officer, to the caution of his bank manager or the sympathetic encouragements of his friends and family.

As if advice (much of it unsolicited) from those associated with the farming industry were not enough, the farmer is also liable to be told what he should do by countryside well-wishers with no agricultural connections, who think, sometimes with some justice, that they should have their say.

The professional planner, whose activities in towns, new or old, can hardly be said to have been free from mistakes, is now turning his attentions to rural problems which have rarely been correctly solved by the centralisation of power, however well intentioned. The prospects for food production are bleak if the type of mentality which thought that tower blocks were an acceptable form of human habitation now has the final word on farms and farming.

A farmer might be forgiven if his reaction was on the lines of 'to hell with the lot of you, let me get on with it', but he knows that within the cacophony of noise there is a tune to which he should listen. His difficulty is to pick the right advice, not perhaps always the advice he wants to hear, but the advice which will ease his worries, lead to greater productivity and help him to avoid mistakes.

The question of motive

In trying to decide who he should trust, the farmer would be wise to give some thought to the possible motives of his advisers. Uninvited advice is rarely altruistic, and even invited advice will not always be impartial. There are few people who can solve a difficult problem, and fewer still who have the time and opportunity to communicate their knowledge freely to others. There are far more who think that they know the right answer and are so convinced that they and they alone are right that they put forward their opinions in no uncertain manner as often as they can. Their motives are often admirable (although at times tainted by selfishness masquerading as a moral principle), but, as will be discussed later, an excellent motive is not enough to guarantee the correct advice.

The main sources of advice are politicians, economists, bank managers, academics from universities, scientists from research stations, advisers employed by governments, international agencies, commercial firms, or by the farmer himself as a personal consultant, fellow farmers or members of the family, anxious 'Friends' of this, that and the other, merchants and dealers, and last of all on a long list, the consumer. Each and every one of these has his own motives for expressing an opinion on farming problems.

A careful scientist reading a paper on a controversial subject always likes to know who funded the research, if only because it is far easier to find the evidence you are looking for, and the paper might not contain all the relevant facts. It is thus pertinent in the present context to ask whether the source of the payment to the adviser could affect the proffered advice.

One who is not paid is the consumer, but he (or she) still has a financial interest because he does the buying and can give powerful indirect advice by refusing to buy the food product. For example, the consumption of bread has fallen in Britain over recent years. This may be due to a change in eating habits or a combination of several other reasons, but it is just conceivable that the housewife has decided that anything with the texture of a feather bed may not be all that nice to eat, is nothing like the bread her grandmother used to bake, and is not worth the high price.

At the other end of the prestige scale comes the politician, who may think that he rules the country but who, in all but the most rigid dictatorships, is really employed by the public and can be dismissed at the next election. It must be assumed that he has the best interests of his country at heart (although this at times is a little difficult to credit), but such a commendable motive does not guarantee that he has the interests of every farmer foremost in his mind. He may think that the industry as a whole is too prosperous, is receiving too much support, or even that some portions of it are expendable. He may wish to put policies into force to keep down the price of food, or be merely making a political party point to gain some ego-inflating publicity, or he may even be at his wit's end to provide more food at any cost. The democratic process may not always be successful in selecting a good government, but it is generally pretty efficient in dismissing a bad one. Even a complete dictator, free from any threat of deposition except by violence, must put forward policies which will ensure enough food for his people. It is only ruthless cynical authorities that might welcome famine as a solution to the disposal of unwanted millions.

It is therefore to be hoped that politicians could be said to be on the side of the angels as far as good intentions are concerned, trying to provide sufficient food and avoiding embarrassing surpluses which cannot be sold to other countries. They are doing their best to arrive at the 'right' answer, and they do not like to be proved wrong any more than anyone else. The same can be said of their advisers, such as economists, who are attempting to find answers to very difficult and complicated problems. Revolutions are said to result in a trivial shift in the emphasis of suffering, a property shared by many economic policies, which seem only to ease one constraint by the creation of another. It is perhaps no wonder that they have to be changed so frequently.

Another motive has to be considered in regard to bank managers who offer (or refuse) loans or overdrafts to the farmer. The manager making the decision whether or not to lend the money for a farming enterprise is mainly concerned with the safety of the money concerned, plus a little interest along the way. He may be prepared to take a calculated risk, he may make mistakes, but his main motive is to make money for his employers.

Turning next to advice from research workers who put forward their views by published articles, by lectures or by talks on radio or television, their main motive must be thought to be the maintenance of their own professional reputation or the reputation of the establishment to which they belong. They are likely to be advocating the soundest ideas of which they are capable, the 'revealing light of a clear intellect and an unbiased judgement', if only because they would be ashamed to be found out to be wrong. This does not mean that they are infallible.

If events or further research do prove them wrong, they normally take the first opportunity to correct their opinions, although stubbornness may grow with age, and youth be blinded by overconfidence. Some research stations may be privately funded with specific interests in mind, such as the benefits of one particular style of farming or the use of a particular range of commercial products. Their standards of research may (or may not) be excellent, but they do involve a certain type of motive which should be taken into account when considering their results.

The staff employed by any government in advisory or extension services have one clear motive, that of trying to improve the national standard of the agricultural industry. They also should have one additional motive in their favour as far as a farmer is concerned. Centrally imposed agricultural policies are designed to help the country as a whole, but the adviser is also trying to help the individual farmer, and should be looking at the problem from the farmer's point of view. If he does not do this, he will soon lose the farmer's confidence and credence.

The extent to which the government-paid adviser is influenced by political policies will vary from country to country, and so will his duties, which can range from simple advice to imperative directions. In general, it can be said that the motives behind such advice are sound.

Weather forecasters who are public employees do not normally issue any advice on matters arising from the effects of future weather. They may issue warnings of a danger, but do not say what action is recommended. Other public authorities can and do offer advice based on the probabilities of the weather forecast. These include the agricultural adviser who, with knowledge of his special subject together with information about the past, present and possible future weather, can issue advice on the actions to be taken to offset attacks by pests and diseases. A high degree of scientific integrity is involved, and the motive is again clear, namely to provide the best possible scientific advice to as many producers as possible with the aim of helping them in their problems.

The main motive of advisers employed by commercial firms might be thought to be the wish to increase the use of materials produced by their employers, but this should not condemn them out of hand. It is very much in their interest that such materials should be used correctly, and thus be seen in the most favourable light. They are unlikely to be able to sell a useless product more than once to the same person. Although this type of adviser would be reluctant to suggest that the products of a rival firm are better, at least he would be trying to ensure that the best possible results are obtained from his own brand.

An independent adviser employed by the farmer has, it is to be hoped, no such restrictions on his range of advice. His aim is to give a good service to his employer in the hope that he will be consulted on a later occasion or be recommended to other farmers. His motive may be the profit from his fees, but his future income depends on his ability to satisfy his customers.

Advice from family and friends can always be regarded as well intentioned. Even if rival farmers in the same line of business keep their innermost secrets to themselves, they are hardly likely to offer misleading advice to try to steal a march on their competitors. The great value of advice from close friends is that it is personal and has the interests of the farmer himself firmly at heart. Success in farming, as in other walks of life, can be bought at too high a price, and the onlooker can often restore a sense of proportion which is not always obvious to the person concerned.

Advice from outsiders, especially those genuinely concerned with the production of the natural resources of a region, can be said to be prompted by the best of motives, although at times there seems to be more than a touch of self-interest. A desire to keep things as they were is understandable, but this should not preclude all types of change but only changes for the worse, and especially those which cause irreparable damage.

The advice from merchants or dealers, the buyers of the farmer's produce, must always be influenced by the chances of personal profit. It can be advice aimed at an increase of production rather than productivity, and it is not always the farmer's profit that the adviser has chiefly in mind. Much time could be spent on trying to analyse the different merits of a fixed-price contract and a free-bargaining system, but the middleman between the producer and consumer generally observes the first law of parasitism: 'Keep the host alive'. It should also be said that not all of the intermediate handlers of food produce are hard, unfeeling operators, and many of them in the past have helped farmers over difficult financial periods.

In general, this analysis is encouraging, with some reservations regarding the suppliers of materials to the farmer and their salesmen. It might be thought that a good product sells itself and that it is only the poor products that need a 'hard sell', but this is not always true.

Much depends on the way of life in the country concerned. In some, the greatest respect is shown to the one that shouts loudest; in others, extravagant claims are greeted with suspicion and may well be counterproductive. Advertising campaigns may or may not be justified, either in their truth or in their results, but it is a pity that sometimes the true value of a new material used in agriculture is only found out after it has been in use on a field scale for some years.

The farmer cannot be blamed for getting tired of being treated like a guinea pig, with manufacturers learning their lessons at his expense. On the other hand, he must admit that he does stand to benefit considerably from a new product that lives up to its initial promises, or even up to its publicity.

The question of accuracy

In the end, the source of advice is irrelevant; the only important point is whether it is accurate and helpful to the farmer. As nobody, however clever or well intentioned, is likely to be right every time, the past record of sound advice from the various sources can only be a general guide to reliability and not a guarantee of future accuracy.

The question of the usefulness of politically based advice is one which might invoke hollow laughter, as politicians only rank second

to the weather on the farmers' list of traditional enemies. Indeed, a
good case could be made from the thought that some of the most
successful agricultural nations have had the least governmental
control, and at least one of the strictest, centrally controlled, political
organisations has had a succession of food-production crises.

Perhaps the politicians are not always helped by their favourite
economists, who may have done their sums correctly but seem to run
into trouble with their forecasts, and who are often in the unenviable
position of finding changes taking place in a critical factor within
weeks of their day of decision. The truth of the matter is probably that
agriculture is the most difficult industry to control centrally, and that
uncontrollable factors such as the weather can make fools of everyone.
The difficulties lie more in the immensity of the problem than in the
incompetence of the policy makers, although there is no shortage of
the latter.

No sane scientist or technologist would claim he was always right,
but the evidence in their favour is the general increase in total
production over recent decades, which is a credit to them and to the
farmers who have taken their advice. At least they could not have
been wrong most of the time.

It has already been suggested that opinions have to be changed if
new evidence arises which proves that previous lines of thought and
conclusions were wrong. It is not often realised that scientists
employed by commercial firms have to change their minds more
quickly than most. A university will still remain in being if one of its
professors continues to cling to an outmoded hypothesis despite
evidence to the contrary (having nothing to lose but his faculties), but
a manufacturing firm will go bankrupt if it does not correct its
mistakes at the first possible moment and fails to keep up with the
latest developments.

Sometimes, this commercial pressure can be too great, and new
products are brought onto the market before they are fully tested, in
which case the farmer may be the first to suffer if any mistakes have
been made. It is always something of a gamble whether it is wise to be
one of the first to adopt a new idea or new product, or whether it is
safer to let someone else try it out first. The farmer has no real guide to
the correct decision and has to rely on his instinct, tempered by the
amount of money he is putting at risk and tempted by large profits
which might accrue if he is first in the field. It is ironic to realise that
the manufacturer is facing an almost similar problem.

The reliability of private consultants is perhaps reflected by their
reputations, although this may also be an indication of their personalities. The farmer may have to choose between the enthusiasm of
youth and the experience of age, and hope for a combination of both.
It may be difficult for a private consultant to keep in touch with all the

new developments which are taking place with increasing rapidity in the various branches of farming. He may be working very much on his own, and new knowledge often comes first from conversations with colleagues rather than by perusal of published results. He may not have rapid access to complex chemical analysis facilities or the specialised diagnostic techniques essential for the precise identification of some limiting factors. He may therefore be tempted to err on the side of caution, rather like a bank manager who prefers to rely on certainties and ignores the outside chances.

The advice of neighbouring farmers may be sound if it is based on local experience, but when a totally new project is under consideration, there is no way of knowing if their judgement is any better than that of anyone else. It is always worthwhile to listen to the opinion of others, but it is foolish to rely exclusively on their advice.

Merchants and dealers, through their many contacts with other farmers, can often play a useful part along the agricultural 'grapevine', helping to pass on valuable information as to what is happening elsewhere. They should also be able to offer some informed opinion regarding future demands and potential markets for a new product, but they cannot be right all the time, otherwise they would be millionaires. Any advice from this quarter regarding the difficulties of marketing a proposed crop or commodity should be taken very seriously. After all, that is the aspect of the subject they should know more about than anyone else, and if they cannot see the way to some sort of profit for themselves in this direction, the farmer would be well advised to think long and hard. It is no use growing a crop if it cannot be sold.

It is said that the customer is always right, but, right or wrong, he certainly has the final word. If he or she does not buy a product, then the finest production techniques in the world have no value to the farmer. As economists know only too well, consumer reaction is the most difficult factor to forecast with any degree of certainty.

After all the advice (solicited or uninvited) has been given, it is the farmer who has to make up his own mind. He then decides what to do, subject to any governmental controls that may have been imposed. Both education and experience may help him in his difficult decision-making process, for each tends to induce a state of mind which enables a listener to detect when someone is talking nonsense, and there may be quite a lot of it about.

International advice

In less parochial fields, specialised agencies of the United Nations, such as FAO and UNDP, have made many expensive and extensive attempts to advise the 'underdeveloped' nations on their agricultural production. Not all such attempts have been successful, although the track record of the World Bank is better than most.

It is difficult enough to solve agricultural problems in familiar conditions, but when dealing with different crops, soils and climates on farms in different social regimes, the problems are multiplied. Tribal customs are not universal laws, no matter what the members of the tribe may think. Only the best and very dedicated advisers have a hope of appreciable success; the good that they do may disappear on their departure. This type of international aid must continue, but the difficulties are enormous and only appreciated by those who have had experience in foreign fields.

Nature can be a very cruel mistress, and gratitude almost ranks as an endangered species. The most disheartening experience of all is the kind of success which brings food to a distressed area, raises the standard of living, and yet results in a population increase to the extent that within a few years the problem is worse than before any improvements were made.

13

Social, political and economic factors

The social, economic and political factors affecting agriculture should be under the control of man, but whether they are under sensible control is a matter of opinion, leading at times to heated and acrimonious debate. They are so closely intermingled that it seems logical to discuss them together.

A reasonable starting point would appear to be the interactions between supply and demand, because it is a vital factor of any industry that offers its goods for sale in the market place, and agriculture is no exception.

Supply and demand

As food is essential for life to survive, it might be thought that the need for the major agricultural products of a given population could be calculated with some confidence. Unfortunately, need and demand are not necessarily synonymous, and this gives rise to complications. If there is insufficient money to pay the asking price, then demand will be less than the true need, resulting in malnutrition or even starvation. On the other hand, in an affluent society demand may well exceed need, even at the cost of introducing diseases due to over-indulgence.

The degree of prosperity of any section of a community will have a qualitative effect as well as a quantitative one. Whereas the poor may be prepared to survive on a diet which can be produced cheaply, the rich are anxious to consume and are prepared to pay for luxury items which are costly to produce and to transport to the point of sale.

Even a small increase in the amount of money available for expenditure on food can have a similar effect, increasing the demand for out-of-season items which hitherto were only eaten during their season of local production. Nevertheless, even with the fluctuations due to the various purchasing powers of the consumers, the demand for most agricultural products can be estimated more reliably than it can for many other less essential commodities.

The supply cannot be calculated with anything like the same

degree of accuracy, and previous chapters have indicated that factors outside the control of man make accurate predictions of yield extremely difficult, so that perfect planning of production is almost impossible. Even when it is realised that supplies will fall short of demand, it may not be possible to repair this deficiency, and in any case extra supplies will take time to produce.

There is no way in which an agricultural production line can be instantly started or stopped. Except for a few commodities for which demand always exceeds supply, the unrestricted operation of market forces therefore tends to result in a pendulum effect, swinging between surplus and scarcity, but seldom in balance.

The period of swing of the production pendulum varies according to the type of commodity. With annual crops or with livestock species capable of rapid reproduction, such as pigs or poultry, the period of the cycle is short. For other products, such as beef or orchard fruits, in which three years may elapse between the start of the production project and the appearance of supplies on the market, the cycle of shortage and glut tends to be on a much longer timescale.

A very different situation occurs if supply exceeds demand over a wide range of commodities and if this imbalance persists. The primary producers cannot sell all that they supply to the market and cannot recover the costs of production. They then tend to revert to a low-input, low-output system in order to try to survive financially. This reaction was typified by changes in British agriculture during the latter part of the 19th century and in the period 1918–39, between the two world wars.

It is difficult, if not impossible, for a farming industry to recover from such deep depressions of trade solely by its own efforts. The outside intervention of factors other than those of increasing demand is necessary to raise productivity, and this creates difficult problems which will be discussed later.

Political control

The threat of starvation in two world wars, when food imports were severely restricted, made governments of countries such as Britain realise that it was imprudent and improvident to allow market forces to jeopardise home food production. Moreover, by the end of the second conflict, the rising standards of living and demands for higher wages by workers in what came to be known as 'Third World' countries led to less plentiful supplies of cheap food imports. Another economic factor was the lack of foreign exchange money to pay for such imports. Successive governments therefore tried to raise the output and productivity of home-based agriculture. Many countries faced similar problems, which were often accentuated by rising populations and the diminishing availability of good farmland.

There were five main features of the British policy. First, with the aim of stimulating production of essential foodstuffs such as dairy produce, meat, eggs, cereals, potatoes and sugar beet, subsidies were paid directly to the farmers who produced them, so that they were at least partially protected from the effects of either low world prices or increased production costs. Such subsidies also ensured that the poorer sections of the community could obtain home-produced food at prices they could afford.

Secondly, capital grants were paid to encourage improvements for farm holdings and investments in new technology. Thirdly, the government expenditure on agricultural research was increased in the hope of maintaining or even increasing the rate of improvement in production. Fourthly, the National Agricultural Advisory Service (with members in every county of England and Wales) was set up to identify the factors limiting productivity, to translate research results into farming practice, and to keep farmers in touch with new technological developments. Such services were free to the individual farmer, and similar facilities were provided in Scotland through specialists attached to universities. Fifthly, there was an expansion in the opportunities available for full- or part-time education in agriculture, horticulture and forestry.

Although this policy was not without its critics, who were concerned regarding the principles involved and also its method of operation, it may have been more than a coincidence that productivity in agriculture increased in the post-war period in Britain more rapidly than in other industries, and at a greater rate than it had done in war time when the industry was under strict governmental control in almost every respect. At the same time the public had an ample supply of all essential foods once bread rationing had ceased, and these foods were available in the shops at moderate prices which compared favourably with those prevailing elsewhere in Western Europe.

Multi-governmental control

A change of policy was necessary when Britain joined the European Common Market. The basic objectives remained much the same: namely, to produce as much food as possible for the needs of the Community within its own multi-national boundaries, and to provide it at as low a price as possible by fostering a more efficient agricultural industry. There was, however, a fundamental difference of method in that direct subsidies to producers were eliminated and instead the farmer was expected to obtain his due reward in the market place.

Even so, the farmer within the Community was not exposed to the full force of world competition. Import levies were chargeable on products from outside the EEC which could be produced inside its territory. Furthermore, if market prices for many commodities fell below a predetermined level, the farmer had the right to sell his products to an Intervention Authority at that agreed minimum price, providing that they reached the required levels of quality.

By this arrangement the farmer had a virtually guaranteed market for whatever quantity of a product he was able to produce, even if there was a surplus to consumer requirements. Providing that his costs of production are below the intervention price, he is able to make a profit.

Critics of the policy condemn it on the grounds that consumers have to pay higher prices than those prevailing on world markets, that it encourages over-production, and that the large unwanted surpluses of some products such as wine and dairy produce can only be disposed of at considerable loss to the Community. It is also pointed out that the cost of agricultural support is an intolerable drain on the EEC budget, which cannot be allowed to increase indefinitely.

Defenders of the policy argue that, like Christianity, it has not yet been tried. Because there is no common unit of currency throughout the member countries, no uniformity of interest rates on borrowed money, and because each member state pursues its own fiscal and taxation policy, the rewards which farmers receive in real terms differ in each country. Such rewards are as much, or more, dependent on the individual economic strategy of a particular government than on a farmer's technical efficiency. The introduction of the 'green pound', enabling agricultural prices to be adjusted separately within the countries of the Community, has not seemed to provide a satisfactory answer to such anomalies.

It is further argued that, if intervention prices were related more closely to world market prices and less to the production costs of the farmers, then the policy would work towards lower prices to the consumer and would tend to eliminate the least efficient producers, thus removing (or at least reducing) the risk of large unwanted and unsaleable surpluses. This hypothesis may be an over-simplification of a complicated problem and an unacceptable example of wishful thinking. It seems more logical to suggest that there are a number of options open to farmers subjected to such a policy, and that there is no certainty that all will select the same option. The trouble with economic problems is that although the questions tend to remain the same, the answers seem to keep changing.

If prices were lowered or maintained at a level which farmers regard as unprofitable, then the most likely general reaction will be the same as it always has been, to apply political pressure to get the prices lifted. As governments try, with inadequate ability and indifferent success, to influence every type of business, they must keep in mind the voting power of the participants in such businesses. This may not be true in 'Democratic' countries, but it is at least partially true in democratic ones. It follows that success in agriculture does not entirely depend on the laws of supply and demand, but also on the votes in parliamentary elections of the industry as a whole.

This voting power varies in intensity from country to country according to the proportion of the population which is associated with the agricultural industry, and it also varies in relation to the proximity in time of the next political election. This type of pressure explains why farm prices are always likely to be a subject for bargaining, almost horse trading, among member states, whatever the level of supply may be.

If a price level is fixed which eliminates the profit margin, or which erodes it to an extent unacceptable to the producers of that commodity, it is unrealistic to believe that those who are most affected will automatically give up its production. As long as a guaranteed market remains, some will try to maintain their income by increased efficiency aimed at a higher output and a tolerable income. Some theorists maintain that an increased efficiency can be obtained by lowering production costs without reducing output, but in practice this ideal is seldom realised.

It is outside the power of the farmer to lower his rent or his interest charges on borrowed money, and impossible to reduce the rates of pay to his staff, though he may be tempted to reduce their numbers. The replacement of labour by improved technology seldom reduces costs, although it may increase production. Thus a policy of reducing intervention prices may well stimulate an increase rather than a decrease in surplus, and this process will continue as long as there is no limit on the quantity that can be sold at the intervention prices.

If a policy of lowering prices is put into effect for long enough, then undoubtedly a point is reached when the least efficient producers are losing so much money that they cannot continue. Two questions can then arise.

(a) Is the decrease of production due to some farmers giving up production greater than the increase in output of the more efficient striving to maintain their income?
(b) Are the land, buildings and equipment of the retiring farmers sold to the more efficient ones?

If the answer to the second question is yes, then output will continue to rise and it may become necessary to impose even more drastic price cuts in an effort to reduce a surplus, because with an increased size of business the more efficient may be able to survive on a smaller profit margin.

Ultimately, if the process of price reduction is continued, even some of these more efficient farmers will fail to make sufficient money, and will begin to look for alternative sources of income. They do not necessarily cease to farm, but are more likely to switch production to other commodities which appear at the moment to be more profitable. As long as their new preferences are not in surplus, the problem is at last solved; but if enough farmers change to the same new product, then all that finally may be achieved is the creation of yet another problem.

It therefore seems possible that a price policy aimed at reduction of a surplus is likely to be slow and uncertain in producing desired results, even if no other factors intervene. It also involves the risk that land released from the production of a commodity which is in surplus may not be used for producing a type of food that is needed, but may pass out of agricultural production altogether. This may be far too high a price to pay for success, especially as there is already increasing competition for the use of good land.

Competition for land use

As populations grow and modern living increases in complexity, more and more land is diverted from agricultural use to other purposes. New housing estates and industrial developments require land, and an increasing amount of space is taken up by new roads, motorways and airports all of which make large inroads into farming areas. Furthermore, the demand for amenity space, parks, reserves and sports grounds increases as leisure time expands.

In theory, the planning authorities take the needs of agriculture into account when making decisions about the uses that can be made of land. In practice, offices and factories which employ more workers to the square metre than do farms per hectare, as well as making a far larger contribution to the local rates and taxes, tend to become an irresistible pressure group to both local and national governments. The annexation of large areas of farmland for a new town, a reservoir for water storage, or a new major airport may attract considerable concern and active opposition, but the slow encroachment of bricks and concrete in smaller schemes passes almost unnoticed, except by those immediately concerned. The sum total of such local losses can be far more than most people realise, and if every year an equal area of land were permanently engulfed by a tidal wave or lost by coast erosion, it would quite rightly rank as a national disaster. The current loss of agricultural land to other uses in Britain is equivalent to an area the size of the county of Surrey every two years. More important still, it is often the land with a high production potential that is taken over.

All small countries with increasing population densities face similar problems, and not all of them have the opportunity, so ably taken by the Netherlands, to create new productive agricultural land from areas previously covered by salt water. Even those countries which are large enough still to have vast areas of land fit for cultivation have to remember that it is always decreasing in area as activities increase which take the best land for other purposes.

This loss of land is a direct cause of lost food production, but there are other indirect pressures on the use of farmland which may also reduce productivity. The beauty of the countryside is an amenity which is enjoyed by the population as a whole, and as cities get more and more ugly its restful environment becomes more valuable and sought after. Most urban country lovers (and they form the bulk of the electorate) are bitterly opposed to changes in the landscape which alter the appearance of what, to them, is the traditional rural scene, often forgetting that if the farmer had not altered the landscape in the first place, then there would not have been any rural scenery to enjoy or admire.

In most countries in Western Europe there is very little undisturbed natural vegetation still in existence. The rural pattern, so much admired, has largely been created by man cultivating the land and tending his stock, unhampered by the carefully prepared plans of the office-based theorist. The result has been pleasant to the eye, sometimes beautiful, and this beauty is now being destroyed by the remorseless invasion of industries and urban 'development'. Even those who come in their motor cars to enjoy the country they admire are bringing about a deterioration, and car parks and caravan sites have to be very carefully sited so as not to spoil the picture.

These facts having been largely ignored, there now is often a strong resistance to a farmer making further alterations to the appearance of a landscape, even if such changes will enhance productivity and food output. This is very understandable from a nostalgic point of view, as most people remember with affection the places where they were young and happy, and they hate to have their memories shattered, if only for the reason that it brings intimations of mortality.

Most resented by the protesters, who do not earn their living from the land but merely eat the food produced from it, is the ploughing and cultivation of old established areas of grass on the moorland fringes, or the removal of hedgerows which formed the attractive patchwork pattern of small fields to form larger areas more easily worked by modern farm machinery. There are often good agronomic reasons for the retention of hedges as windbreaks to improve the microclimate, but regrettably these are rarely included in reasoning based on less materialistic points of view. If it could be shown that the presence of hedges improves the chances of higher yields, then a farmer would be all too pleased to retain them.

Other inconsistencies seem to arise: lakes are admired but new reservoirs are detested; forest plantings are called all the emotive insults imaginable, even when the hills on which they are introduced were once covered with trees before man removed them. The heart has its reasons, and is little troubled by history or logic.

In addition to those opposed to visual change, there are those who are disturbed about the threat to the continued existence of wild species of plants and animals, birds and insects by the introduction of new agricultural practices or the destruction of special habitats. This objection is more soundly based than one founded on sentiment and self-interest. The drainage of wetlands, the discharge of excess nitrogen and phosphates into streams and lakes, the removal of hedgerows, the felling of copses, and the cultivation of scrub or heathland can cause major changes in the ecological conditions to such an extent that some species may become rare or even extinct, chiefly because of the disappearance of their natural habitat or source of food.

Furthermore, the chemical control of weeds and pests may inadvertently destroy harmless plants and animals, although probably not to the extent imagined by the credulous, to whom pesticide is a four-letter word. Biological organisms which may be an enemy to a farmer can be a priceless treasure to some naturalist, but it is a pity that some such enthusiasts do not realise that they owe the world a living and not vice versa.

The possible threat to wild species must be taken very seriously, and be correctly assessed. Any complete disappearance could lead to the loss of irreplaceable genes which could be of value in more ways than one. The loss of old cultivated strains of plant or domesticated animals might handicap any future breeding programme. This growing interest and concern for sensible conservation will undoubtedly increase the pressures on farmers to restrict or even abandon practices which increase productivity but which present a real or imagined threat to the natural world as we know it. Some form of compromise is clearly essential, and it is to be hoped that future changes are determined sensibly and logically and not swamped by either emotion or greed.

There are also some more direct conflicts between urban and rural interests. The extension of industries into the countryside not only removes land from production, but also can give rise to industrial waste products and effluents which may have a serious adverse effect on neighbouring crops and stock. Smokestack emissions and water discharges from certain types of factory can be toxic, and although levels may be controlled by law, there can be accidental excessive discharges, and in some cases there may be a slow build-up of pollutants in the soil until they reach dangerous levels.

This slow build-up may lower output by making plants and animals less thrifty, perhaps to the extent that specially susceptible species may have to be abandoned. The discharge of toxic or contaminated liquids into watercourses may render the water unfit for drinking by stock, for crop irrigation or for the washing of produce prior to marketing.

If any water becomes seriously polluted by human sewage or animal waste, there is no alternative to costly purification or the total prohibition of the use of the water in agriculture, because there would be an unacceptable recurrent risk of outbreaks of infection such as that due to salmonella.

The increasing awareness of these problems has led to a more effective sampling of water quality and stricter control of the purity of watercourses, but part of the cost of such improvements has to be borne by the farmer in higher charges for the abstraction of water for agricultural purposes.

On the other side of the picture, some forms of pollution caused by the action of farmers may appear to threaten the health or comfort of the rest of the community. Apart from the suspected ecological dangers arising from the changes in farm practice, the main complaints against the farmer are concerned with an excessive use of chemicals.

These complaints fall into two distinct categories. The first concerns the over-use of fertilizers, particularly those including nitrogenous materials, with the result that the excess enters into water supplies and so threatens the health of the public, especially that of young children. The second type of complaint deals with the use of toxic crop-protection chemicals which can create a health hazard to those living in the vicinity, and the residues of which could contaminate human food supplies.

In Britain, the finding of a recent Royal Commission on Pollution in Agriculture was that the industry was innocent of dangerous practices, or, at very least, the charges were not proven. It was agreed that although vigilance over the nitrite levels in water supplies must be maintained, there is no evidence that present rates of fertilizer usage are dangerous. It might also be remarked that with the present high cost of artificial fertilizers, no farmer is likely to use more than he needs, or at least not deliberately.

It was found that there had been isolated cases of the misuse of agricultural chemicals which caused damage to neighbouring crops, but there was no evidence of indiscriminant spraying causing a threat to the health and safety of the public at large. The amounts of plant-protection chemicals consumed in food were much less a hazard than the inhalation of the chemical discharges in other industries, or from the exhausts of the ubiquitous internal combustion engine, or the ingestion of chemicals used in food preservation, or the self-induced over-indulgence in some pharmaceutical products.

As in many other cases of public concern, the complaints lacked a sense of proportion, and sometimes showed no understanding of the order of magnitude of the factors involved. This is not to say that such complaints should not be taken seriously, but they should be carefully considered, and the fears of the public regarding something they do not quite understand should, where appropriate, be put at rest.

The Royal Commission concluded that the most important unresolved problem emanated from large-scale intensive animal units, especially those concerned with the rearing of pigs. The safe disposal of waste products from such units is feasible but expensive, and there is no simple practical solution for getting rid of the smell. Although such odours are not dangerous to health, they can and do persistently lower the quality of life in the neighbourhood. Further intensification of large livestock enterprises in close proximity to populated areas is thus likely to be strongly opposed. Conversely, the presence of such units in the open countryside may be a defence against urban encroachment. If bacon is wanted for breakfast, pigs must be reared somewhere.

In intensive arable areas, the practice of burning cereal stubbles brings forth an increasing volume of noisy protest and complaints from the non-farming population and from organisations with impressive names. Even when the burning is carried out according to the sensible agreed code of practice, a sudden change of wind direction or strength may produce a smoke cloud dangerous to traffic on adjacent roads, and a deposit of fine ash over clothes on the washing line or drifting through open windows does not endear the farmer to the housewife.

The burning of stubble, a cheap and convenient process, can also be criticised on agronomic grounds, but even practices which the farmer knows are essential to maintain or improve productivity, but which are a real or imaginary threat to others, are likely to meet with increasing opposition. This opposition grows with increasing and sometimes ill informed publicity, especially when the agricultural community represents a declining proportion of the population.

The urban or suburban public may think that the activities of farmers cause them harm or constitute a public nuisance, but the farmers are well aware that they themselves are liable to suffer damage and annoyance when strangers appear in their community. Increasing leisure and possession of their own means of transport enable an increasing number of people to penetrate into the countryside, seeking pleasure and relaxation. Even if they all carefully observe the 'countryside code' of behaviour, the sheer numbers of weekend or holiday traffic can seriously hinder the normal flow of farm movements of both equipment and stock. A farmer and his family would be well advised not to fall ill over the weekend, because their doctor is almost certainly fully occupied in attending to the victims of motor accidents.

Too many visitors to the countryside are either unaware of, or choose to ignore, the fact that agricultural land is a production line for the food they eat, and not an area for their unrestricted enjoyment. To them, a grass field is a pleasant place for a picnic, not a source of fodder for the cows who produce their bottles of milk on the doorstep. Wanton or accidental damage occurs in some popular country areas close to large residential zones as regularly as it does in the towns and cities themselves, although it seldom attracts so much attention in news reports.

If a party of farmers and their friends broke into a factory, damaged the expensive machinery, and then indulged in all the biological activities of which the human species is capable, including ingestion, excretion and reproduction, leaving a mass of debris behind wide-open gates and doors, it would no doubt be regarded as newsworthy, and the television cameras would be swarming all over the scene of the vandalism. Yet this happens on some farms in popular tourist areas nearly every weekend, without causing any comments except the unprintable ones of the farmer suffering the damage.

In extreme cases, this damage by uninvited visitors and their uncontrolled children and dogs may cause such financial loss that the farmer is forced in despair to change his farming system and, for example, abandon such specially vulnerable commodities as sheep or fruit. The wolf used to be the worst enemy of the lamb; nowadays it is the domestic pet, the killer dog who savages the young lambs or causes the ewes to abort.

As the amount of leisure time is liable to increase in future years, this conflict of interests is not likely to diminish unless education is more successful in teaching a sense of personal responsibility than it so far has been, or until the rising cost of motor fuel curbs the pressure of inconsiderate visitors to the countryside.

Energy

A drop in the number of unwelcome visitors is probably the only benefit that agriculture will gain from rising fuel costs. As in every other industry, the increasing expense of energy is a serious threat to productivity. The more advanced the farming system, then the more dependent it is on reliable supplies of electricity, petrol or diesel oil. A reversion to the use of draught animals or to man himself as a source of power does not offer a feasible solution, even if soaring unemployment makes cheaper labour available. The loss of power and speed of operation would inevitably result in both a lower output and less productivity.

If, in the future, there is a real shortage of energy supplies, then the effect on food production will depend on how effectively agriculture can compete with other industries. In such circumstances the outcome will depend on the answer to the old question 'guns or butter?', and whether starving in a spacecraft is preferable to walking and having something to eat.

The increasing importance of the energy factor has led to attempts to formulate energy balances for food products. In this way it is hoped to compare the efficiency of the production of various commodities and farming systems in terms of the calorific value of the food produced relative to the amount of energy needed to produce it.

Not surprisingly, the systems in which animal products are involved are relatively inefficient by such standards, because the interposition of the animal into the food chain results in an additional energy consumption without any compensating gain. However, it is unlikely that this type of evidence is sufficient to persuade the affluent to forego their steaks and become wholly vegetarian in their eating habits, especially if it includes the eating of processed grass.

Moreover, like financial balance sheets, the energy balance sheets must be examined with care and interpreted with caution. The food that we eat supplies not only energy, but also the proteins, major and minor chemical elements, and the vitamins which are the raw materials necessary to the body for growth and healthy existence. It is possible to provide some of these essential items from inorganic or synthetic sources, but in so doing an item from one column in the balance sheet is being transferred into another without significantly changing the final totals.

Accurate energy assessments are difficult to make. The total energy available in the end-product can be calculated on a calorific scale with relative ease, but calculations of the energy used in its production are much more difficult and liable to error. A considerable amount of the energy involved may be consumed off the farm. The production of fertilizers, crop-protection chemicals, machinery and equipment requires energy. To this must be added the energy used in conveying these materials to the farms, and the energy used to handle, transport, store, process and finally cook the end-product. The energy required to bring the finished food product to the mouth of the consumer may well exceed that expended by the farmer in its production, but it is very difficult to calculate accurately, and it can be subject to many variations.

Another difficulty in the preparation of a reliable and completely consistent energy balance sheet is that the essential energy source on which the whole food-production system depends, namely the Sun, may be free, but it is unpredictably variable in incidence, except in those areas where there is no moisture in the soil to grow anything at all. All agriculture, and indeed all life on Earth, depends on the ability of plants to utilise Sun energy and convert it into food for animals or men. Even the complicated food chain in the sea and its inhabitants depend basically on warmth from the Sun. The efficiency with which any food-production system uses solar energy is therefore the most important parameter in any energy balance.

The existence of mankind does not only depend on the growth of existing plants, but also on plants which grew in previous aeons and which were converted into the fossil fuels now so essential to a modern way of life. As the reserves of these fuels inexorably diminish, searches are now being carried out for alternative sources of energy. It seems to be of extreme importance that serious consideration should be given to try to short-circuit the long process of coal, gas or oil formation by growing crops for immediate conversion into some form of fuel, probably alcohol, for use by machines. This adds urgency for the precise solution of the energy equations of the plant-production systems.

Scientists and engineers are also examining other possible sources of additional power, such as the wind, the potential and kinetic energy of water, and geothermal heat from the deeper strata of the Earth. Like the growth of plants, wind and water energies are also manifestations of the heat of the Sun; the inner heat of the planet has a more complicated origin. Whether politicians and administrators have sufficient foresight and scientific awareness to encourage such research is a question to which only our grandchildren will know the answer.

Labour

The quantity and quality of labour are important factors in all industries, and agriculture is no exception. As much work on the farm has to be done without continuous supervision, it is not unfair to suggest that quality of individual work is a major factor in productivity. The agricultural industry in developed countries has a remarkable success record, second to none. A massive increase in production and productivity has been achieved over a period when there was a sharp decline in the total numbers of the labour force.

This is to the great credit of all involved, but the farm labourer is often still poorly rewarded in comparison with workers in other industries, both in terms of basic rates and real income. This is all the more remarkable when it is realised that the farm labourer is no longer an unskilled or semi-skilled employee carrying out time-consuming but relatively simple tasks. In many cases he is now a highly skilled technician, who frequently has to exercise judgement and take instant decisions, with little chance of consulting his superiors. Like his predecessors, he is usually expected to work irregular hours at anti-social times in what may be unpleasant weather conditions.

The illusion of an open-air, healthy life is rather shattered by the statistics of the occupationally induced diseases such as farmer's lung, rheumatism and arthritis among farm workers. Despite such risks, some workers may genuinely prefer the relatively free and varied life on the farm to the monotonous discipline of the factory floor; but they should not be penalised for their choice.

The dispersion of farm workers into very small groups, with those within one area often working under very dissimilar conditions and even doing entirely different types of work, makes it difficult for them to unite into an organisation which can present a common front to their employers. The absence of any alternative employment in some areas, and, to some extent, the tied cottage system offering housing to a family man, have contributed to a state of affairs where the farm workers appear to accept a minor role; but this is not the complete explanation.

A more important reason is perhaps that in farming, far more than in most other industries, there is a close personal contact and relationship between employer and employee. They often have to work side by side to achieve success by overcoming difficulties shared by both. Pride in achievement and, in the case of the stockmen, genuine concern for the welfare of his animals, tend to diminish industrial tension and resentment.

Nevertheless, it will be surprising if farm workers do not eventually realise how indispensable they are, and demand a higher financial reward as the numbers of staff decline, even at the cost of dearer food for everyone. On the other hand, many industries could learn valuable lessons from the staff management on the best farms.

The discussions in this chapter have been for the most part inconclusive, which is inevitable when the problems admit of no simple solution which will please everybody. The best that can be hoped for is that any policies that are adopted take into account all the factors involved in an impartial manner, and are flexible enough to be changed quickly if the results indicate that mistakes have been made. All dogmas, those accredited mendacities, spell danger.

Mobility of men and ideas

On some occasions, the social and economic pressures in one country may have a positive and enduring effect on the productivity else-where. Several years ago, Italians, who were accustomed to rural work in hot conditions, were readily prepared to accept casual work in the glasshouses of the Lea Valley in England for wages which were higher than they could earn at home. Not all of them returned with their savings to their native land, and the more enterprising among them managed eventually to acquire horticultural nurseries of their own, with the result that there still persists in the industry a colony of Italian origin.

The thriving glasshouse area of East Yorkshire in the north-east of England probably owes a great deal less to the climatic advantages of the area, which are limited to say the least, than it does to the well-established sea links between Hull and Rotterdam. Because of the difficulties in acquiring suitable sites for glasshouse nurseries in the Netherlands, some Dutchmen bought land more cheaply in Yorkshire than they could at home, and some even brought their glass structures with them.

A more important effect was that they brought new ideas for greenhouse and glasshouse construction, and also introduced tech-niques and expertise which they had perfected in the unrelenting competition for survival in Holland. If their success was perhaps initially resented by a few of the local inhabitants, other Yorkshiremen were not slow to adopt the new ideas and methods which were applicable to the local environment, with consequent profit to the community as a whole.

The intense competition for land in the Netherlands, and its close links with other East Anglian ports, have also been important factors in the expansion of the bulb crops industry in southern Lincolnshire, to the point where the export of daffodils from the district of Holland, Lincolnshire, threatens to surpass that from the province of Holland in the Netherlands.

One of the fears on joining the EEC was that there would be a mass invasion of England by land-hungry Dutchmen who might buy most of the farms which came onto the market. Although they have undoubtedly been present at some auctions and have occasionally been successful in their bids, there is as yet no sign that their infiltration has reached excessive proportions or has tended to raise unduly the prices of land. Perhaps comfort should be drawn from previous examples of international mobility suggesting that new-comers bringing new ideas and even new commodities may provide a welcome stimulus rather than unfair competition.

It would be pleasant and mutually advantageous to see a reverse migration, with British farmers who have acquired land in Europe having a similar leavening effect by introducing their own particular expertise, providing, as it were, a free demonstration farm. So far, only a few have been able to overcome the legal, fiscal, social, politicial and linguistic difficulties which prevent the Common Market being truly common to all.

The invasion of new farming ideas is not new, being common throughout historical time, although in the past it usually followed less peaceful invasions by armed force. Farming in the British Isles was successively affected by arrivals of Iron Age tribes, Romans, Saxons, Angles, Danes and Norwegian Vikings, culminating with the Norman triumph in 1066, a race which can only be described as a cross between Viking sires and Gallic dams. The effects of each of these invasions can still be seen in the pattern of British farms.

On a slightly less aggressive scale, the vast productive areas of Australia and New Zealand were opened up by settlers and colonists from the British Isles. Many Canadian farmers are descendants of the English, Scottish or French. Immigration over a period of some 300 years has influenced the agricultural scene of the United States of America, beginning with the English settlers along the east coast and continuing after Independence with the influx of farming families from almost every country in Europe.

The influence of 'in-comers' is often resented because they offer a threat to the existing inhabitants, but the civilised entry of new ideas into any system of land use can only be welcomed, and can lead to greater food production, no matter from what source such ideas originate. The only real danger which must be understood and avoided is that of permanent damage to the land potential.

Part V

The resultant problem and possible solutions

14

Interactions between factors

For convenience and simplicity, groups of related factors have so far been considered almost as if they acted independently of each other. In reality, all the factors are operating at one and the same time, and so there are complex and continual interactions among them. An attempt will now be made to examine these processes.

Furthermore, only passing reference has been made to another factor, namely time, the interaction of which with each and every other factor is often of critical importance. The time of the growing year at which a factor operates may be as important as, or more important than, its magnitude. For example, the average values of the weather factors, such as temperature, rainfall, sunshine and wind speed, may help to indicate the general suitability of a site for a particular farming enterprise, but unless these have been specially compiled with a special purpose in mind, they may be useless in indicating the true potential.

Prolonged periods of frost when fruit trees are dormant are of little significance to the grower, except that they could limit his activities on the land. A single night of sub-zero temperatures when the trees are in full blossom, a period which will vary from year to year and from place to place, can be a complete disaster, with a total loss of crop and annual income.

The frequency of occurrence of such late spring frosts may often decide the commercial viability of a site for fruit growing, even though the soil type, the soil-moisture regime and the incident sunshine are optimal for such an enterprise. The time factor is critical, but it is not the time indicated by the date on the calendar. It is the time on the phenological scale of crop development, which itself is determined by previous weather factors such as the extent of winter cold.

The interactions between the various factors are so numerous that it is impossible to deal with every possible combination. Some general idea of the major complications which arise can be given, and with the aim of explaining how many factors are involved, two specific examples will be considered in detail.

Production problems

The environmental factors of weather and climate react with the site factors, altitude, aspect, drainage and soil type, to determine the range and potential yields of commodities which could be produced. They set a potential ceiling on the productivity level of individual commodities and probable variability of such levels from season to season. They also determine the extent of the choices available to the producer and the scope for possible changes in production plans dictated by a changing market. These same environmental factors also determine the range and intensity of the unwanted organisms, weeds, pests and diseases which may cause loss in yields.

If the climate and situation are particularly suited to certain commodities, then there is a sensible tendency for the production thereof to be concentrated in that area. This has a profound effect in two ways on the incidence and persistence of pests and diseases and the prevalence of weeds. Airborne travel of these unwanted organisms is over shorter distances from initial foci to second-stage infection. Moreoever, once established, such enemies to production have large host populations in the immediate vicinity on which they can multiply, and failure to control them on one farm can threaten production on all the others.

The balance may change with the arrival and build-up of competitors and predators to the pathogens. It might be expected that an equilibrium would eventually be reached, and this might indeed be the case but for the fact that changes in weather conditions, sometimes small in magnitude but large in effect, continually alter the balance. It also should be remembered that there is generally a time lag between the upsurge of a pest and the arrival of the predator.

Although there may be a general tendency for some types of unwanted organisms to occur more frequently in a given area and so be more damaging to production than others unsuited to the environment, this state of affairs is more dynamic than static, and the spectrum of adverse factors is continually changing in both type and intensity. As the current problems are largely determined by the weather, the changes could only be foreseen accurately if precise detailed long-range weather forecasts were available, together with a complete knowledge of the organisms and their life cycles, a state of affairs improbable to say the least.

Difficult though the situation may be, there are technological and scientific developments at the disposal of the farmer enabling him to counteract the depressions in food production caused by unwanted organisms. These may act directly against the pathogens, and can only be effective if the farmers are willing and able to adopt and pay for the necessary control measures. Even so, there is no prospect of a final outright victory over the enemies to production. If one enemy is all but eradicated, another new species or mutation of the same species will tend to take its place. The ever-changing environment resulting from the interactions of weather, site and farming system provides endless opportunities for the continued variation of pest, disease and weed populations. The enemies are also often able to change their tactics more quickly than the farmer can change his defences. The best that science can do is to keep abreast of the constant change and try not to allow any enemy the chance to cause catastrophic losses.

Scientific developments are not likely to be able to change either the weather or the micro-environment to any major extent to the benefit of the farmer, although in some matters, such as irrigation or shelter, they can be very useful indeed. Even if it were known how to control the growing conditions perfectly, the amount of energy needed to do so would be prohibitive unless unforeseen sources of cheap energy became available. Completely controlled environments consume more energy than they produce in terms of food, and with the present trend in energy prices, their costs may become prohibitive.

Although the aim of technology is to help the farmer, the misuse of new techniques can cause serious environmental changes, some of which may be permanent. The power that is used to remove an existing pattern of vegetation can, if used in the wrong circumstances, produce a soil condition which is liable to wind or water erosion so that it becomes virtually sterile. The use of heavy high-powered equipment on a saturated soil may enable the completion of an urgent task, but only at the cost of reduced yields for several succeeding seasons because of soil structural damage.

What science can and does do is breed new races of plants and animals with higher output potentials and which are better adapted to the environmental conditions of a given area. It may even produce breeds and varieties which are less sensitive to fluctuations in seasonal conditions, and are thus more consistent in their performance. This stream of new biological material offers new opportunities, but it places a constant strain on all those involved in the chain between breeder and producer, facing them with a series of important decisions concerning choice and subsequent action.

New developments in improved machines and techniques helping the farmer, with more power, speed and precision, to carry out operations with less manpower and more certainty, are no less important. The adoption of new technology has thus brought about increased productivity and has enhanced the total output of food, despite the loss of large areas of good agricultural land. It is useless to speculate on the levels to which output might have risen without this diminution of land resources. It is unwise to be complacent and assume that reliance can be placed on further advances in science and technology to make good the deficit caused by future losses of cultivatable land.

Any investment in new technology is expensive to the farmer, and usually involves not only the purchase of new equipment, but also the continuing cost of maintenance and the subsequent replacement as it wears out or becomes obsolete. Keeping abreast of advances in new technology therefore depends on the existence of a buoyant demand for the produce, and on profit margins large enough for the producer to earn a living and also be able to spend more money to keep his system up to date.

It follows that farmers will tend to invest in new techniques when profit margins are high (particularly if doing so also reduces their tax liability), even though there is an obvious danger that if too many of them follow the same course, then supply may outpace demand. Conversely, although there may be a strong demand for increased output after disastrous harvests, farmers are then less likely to have the necessary available capital to buy the new aids which would help them remedy the deficiency of supply.

In such circumstances, an economic policy which rigidly insists that returns to farmers must be made only through the marketplace and debars them from access to cheap credit or equipment grants would have obvious disadvantages, and possibly disastrous results. It is a waste of national resources if a farmer who needs to improve his farming system is not able to do so because his present income is too low.

The replacement of men by machines has consequences which are not always foreseen. As machines become complex and are capable of greater outputs of work, they need highly skilled operators to use and service them. The farmer therefore becomes more and more dependent on the few men who remain on his staff, and has no immediate replacements if one is absent. Unless the farm is very large or is run in conjunction with another, he can generally only afford single units of specialist machinery. If the one such machine breaks down, then the necessary repairs cannot always be carried out on site, and often need expert attention which is only available from a distant servicing depot.

In such an emergency, neighbouring farmers may be able to provide temporary assistance if their own programme of work permits, or the farmer may be able to call in the help of contractors, which may be a costly procedure. A complete disaster might be avoided, but at very least it means that the precise timing and the speed of action which are the major advantages of a mechanised system have been lost.

Farmers are under increasing pressure (chiefly from the manufacturers) to consider the use of electronic computers to obtain rapid answers to complicated calculations. It is doubtful if there are more than a few who need a computer of their own, but there may be several who could benefit from access to a machine at an advisory centre. It must, however, be remembered that computers cannot work miracles, they can only obey the programs fed into them. The infallible rule 'Garbage in, garbage out' can lead to a fine selection of wrong answers.

Other problems arise from the fact that the high capital costs of low-labour, highly mechanised systems tend to make it more difficult to change the pattern of a farming system to meet changes in demand or in market prices. The making of a drastic change means the disposal of expensive equipment at a loss, and the replacement of it by more expensive equipment of a different type. Farm buildings may have to be modified, and certainly the farmer and his staff will have to acquire the new skills necessary for the efficient and profitable operation of the new system. The farmer may also have to develop new expertise in the methods of handling and marketing the new end-product.

It therefore follows that as a system with a high running cost and requiring a large capital investment becomes progressively less profitable, it becomes more difficult to change it. Paradoxically, it is when a system is running most successfully at maximum productivity that it engenders the best opportunity for change. With demand, environmental conditions and technological advances all capable of rapid unpredictable variations, it means that the ideal moment for planning and carrying out any change in a farming system is much easier to recognise in retrospect, and very difficult to take advantage of at the time.

Financial problems

The interactions among market demand, price levels, running costs and size of business do not form a consistent pattern. The degree to which prices and profit margins fall is an important but varying effect. If the fall in profit is about 10 per cent, then the large-scale operator with a large income may have to lower his standards of living for a little while, or draw on the profits of previous years, but he does not suffer serious hardship. For the small farmer, who may be equally efficient within his own area limitations, the same percentage drop may bring his already low income below subsistence level, and he has no reserves on which to call.

If, however, the price decrease continues, and especially if it drops low enough to give a net loss to the producer, then the impact of severity is reversed. The large business, having to meet bills for maintenance, fertilizers, chemicals, energy and labour, plus tax demands on its previous profits, together with high fixed charges for rent and interest payments on loans, may soon have difficult and even unsolvable money 'liquidity' problems. The small farmer, producing much of his essential food himself, does not have the same unavoidable outgoings. He can tighten his belt still further, try to supplement the family income by providing facilities for tourists, or by one or more members of his family finding other employment outside the farm, and so will be able to carry on farming. Moreover, as the small farmer operates on a less expensive scale, he may be the more able to modify the pattern of his farming to meet the needs of the times. Although in this way his general position is far more flexible than that of the large farmer, he may be in a locality where the environmental conditions limit his choice of farming type.

A number of large farming 'empires' now present in Britain were founded by small farmers who managed to survive the agricultural depression of the 1920s and 1930s by sheer hard work and the acceptance of a low standard of living. They then had the vision and determination to take full advantage of the more favourable conditions in the war-time and post-war years.

In consideration of financial problems, a word of caution should be introduced concerning the careless use of the mathematical term 'percentage'. It is essential that anyone hearing or reading this word should immediately ask the question 'Percentage of what?'. For example, a farmer who has spent 90 units in producing a commodity which sells for 100 units has made a profit of 10 units on an outlay of 90, or approximately 11 per cent. If now his costs increase by 10 per cent, while his income remains the same, then he has spent $90 + 9 = 99$ units and received 100 units, giving him a profit of 1 unit. His old profit was 10, so that his profits have decreased by 90 per cent due to a 10 per cent rise in costs. Suppose now that the price he receives for his commodity falls by 10 per cent to 90 units, which is equal to his outlay. His profit is nil and has decreased from 10 units by 100 per cent. The important lesson is that the profits to the farmer are about 10 times more sensitive than costs or prices because they are fractions of a smaller number. Equal percentages are not equal in significance, unless they refer to the same circumstances.

Labour problems

It has already been mentioned that mechanisation on the farm may cause labour replacement problems by diminishing the number of potential skilled workers in the rural population. In addition to this manpower scarcity, there may also be a reduction in the availability of part-time seasonal workers who are needed by the farmer at peak work periods, such as harvest.

Until efficient and reliable harvesting equipment is invented for commodities such as fruit, the farmer who cannot find harvest workers may be forced to change his cropping system. The alternatives are to increase costs by transporting casual workers from further afield, or to develop a 'pick your own' system, inviting the public to harvest the crop they require and pay him for the commodity and the privilege of picking it. The farmer gets the money, and the public get fresh produce of their own selection.

Changes have also taken place in the industries which support the farmer. The blacksmith who was able to repair or even make essential farm tools has tended to disappear from the village smithy and be replaced by an engineer in a more distant town. As equipment becomes more specialised and complex, this support industry evolves into several different engineers and electricians at different service centres. Admittedly such support services serve the same essential function as the village blacksmith in keeping the farm machinery moving, but the extra distance between the farmer and the repairer has to be paid for in both cash and delay; crop losses due to such delays may even be the more expensive item in the cost to the farmer. Larger farming companies may overcome this problem by employing their own engineer or mechanic, but he cannot operate efficiently without a further investment in a well-equipped workshop and a good stock of spare parts.

A similar pattern of change tends to emerge with all other associated industries, whether they supply the farmer or buy produce from him. Depots tend to get larger, but also they tend to get fewer and farther apart. They may carry a larger range of commodities and handle them more efficiently in larger vehicles or delivery vans, but only at an ever-increasing cost. Moreover, many farm approach roads were not designed to carry heavy lorries, so that the farmer either has to widen and reinforce them or provide loading points on the main road and complete the movement of goods with his own vehicles. In olden days, few farms were further away from a market town than the distance that could be covered by a horse and cart in half a day. In modern times, food often travels the length of a country or the breadth of a continent to find its market.

Social problems

The changes in village structure may also result in a build-up of sociological pressures. A declining population can bring about the closure of the village school, and even if it is possible for it to be kept open for infants, the older children will all have to finish their education elsewhere. Transport will be provided to carry these children to the larger schools with broader and better educational facilities, but this possible gain may be at the cost of producing a new generation which no longer identifies itself as part of the local agricultural community. Time spent in school buses will have replaced the time spent in learning the practices and lore of the countryside during playtime or part-time work on a farm. Children who have acquired a taste for town life may no longer wish to spend the rest of their lives on a comparatively isolated farm with few opportunities for communal leisure activity. One of the problems of the future may not be that food cannot be produced from upland marginal farmland, but that no one will be willing to undertake the work and conditions of living.

If the lost village population is wholly or partially replaced by urban residents or weekenders who spend their working days at another residence in towns, then a different sort of problem may arise. The newcomers may not like to have their pure country air polluted by the aroma of pig effluent, over-ripe silage or chemical sprays, nor may they be tolerant of a village street contaminated by mud or manure. As they neither benefit financially from such episodes nor depend on those responsible for their employment, they are apt to voice their disapproval in ways which cause more than a little friction, and they may even, on health or amenity grounds, try to get the objectionable practices restricted or completely stopped.

Sometimes the boot is on the other foot: it is the newcomers who object to any improvement which might change the face of a village, as they wish to preserve its 'olde worlde' charm which they find so attractive. For example, some have been known to object to the introduction of street lighting for which the native inhabitants have been fighting over a period of many angry years.

These local differences of opinion are but a small part of the wider struggle between those who wish to use the land to produce more food and those who enlist under banners of preservation and conservation. This does not imply that all the population is divided into two distinct, opposing camps. The majority wish to have a foot in both, considering changes in land use which give them pleasure and/or profit to be sensible legitimate advances, but those brought about by other people to be foolish, selfish exploitations which should be halted immediately if not sooner. It is true that there are those who try to reach a balanced impartial view, but their voices are seldom heard, and if heard, seldom listened to and understood.

The possible consequences of any change in land use often receive too little consideration, and in any case the end results may be very difficult to foresee. It may seem reasonable for town dwellers to demand more and better roads so that they may travel more quickly and safely to the country or seaside to enjoy their hard-earned leisure. Unfortunately, to satisfy this demand, the surrender of a few thousand hectares of agricultural land is required. The food production thereby lost cannot easily be made good by bringing less valuable land elsewhere into cultivation. When the new roads are at last completed and the urban dweller reaches his destination, he may be disappointed and surprised to find that farmers have made considerable changes to the landscape which he used to enjoy. To be fair, they also object when a new motorway cuts across the middle of their favourite view; but a country, like an army, depends on its lines of communication.

The changes on a farm cannot be explained as a simple cause-and-effect relationship. New technology is seldom the result of a conscious effort to bring the less favourable areas into cultivation to make good the losses incurred elsewhere. It is rather in the nature of a continuing firm demand which makes it possible to make good the decrease in food supply by increasing production. This increase needs expenditure on new machines and techniques, and in so doing changes the farming systems and alters land use and appearance.

This process is only possible if the new system can bear the costs of development and still be more profitable than the system it supersedes. The population as a whole may benefit in that food supplies are being maintained, even if they cost slightly more to cover the cost of the new developments. It does, however, appear inevitable that some of the consumers will object vociferously to the change in land use, and seek to prevent any repetition of the process, and if the change in use was ill advised, they have every right to do so.

The infinitely variable pattern woven by the constant combination and conflict of different factors influences the apparently simple everyday decisions as well as the major agricultural issues. It is impossible to describe, or even refer to, all the cases in which complications arise, but as an example an attempt will now be made to examine in detail the factors involved and the decisions that a farmer has to make when faced with the problem of the control of one single crop disease.

A disease problem

Over a series of years with wet summers in the 1840s, the potato crop was devastated by a new disease known as potato blight in most of the main growing areas in Europe. In Ireland, badly overpopulated and seriously undernourished, the potato was an essential staple item in the diet of most of its inhabitants. The widespread starvation which occurred there when the disease destroyed the potato crop was an important contributing cause to immediate civil unrest. The consequent emigration of many of the surviving Irish to Great Britain and, especially, to the United States of America left behind it a political aftermath which lingers on to the present day. For not the first time in history, the invasion of a new unknown pathogen affected the destiny of a nation.

It is not surprising that, although initial progress in understanding was painfully slow, potato blight is now one of the most thoroughly investigated and best understood of all the temperate fungal plant diseases. Considerable research effort still continues to try to produce high-yielding varieties which are resistant to this disease, and to discover more effective chemicals with which to combat its incidence.

The disease is carried over from one growing season to the next in potato tubers which are infected but which do not rot and break down. There are three main sources of this carried-over infection: the tubers which are left in the soil when the crop is lifted in the autumn (probably the main cause of the successive Irish epidemics), tubers discarded but not destroyed when the crop is graded prior to marketing, and infected seed tubers planted the following spring.

Some, but not all, of these infected tubers grow the next year, and under warm moist weather conditions the fungus develops a crop of spores on some of the leaves. These spores are then dispersed by wind and rain splash to nearby potato plants, which they infect if the leaves are moist and temperatures are suitable. After further incubation, a fresh crop of spores is produced and if the same warm moist conditions persist, the infection continues to spread throughout the crop and the crops in neighbouring fields, and the disease becomes epidemic.

The infection of the next generation of tubers takes place by the washing down of spores from the leaves by rain onto the tubers in the soil, or by lifted tubers coming into contact with the spore-carrying infected plant tops at harvest. Many of the infected potato tubers rot completely, but some survive to carry over the disease to the next growing season.

The amount of damage and loss of crop caused by the disease each year is the resultant of a complex function in which time interacts with the disease, the weather, the site, the husbandry practice, and with the control measures. The timing of the autumn rains is very significant. If a series of heavy storms occur before the potato harvest while the infected plant tops are still alive, then not only is there an immediate loss of crop, but also a high carry-over of disease inoculum to the next season.

Infected seed potatoes provide the most dangerous source of the initial foci of the disease attack the following year, because infection from within the crop is likely to be far more effective than infection from outside sources by spores carried on the wind. In order to minimise the chances of infection with virus diseases, most seed potatoes are grown in windy areas of high rainfall, such areas being unfavourable to the aphids which carry the most important potato viruses. Seed potatoes therefore tend to be at greatest risk when the weather in these specially selected areas is favourable for potato blight, higher temperatures than usual often being the critical factor.

The other important time–disease–crop interaction concerns the occurrence of weather conditions which enable the primary infected plants to produce spores, and also allow these spores to reach other nearby plants under warm moist conditions which last long enough for the transported spores to germinate and infect their new hosts.

If these weather conditions occur early in the summer and then re-occur at frequent intervals over the following weeks, the potato tops are quickly destroyed and there will be a serious depression of yield or even a total failure of the crop. If the first infection conditions are followed by dry or cool weather, then the progress of the disease is halted and little damage is done to the yield. If the first infection conditions do not occur until late summer, the decrease in final yield is also negligible.

On the other hand, a late attack increases the risk of the disease being transferred from the leaves to the tubers at lifting, and a long drawn out attack increases the chances of spores being washed down by rain to the tubers. Although the late attack may have little effect on the weight of total crop lifted, it may reduce the amount of saleable or storable tubers, and the time taken to separate the diseased tubers increases the labour costs. In addition, the amount of inoculum carried over until the next year is likely to be above normal, and this increases the danger of an early epidemic in the following crop.

It is somewhat paradoxical that warm wet summers which favour the development of potato blight also encourage the rapid bulking of the potato tubers. In such seasons, although the yield is diminished below its full potential by the early death of the plant tops, the total harvested yields may be greater than those in a hot dry summer when the disease is absent but when lack of soil moisture curtails development.

A second paradox is that if the disease reaches epidemic proportions quickly, then it may destroy the tops before there is time for many spores to be washed down to the tubers. In this case there is little loss of saleable potatoes and a minimum of inoculum available to infect the succeeding crop.

It can therefore be seen that the interactions between the amount of inoculum, the rates of development of the crop and the disease, and the crop growth stage at which infection occurs form a complex function which cannot be interpreted in advance, because the precise details of the controlling weather cannot be forecast with anything like the required degree of accuracy. Even with hindsight, the derivation of a weather–disease–yield relationship is very difficult.

The problem facing the farmer

Faced with the threat of blight, the farmer has to consider the questions he must answer in order to arrive at the most economical method of combatting the disease in his particular circumstances. First, he must decide on his best strategical approach, which can vary from doing nothing at all to adopting the most comprehensive and expensive protection programme.

This decision largely rests on his opinion of the interactions of the general climate of his farm, the local climate of the potato field, the concentration of the crop in the immediate neighbourhood, the expected maturity date of the variety of potato grown, the amount of money he has available to spend on plant protection, and the expected selling price of the crop. The type of summer climate in which potatoes flourish, namely, mild weather with no late frosts and frequent rain or showers to replenish soil moisture, is also likely to include warm, high-humidity periods which are so favourable to the infection and spread of the disease. It thus follows that the maximum disease risks occur in the areas where the crop is most popular.

It is theoretically possible to divide an area such as the British Isles into zones of equal liability to blight, but the climate within such zones cannot be regarded as totally homogeneous, and much could depend on local variations which would increase or decrease the risk. The areas usually considered to be at maximum risk are those in the west and south, including much of Ireland, the Devon and Cornwall peninsula and the Welsh counties bordering the Bristol Channel. Areas in north-east England and east Scotland are least liable to serious blight attacks.

Farmers living in the blight-prone areas rightly accept that an annual protective programme is an essential insurance against loss of yield. For farmers at the other end of the scale, such a programme would be a waste of money, as they need only fear a damaging incidence of blight once or twice a decade. Occasionally they might have to take some action and adopt swift measures to curb the disease, but their strategy would probably be based on the use of curative sprays.

It is the potato growers in the centre of the range of risk who face the most difficult planning programme. The issues are not clear cut, so that the rich and the poor, the optimist and the pessimist will come up with different answers. Much will depend on the total area at risk and the extent to which the farmer depends on the money from the sale of his potatoes in relation to his total income. The success or failure of any decision will rest entirely on the future weather.

If the potato grower decides that he should take precautions against the disease, he has to make the choice of relying on husbandry techniques, selecting a less susceptible seed variety, or using a protective or curative chemical control programme, or any combination of such options.

There are three main husbandry precautions that can be taken. The risk of fungal spores being washed down by rain to the tubers in the soil will be reduced if a good cover of the developing crop is created by special cultivations between the rows to provide high clod-free ridges. Although this extra cultivation of the soil may increase operating costs, it will almost invariably increase the marketable yield, because the absence of large soil clods at lifting time lessens the mechanical damage to the crop. If the weather is dry at harvest time, this damage may become excessive and result in a large number of tubers being unmarketable. Such cultivations also help to reduce the competition from weeds.

The second important husbandry technique is the destruction of the top growth before there is time for the spores to be washed down into the soil and onto the tubers below. The timing of this operation may be a matter of very considerable difficulty. If it is carried out too soon, the tubers do not have the opportunity to develop to their full potential, and the yield is reduced by curtailing their growth period. If it is delayed too long, especially if there is a change to wet soil conditions which will delay the operation still further, then heavy losses through tuber infection may well result.

Thirdly, attention to hygiene is important. Disease-free seed must be used even if extra expense is incurred. The ground must be cleared as far as possible of diseased tubers from a previous crop. Even 'ground-keepers' in an adjacent field or the site of an old potato clamp can provide a source for a disease attack the following year. If infected tubers still survive in the soil, efforts can be made to destroy their new growth before the disease can be dispersed from them. Potatoes which emerge from places where they have not been planted are a menace, not a bonus.

Choice of seed may provide a different form of defence. In some areas, early maturing varieties can be sown which can be lifted and sold before the disease normally appears or has a chance to depress the yield. This choice is not open to growers in the western and southern areas, where disease incidence is at its earliest, but in any case they would often prefer to grow the early potato varieties to make use of their early springs and to catch the lucrative high prices despite the lower yields.

Climate does not allow growers in other zones to compete with these southwestern growers in the production of this expensive first early crop, but the planting of second early varieties to fill the gap between the first earlies and the autumn main crop may provide a commercial solution. This plan is only possible if sufficient labour is available during the summer months, when there may be other crops making conflicting demands on the available sources of manpower.

The risk of a late spring frost is also a factor which restricts the choice of early potatoes to avoid blight. Growers on the western coasts may be relatively free from such a hazard, but further inland the dangers may be high in a dry spring, especially in a valley where the soil is best.

The planting of potato seed completely free from blight infection will do much to reduce the risk of disease, and will create epidemiological conditions in which other defence measures are more likely to be successful. Unfortunately, seed production areas which can reliably and consistently guarantee freedom from both potato blight and virus infection are not easy to find.

Some potato growers overcome this difficulty by buying virus-free seed each year and multiplying it under their own supervision, but this is only possible for the large-scale producers. It requires sites which are isolated from other sources of blight infection, scrupulous attention to hygiene, early destruction of the tops before any infection can occur, and may also necessitate an intensive chemical protection programme.

The farmer may also choose to grow only those varieties which have a high degree of genetic resistance to the disease, provided that they also satisfy his needs in respect to yield, quality, and market requirements. Some varieties have tops which are highly resistant to infection but are not immune to the disease, and possess tubers which are very susceptible. The growing of such varieties demands special vigilance, because if the tops are not destroyed as soon as they become infected, one heavy storm can transfer the spores to the tubers, with disastrous consequences. Even when some varieties show promising properties of resistance to both top and tuber blight, there is always the risk that new races of the fungus will emerge which can overcome this resistance. This means that during an epidemic, even such varieties have to be treated to make sure that they are kept disease free.

The final defence against the disease is the adoption of a chemical control system, but a number of correct decisions are needed to do this successfully. A choice has to be made from the available selection of spraying materials, all of which claim to be the best if the advertisements are to be believed. The farmer has to weigh proven past performance against cost, and also has to be alert for possible side-effects which can be harmful to some potato varieties or, in certain weather conditions, to adjacent crops. After selecting the materials there are then three critical questions: when to start spraying, how many applications are needed and at what time intervals, and when to stop spraying.

Plant pathologists and agricultural meteorologists can combine forces and issue warnings when the weather conditions have occurred which were favourable for the first infections by the disease. Errors in such forecasts are almost always on the premature side, so that the grower can, with some confidence, delay spraying until they are issued, provided that he has sufficient staff and spraying equipment to treat all his potato crops within about a fortnight, allowing for days when wind, rain or saturated soil make the operation impossible.

The decision regarding the optimum interval between spray applications is more difficult to make. Almost all the chemicals available for use depend for their efficiency on the placement of a film of the material on the foliage, thus inhibiting the germination of the fungal spores. Under the warm, wet, high-humidity conditions which are most suitable for disease spread, the crops grow vigorously and so develop new unprotected foliage. During rain, the existing chemical deposit on the old leaves tends to be washed or leached away. Further problems arise when the soil gets wetter with successive rains and it becomes more difficult, if not impossible, to operate tractor-drawn spraying machines, so that the risks of damage to the crop and to the soil structure increase.

The sprays can be applied speedily and efficiently from low-flying light aircraft, but this expensive solution is only possible if aerial spraying contractors operate in the area, and if they are not already fully employed by other farmers. Conveniently situated landing strips have to be available for the planes, and the crop fields have to be free from hazards to low flight, with no nearby obstacles such as electricity pylons, tall trees or steep hills. Although they take less time to spray a crop than machines moving along the ground, aircraft cannot operate safely in adverse weather conditions such as heavy rain, strong winds or poor ground-to-air visibility.

The best compromise to obtain the maximum protection at the lowest cost and to avoid crop and soil damage is not easy to reach, especially when the weather in the weeks ahead is so uncertain. The sprays seldom, if ever, provide a complete protection of the foliage, but they can often prolong the period available for the bulking of the crop by several weeks, during which time sufficient extra yield may be obtained which will bring the farmer his year's profit. Without the extra yield gained in this manner he would have had no profit at all.

Leaves infected with blight die off quickly if they are not sprayed. Spraying will cause them to die off more slowly, but this gain is offset by the longer time it provides for the spores to be washed down into the soil. The decision of when to stop protective spraying and when to destroy the tops, either mechanically or by another chemical spray, is therefore again critical for success. For a previously sprayed crop, the optimum date for haulm destruction will certainly be different from that for a crop which has had no such treatment.

Finally, the farmer has to weigh the increase in costs of his chosen strategy against the potential financial gains. The costs will vary with the disease and weather conditions, and be subject to the apparently inevitable inflation, but they can be calculated with some degree of accuracy. The prediction of the ultimate income and the consequent financial benefits is more difficult. Only in the seasons when the onset of potato blight causes a definite shortfall in supply can the farmer expect higher prices to cover his increased costs of control measures.

If there is a serious shortage of potato supplies in a country as a whole by the end of a season, then the enhanced profits arising from higher prices may well cover the disease control costs of the farmer for a number of seasons, unless the authorities decide to import stocks from elsewhere to bring the sale price down. If the grower is attempting to market a well presented, uniform, unblemished product of the type now required by bulk buyers such as supermarket chains, a small percentage of blight-infected tubers in his sample may destroy a reputation that has taken years to establish, even to the extent of losing future contracts.

The crop losses due to potato blight in England have tended to decline over the past 30 or so years, so that it might be concluded that because most potato growers have made sufficient profits to remain in business, they have proved their ability to solve the complex problems of disease control which have been outlined in the previous paragraphs. Even so, there still remains the major question of how modern techniques and know-how would face up to the challenge of a repeat of the weather conditions of the 1840s, with three successive years of severe blight attacks.

It seemed that this challenge might have to be met in 1983. The wet autumn of 1982 helped to provide ample inoculum for the following season. In 1983, the cold, wet, late spring delayed planting on many farms, and even where it had been possible at the normal time, the ensuing growth was slow. Warmer but still wet conditions in June led to a wide scatter of blight outbreaks, some earlier in the season than farmers had ever previously experienced, and these attacks occurred on crops which had scarcely started to bulk.

Everything was then set to discover whether modern prophylactic techniques could stop potato blight being the major cause of one of the most disastrous potato harvests of the present century. Then came one of the warmest and driest July months on record. Even where no remedial action had been taken, the spread of the disease was halted. August was nearly as dry as July, and this ensured that the contest between the disease and the crop defenders would not take place. By early September, some potato crops were drying off prematurely, not from blight, but from sheer lack of soil moisture.

The unpredictable weather had once more proved to be the final arbiter in what actually takes place on the farm, and this underlines the difficulties confronting farmers in the making of decisions and scientists in the making of agricultural prognostications. It also shows that if the weather produces the most adverse conditions at every critical stage in the life of a crop, then any indignant talk about unacceptable surpluses is sheer folly.

The problems concerning the defence of the potato crop against attacks by blight have been considered in great detail, but there are many other pests and diseases to which the crop is liable. All other crops are similarly threatened, and each threat demands the most careful attention of the grower, involving the making of a series of critical decisions, every one of which has got to be as nearly correct as possible.

The control of potato diseases is elementary compared with the very complex programmes of pesticides and fungicides needed to produce a consistent supply of unblemished desert apples.

Livestock farmers also have their own problems of a similar demanding nature, many of which have increased in magnitude because of the present trends towards the intensive rearing of stock under conditions which favour rapid spread of infection. A constant daily check has to be maintained on all animals, and if any suspicious symptoms are noticed, then the correct decisions have to be made and action has to be taken.

There are two main lessons to be learnt from this dissertation: first, there is no simple answer to any problem, and secondly, that the answer changes in accordance with the circumstances.

Problems of crop introduction

The second detailed example deals with a different type of problem, the interaction of factors governing an apparently simple political and economic course of action.

For many years almost all the sugar consumed in Britain was derived from imported sugar cane grown with cheap labour in distant climates almost ideally suited to the crop. Today the bulk of the sugar comes from sugar beet grown in the country, and very little cane sugar is imported. The reasons for this change are easy to identify.

The major initial incentive was a wartime necessity of becoming as independent as possible of imported food supplies. The realisation of the objective was made possible by a series of unrelated but inter-acting technological advances. Plant breeders developed varieties of sugar beet which were capable of a greater yield, and with roots containing a higher percentage of sugar. They also bred monogerm varieties which made precision drilling possible, and this in turn reduced the labour of singling the crop after emergence. It was then possible to achieve plant populations which were near the optimum in regard to number and spacing.

Agricultural engineers developed the drills and other cultivation equipment required and, most important of all, the machines which could harvest the crop. Chemists devised new materials to control the weeds and so saved much expensive hand labour by casual workers. They also provided new aphicides so that entomologists and plant pathologists could co-operate to plan well timed spray schedules to reduce the onset of sugar beet virus yellows, the major disease threat to the crop. The most dangerous pest, eelworm, was countered by the insistence of the sugar beet factories on an approved crop rotation system as a condition for a contract to grow the crop. The factories themselves improved their techniques of extraction and purification and, with all these added advantages, it would appear to be a simple matter for enough beet to be grown in Britain to make the country independent of external supplies of sugar.

In practice, it was not quite so easy as it sounds, because it raised political, economic and farm management problems which required positive solutions. The remaining contracts for cane sugar would have to be cancelled or allowed to run out and not be renewed. This would have serious economic effects on some of the small nations concerned, and this in turn would have an adverse effect on their ability and willingness to buy goods manufactured in Britain.

If a government is determined to go ahead with the change despite such objections, then it has to make certain that there is sufficient processing capacity available, which will entail the conversion of some factories from cane sugar to beet sugar extraction. New factories may have to be built on carefully chosen sites which are convenient to the major areas of proposed beet production.

Furthermore, there are the economic questions of whether sugar can be produced as cheaply from home grown beet as from imported cane. If (as in the EEC) imports are excluded, then the question changes to whether the British farmer can compete successfully under his climatic conditions with farmers growing sugar beet elsewhere in the Community.

The farmer now faces his problems. To start to grow or to increase his growing of beet, the farmer must have enough land capable of producing the crop and suitable for the operation of modern equipment essential to large-scale cultivations and harvesting. The fields must be of sufficient size, reasonably level, fertile and with few stones; the soil must be able to be worked to a fine tilth in time to provide a seed bed good enough to ensure a uniform high emergence of seedlings. The site must not be liable to wind erosion at the critical time between seed drilling and plant establishment, or extra expense has to be incurred to counteract this danger. The soil must also be retentive of moisture to enable a full root to develop, or an economical irrigation system with reliable water supplies must be available.

The autumn climate may be critical: wet conditions at harvest may make the operations of the lifting machinery difficult, if not impossible, and bone dry soil conditions at that stage would be equally frustrating. Any liability to autumn flooding would rule out a site which otherwise would have been acceptable. To produce the maximum sugar content, the growing crop needs plenty of sunshine, especially in the later stages.

The farm has to be within economic haulage distance of the beet processing factory which can offer the farmer a contract large enough to satisfy his requirements. A newcomer into beet production will need to grow an area large enough to justify the purchase of all the necessary specialised equipment. An existing grower may need only enough area to supply capacity employment of his machinery and labour force. If he is using such facilities to capacity, he would need to double his crop area and contract size to justify the purchase of more equipment.

Any introduction or extension of sugar beet growing will only be attractive to a farmer if it gives him a higher profit than the crop it replaces, and the assessment of probable profit may involve some very difficult and complex calculations. Apart from the uncertainty of future prices for sugar beet and the crops it would replace, its introduction into a cropping programme may have side-effects on the whole of the farm arable system and operational programme.

It may have a beneficial effect in providing a needed extra break in a cereal rotation, but if a farmer is already successfully operating a regime of continuous winter wheat, then the introduction of a one-year break of sugar beet may resurrect a 'take-all' disease problem in his cereals. He may have less time to prepare the land for a following winter cereal because sugar beet does not mature until late autumn, and he may thus be forced into spring sowings if the weather is unfavourable. Any delay in winter sowing or a change to spring sowing is virtually certain to diminish his income from his cereal crops the next season.

The farmer must also consider what effect the change in his farming system will have on the labour demand at the different periods of the year, and the relationship of this with the number of farm work days the weather is likely to allow him at the critical times.

The requirements for pest control are also a major factor, and the farmer should practise a four-year rotation of beet to reduce the risk of build-up of eelworm, so that only one-quarter of his total suitable land can be planted in any one year. The total area of suitable land must thus be at least four times the annual area necessary for economic operation.

The final decision to grow sugar beet or not has to be taken on the available evidence, and it will depend on the interactions of political, economic, climatic, soil, labour, technological and pest and disease factors. If any of these factors subsequently change, then the costs of production and the potential profits will also change. A farmer has thus not only to be able to make complex calculations, but must also be prepared to take a kind of gamble on future developments.

Similar examples could be quoted to illustrate the complicated interactions of factors in terms of any other crop or livestock enterprise. The number and relative importance of each factor will change with each product and with time, so that no permanent solution is possible. Farming may indeed be thought of as the art of the probable.

The future output of food and productivity in agriculture depend on how successful the majority of the farmers are in making the correct forward-looking decisions. They may be guided by instinct, experience or knowledge, they may be given advice from those they consult, or from those they do not, but unless their decisions are correct, food production will fail to meet the demands of an increasing world population.

The problems are very difficult, but the solutions adopted decide what actually happens on the ground at the work face of agriculture. It therefore seems appropriate at this stage to review the nature and multiplicity of the questions that a farmer has to answer in the course of every year.

15

The important decisions

The continual interactions between all the numerous variable factors affecting food production ensure that there is never likely to be a permanent state of equilibrium in agriculture. The picture is always changing, like the patterns in a rotating kaleidoscope, with the additional important complication that no two of the individual farms composing the agricultural pattern are identical.

The influences of climate, soil type, topography, past history, current farming policy, individual ability and financial backing, and a host of other factors, make it inevitable that each farm will have its own particular characteristics. Not only are these basic properties all different, but each is subject to change at different times, at different rates and in different ways. It is no wonder that agriculture is a difficult industry for which to plan or legislate; there is no common formula for success.

The concept of a placid, unchanging countryside as a series of rural paintings, differing fundamentally only according to the season of the year may be a comforting illusion to the urban mind, but it is more like a myth or a mirage. Change, varying in speed and direction from region to region, is the one inescapable certainty in the farming scene. The surprising result in many countries is that so many different factors, acting in various ways on numerous individual farmers, have given rise to an increase in productivity which is the envy of many other industries. Admittedly the progress has not been a steady process, nor has it been uniform in all branches of farming. There have been casualties along the way; but the record invites and deserves admiration.

Farming has had to survive serious depressions, some of them being the result of ill conceived economic policies, and yet it has survived and ultimately prospered. Although some of the credit for this recovery may be claimed to be due to some more enlightened policies and to efficient technological advances or scientific progress, much of the praise must be given to the farmers themselves, who have taken full advantage of the opportunities offered.

The good farmer accepts that change is a normal state of affairs and should not be regarded as an unexpected and deplorable emergency, although at times this is inevitable. His reactions to change are as positive and as skilled as those of a yacht helmsman to shifts of wind and tide, getting the best out of his boat, his sails and his crew. Sometimes he finds he is on the wrong tack, but as soon as he realises this he makes the necessary corrections. Once it is clear that he is making good headway, he is quickly joined by a fleet of competitors, some of which may finally outsail him. To maintain his lead he cannot relax for an instant, because the next decision he makes may be the critical one. To make no decision at all may be equally significant.

Recent changes in the visual pattern of the countryside provide ample evidence of how effectively this process operates. In England, for example, poppies and other weeds are now a rare sight in the cornfields, although all too often they have been replaced by wild oats. The rapid spread of the bright yellow flowers of oil seed rape from the Midlands across eastern England, traced easily by its increasing dominance as a weed on the verges of a motorway, is a clear indication of how farmers have seized a new opportunity to grow a new, profitable crop.

Traditional haystacks are being replaced by silage towers and clamps, affecting at least two of the human senses, sight and smell. There is growing concern and alarm each autumn at the widening spread of stubble fires which illustrate the increasing success of farmers in cereal production and their need to cut the costs of straw disposal. In pastures, the massive off-white beef cattle indicate where the red-coated, white-faced Herefords have receded before the advance of crosses with European breeds in the struggle for more efficient meat production, just as in earlier decades the black and white Friesian dairy cows replaced the old Shorthorn in the drive towards higher milk yields.

For those with eyes to see and with brains to comprehend, these and many other changes illustrate the march of progress, or at least what is hoped and believed to be progress. Other changes, such as those in husbandry techniques, in pest and disease control, and in breeding more productive varieties of crops, are less visually apparent, but they too have been adopted on such a scale that the reduced farming area can now produce nearly three-quarters of the British needs of temperate climate commodities.

It must not be supposed that this success story is a simple one of wise or fortunate innovators seizing a new opportunity and, when it has been proved to be successful, the following of others after them in a blind imitative rush for profit. The variability of potential in different farms and the heterogeneity of skill in the individual farmers present a much more complicated situation.

The enhancement of agricultural productivity is something like waging a war. Politicians and chiefs of staff can define objectives and plan a campaign, scientists and engineers can invent more effective weapons for factories to produce, and create efficient lines of communication to distribute them to the right places at the right times. All these activities are essential, but they are useless unless the commanders in the field make the right decisions and take the right actions when the local circumstances demand. There is a similar chain of command in agriculture. A wise governmental policy, improved techniques, better breeding stocks, the production of essential raw materials and machines, and their timely distribution are all needed, but ultimately it is the decisions and actions of the farmer at the 'battlefront' which determine victory or defeat.

Nevertheless, the farmer does not merely obey orders from higher command. He has much in common with the general at Field HQ or the admiral on his flagship. He must have the ability to make the correct strategical and tactical decisions, often with little time at his disposal and with inadequate information. He must, moreover, ensure that the long-term and short-term plans do not conflict with each other.

He must also avoid the temptation of taking any action which gives him immediate maximum profit if in so doing he impoverishes his land for future use, just as the army general cannot squander his resources of men and material on a tactical triumph but then be too weak to continue the campaign. On the other hand, the most brilliant strategic concepts are useless if a tactical blunder brings about an immediate crippling defeat. The most careful, far-sighted plans of a farmer to meet future demands cannot benefit him if he goes bankrupt before they come to fruition.

Although the many and varied factors already mentioned never cease to operate, their total impact on each decision is different. Daily, or even hourly, changes in weather conditions are of prime importance. A farmer may be well aware of the immediate needs of his stock or crops, but the weather often decides whether he can meet them. Weeds, pests or disease may be threatening to reduce his yields, but rain, wind or saturated soils may prevent him doing anything about it. Pastures may be rich with new grass, but if the soil is so waterlogged that it will be seriously damaged by the tread of trampling hooves, then his cows will have to stay in the yards or under cover and have to have fodder brought to them at extra expense.

Even when the weather is so favourable that all land activity is possible, the farmer has then to decide which work is the most urgent and must be given priority. There are always difficult problems to be solved involving the present and the possible future weather conditions, the conflicting demands of crops and stock, or even individual fields or single animals, and the available resources of labour and equipment. It is all too often true that there are never enough pairs of hands during the week but too many on pay night.

The calculations for future strategy involve other variables which are just as unpredictable as the future weather, and there are always long lists of problems awaiting operational decisions. Each year the farmer has to answer the same important question: 'Is my present system of farming the one best suited to satisfy my future ambitions?'. Even if he is satisfied that his mode of farming is perfectly attuned to his environmental conditions and to the resources at his command, even if there are no foreseeable changes in political or social constraints, some changes may still be unavoidable.

The one forecast he can make which is almost certain to be correct is that the total cost of the farm inputs, made up of rent or loan interest, labour, fuel, repairs and maintenance, seeds, stock replacement, transport, marketing expenses, in fact everything that has to be bought or brought on to the farm, will rise. It is almost equally certain that if there is a corresponding rise in the prices of his produce, it will not become effective until long after many of his bills have had to be paid.

He therefore has to devise a plan for making his system more efficient or accept a fall in his real income. He has to consider the possibilities of improved husbandry techniques, the use of higher yielding strains of stock or plants, the better control of unwanted organisms, the more effective deployment of labour and machines, or any combination of these options. The one solution which is untenable is to maintain the existing system and to alter nothing. If circumstances change, the farmer must change with them.

If the farmer decides that it is necessary to modify his farming system, then there are different and probably even more difficult problems to solve. Any change that he makes cannot have its full effect on his income until at least one growing cycle is completed. If the proposed change is a major one and involves considerable capital expense, he may be committing himself to a course of action over several years, in which case he is forced to try to estimate demand and prices for a long time ahead.

He can reasonably expect that there will be no major climatic change to disturb his calculations, so that he will have to contend only with the range of weather conditions to which he and his forbears are accustomed. The risks he is running on this assumption are greatest if he is operating towards the fringe of suitable conditions for the project he has in mind. He can only hope that there will not be any major change in political policy which will affect the accuracy of his estimates.

For a farmer contemplating change, the list of possible alternatives is restricted by the environmental conditions of his farm and by the technical skills and financial resources at his command. Having decided what appears to be the best policy, he then has to calculate the requirements in terms of additional land, buildings, stock, equipment and labour in order to implement it, and he also has to decide how the project can be financed.

It may be necessary for the farmer himself, or some of his staff, to be trained to acquire new skills. The amount of time and money this requires plus the capital needed to obtain all the essential components needed to operate the new system will all have to be estimated correctly. The effects of this period of change on the cash flow of his business and his financial stability will demand very serious consideration.

Once he has embarked upon his new course of action, the farmer may receive help from private, commercial or governmental advisers, but the conditions under which he works are unique to his farm, and his level of final success will be largely determined by his own technical and managerial ability supported by the capabilities of his staff. Good fortune often comes in agriculture to those who deserve it; good luck is more impartial.

The farmer has one advantage over a field commander of any armed force. In most countries where a degree of personal freedom still exists, no chiefs of staff or political masters can order the farmer to change his own particular strategic plan or prevent him trying to implement it. Nor, if his results do not please them, can they in a free society countermand his orders or remove him from his post. The remarkable outcome is that, with so many independent farmers each following their own chosen strategy and tactics without any major central coordination, enough are so successful that there has been a continual rise in both output and productivity, subject only to those variations caused by the impact of weather-sensitive factors.

For the most efficient use of land in any given environment, there are optimum ranges of size of holding for any system of farming. It therefore follows that the farming structure, or the pattern of distribution of land and resources between different owners and the size and quality of the land farmed by each occupier, is of fundamental importance to the prosperity of the agricultural industry.

Customs of inheritance or out-dated laws which divide holdings between too many heirs can cause fragmentation, converting successful farms into non-viable units. Once such subdivisions have occurred, strongly held but ill conceived political and social pressures may make it virtually impossible to put the pieces together again. It is easy to make comparisons between countries with a highly productive industry composed of farms which are mainly large enough to support the farmer and his family and those countries with a low productivity resulting from a large number of inefficient small holdings, but it is much harder to devise ways of rectifying the situation. Indeed, the ideal farming structure is as difficult to define as the perfect woman, as so much depends on the eye of the beholder.

The size of the smallest viable unit has less to do with its physical dimensions than whether it is large enough in the hands of a competent farmer to provide him with a sufficient income. This income must be enough to satisfy the necessary living standards of the farmer and his dependants, plus a sufficient margin for depreciation, maintenance and replacement of buildings, stock and equipment, plus a reserve to act as a buffer against losses in unfavourable seasons. Replacement costs will vary enormously according to the type of farming system and with the unpredictable expense of having to invest in new methods.

The individual farmer's definition of a reasonable standard of living will be just as variable. The more modest may be satisfied with simple housing, food and clothing, a small car for transport of all types of load, part-time technical training for the son and heir, and few or no holidays. Higher up the scale, food and shelter become more luxurious, and a powerful all-purpose car with radio telephone and a second car for social occasions, a college diploma for the heir, and a holiday abroad, are all included in the recognised standard. In the real upper echelons, a hard tennis court and a swimming pool are obligatory to maintain status, and a selection of motor vehicles plus an aircraft or helicopter to travel from one part of the farming empire to another are all regarded as essential. The stress of controlling it all necessitates at least one month per year in the sunshine of the West Indies or Seychelles, and a winter break on the ski slopes to recuperate.

Some sociologists would prefer a more egalitarian system, with a greater uniformity in size of holdings. They prefer to overlook the fact that the talents and ambitions of farmers are not and are never likely to be equal or uniform. Even if their ideas could be enforced, it would be unlikely that there would be any lasting benefit to either producers or consumers. The historical evidence of attempts to impose such schemes is that the reverse would happen, and that disparities would soon being to reappear. It seems that man, like many animals, seems to feel the need for some sort of 'pecking order'. Without it there would be no 'Hit Parade' or 'Top Twenty' in the popular music of the day.

In Britain there exists a kind of flexible structure with a wide variation in the size and type of farming enterprise. However, over the years and centuries there has never been a state of equilibrium, and there is now a persistent trend towards fewer and larger farm businesses. In the course of this change, the absorption of small non-viable units into larger sized holdings has made a contribution to the success of the industry; but as a position is approached in which only 20 per cent of the farmers are responsible for nearly 80 per cent of the output, it may be timely to consider whether there are any dangers in the continuation of such a trend.

In the past, an important contribution to progress in agriculture has been the rise from the ranks of employees of men with skill, enthusiasm and vision who have established themselves as farmers in their own right. Now, with the average value of farm land nearing £1,000 per hectare, and good land realising half as much again at auction, the chances of young men, able, hard working, and ambitious, being able to purchase a holding of viable size and also finding the considerable working capital to run it successfully are seriously diminished. This state of affairs cannot be good for an industry in which the transfusion of new blood is essential for progress.

At the other end of the scale, the aggregation of land into large areas owned by a single individual or large company may not always enhance productivity. When land is purchased by the managers of pension funds or similar bodies primarily concerned in acquiring an asset with a rising capital value, there may be little incentive to make long-term plans to ensure maximum efficient production. Even when this is a prime objective, big may not always be beautiful, or even efficient. Even when the owner is an able and experienced farmer, there can be difficulties in large enterprises arising from the need for trust and understanding between farmer and worker, a state of affairs which can often be a feature on the best run smaller farms. This mutual trust is an asset impossible to quantify on a balance sheet, but its absence may well cause a drop in the profits column.

When land passes into the ownership of a commercial company with no farming experience, even greater problems may arise. It is not always realised that different farms can have very diverse potentials in the range of products they can produce, and that managers have to be carefully chosen with the skills to match this potential. Having appointed the right manager, it is also essential that he should be closely involved in the planning of farming strategy, and that once this has been decided he should be given full authority to carry it out. Interference with the tactical decisions of an expert farm manager concerning farm operations can be as disastrous as overriding the orders of an admiral in the middle of a sea battle. Even so, it happens often enough to make one suggest that good farm managers should be fitted with Nelsonian (blind) eyes as standard equipment.

Failure to understand the complexities of farming and the need for efficient on-the-spot control may cause some large holdings to disintegrate, and although this may bring financial loss to a few, the community as a whole may benefit from the return to units of a more sensible size. The fields that have to be disposed of are most frequently taken over by more competent owners. A worse peril arises when a large company tries to play safe by sticking to old and tried methods long after they have become outmoded, and is afraid to invest money in new techniques and enterprises. Output may not fall but remain static, and with rising costs, real productivity decreases. When this type of situation arises, the country as a whole suffers because the output per unit area is less than it should be and the cost of food production rises.

There is yet another danger in the reduction of the number of farmers. Progress in agriculture owes much to a few innovators, men of ability, courage and foresight who have been prepared to take the risks of trying out new ideas. It is true that they had to have reached a reasonable level of success before they had the opportunity to experiment, but if the higher ranks of farming are confined to fewer and fewer people, then there will be less opportunities for an innovator to make his contribution to progress.

It is almost impossible to define precisely the ideal structure for an agricultural industry, but it is important to realise that certain attributes are essential. The structure must be flexible to be able to respond quickly to changing conditions, and it must not be out of proportion at either its upper or lower extremities. There is much to be said for a system which allows for both promotion and relegation so that the best can prosper and the worst cannot become a brake on progress. Justice without equality is preferable to equality without justice.

Governments which aim to increase agricultural productivity have fewer effective choices of action than most people realise. They really only have four main courses of action open to them: a policy of 'laissez-faire', the threat of the 'stick', the promise of the 'carrot', or the encouragement of a new idea. All of these options have their limitations.

Laissez-faire, the policy of minimum interference, implies reliance on the response of farmers in a desirable manner to the unrestricted laws of supply and demand. As explained earlier, this can only lead to an unpredictable oscillation between surplus and deficit, which brings few benefits to either producer or consumer. There is also the risk that too much dependence may be placed on the continued supplies of cheap imports of essential foods. Until the world arrives at the Utopian or Arcadian state wherein neither strikes nor wars can instantly sever transport services and adverse weather never occurs anywhere, such a policy is more likely to be suicidal than wise.

Farmers, like other reasonable people, respect and obey laws which are clearly of benefit to all concerned, such as those designed to improve human safety, prevent the spread of disease, or obviate nuisances to neighbours or travellers, even if such laws restrict their own activities, but there is a limit to such obedience. They have survived the vicissitudes of wars and political upheavals over many hundreds of years with a strength of character and an independent spirit unlikely to take kindly to the idea that any state official should dictate to them exactly what they should produce and how they should go about it.

Indeed, it is improbable that even the most autocratic totalitarian regime has either the ability or the power to control the precise level and type of agricultural production. It may set rigid targets for every farmer, but it cannot command the growing conditions or divert the onset of bad weather. Attempts to centralise the direction of detailed farming activities in the past have hardly been conspicuous for their success. In an industry wherein the critical factors are constantly varying, rigidity is a recipe for disaster.

Even if the master plan were perfect, it would not be an easy task to supervise the activities of every farmer and farm worker and decide if they are efficiently trying to carry out the allotted task and reach the predetermined target. An immense army of supervisors and controllers would be needed to attempt such action, and would add very significantly to the costs of production, with a very doubtful gain in output. Nor would it be easy to refute the claims that any shortfall in production was due to the old enemies, weather and pestilence, rather than disobedience or lack of effort. It is almost impossible with most food commodities to check that the amounts produced are the same as those reaching the official market place, especially if there are many hungry mouths along the route.

The 'stick' thus being of limited efficacy, it is not surprising that more hopes of coercion are placed on the use of a 'carrot'. Direct or indirect financial inducements are naturally more popular with the farmer than any form of compulsion, but this does not mean that they are necessarily always effective.

Direct subsidies on individual products which can enable a small farmer to carry on his farming in relatively unsuitable conditions may also at the same time give a completely unnecessary additional profit to the large farm business on first-class land. Furthermore, such financial help may remove the incentive to become more efficient or to venture into the production of new commodities more suited to the local environment. Inducements which aim to switch production from areas of surplus to areas where there is a deficiency are seldom cost effective. The more efficient farmer would often make such a change without governmental aid if it was operationally sensible and economically justifiable. On the other hand, the farmer struggling to survive is possibly encouraged to change to a system which is even less suited to his growing conditions or his husbandry talents. The cynic might argue that if the more progressive are thus made richer and the inefficient go bankrupt, then the industry as a whole has benefited, even if this was not exactly the original intention.

Investment in research and development has a much better record of success than most governmental planning, although how much this success is attributable to wisdom and how much to good fortune is a matter of opinion. The dilemma is whether maximum resources should be concentrated on basic research which could lead to unpredictable advances in unforeseen directions or on the more down-to-earth identification, consideration and elimination of individual limiting factors to production. Usually a compromise has to be arrived at, making the best use of available resources in the light of immediate needs. Problems are rarely solved quickly, each one seeming to have its own time when it is ripe for solution. All that is then needed is for the right man to come along and act as midwife.

In practice, the decision as to the direction of mental and experimental effort often rests with the scientists and technologists rather than with the politician or the administrator. There is no way of controlling or forcing the emergence of new ideas, and no way of knowing whether they will lead to new advances or help to solve existing problems. Much can often depend on serendipity, that pleasant combination of accident and wisdom. Perhaps the most difficult decision is the picking of the right time for the exploitation of a new idea and its introduction into farming practice.

Both those producing the new ideas and those wishing to exploit them have to realise that the most brilliant concept with the best potential use can only be successful in practice if a sufficient number of farmers believe that it is in their own interests to accept it. No outside agency, commercial or political, can raise productivity without the active, whole-hearted cooperation of the farmer. It therefore follows that farmers need to be convinced that the new methods or new policies aimed at increased productivity will be to their advantage operationally or financially, and preferably both.

It also has to be accepted that increase in productivity invariably causes changes in the pattern of life in the countryside. A stable pattern of farming or farm structure is not always an indication of an ideal system, it may be a symptom of a system which is stagnant and in danger of decay. The difficult problem is what degree of change is necessary to maintain progress, and what is likely to be the long-term effects of such a change.

It therefore seems that the best aim is towards a flexible and mutating state of affairs in which farmers will have enough freedom of choice to pursue their own legitimate ambitions without causing irreparable damage to the quality of the environment. Whatever the conditions imposed upon them by the decisions of others, each and every farmer has to make his own decisions every day of the year.

After all is said and done, all the speeches made, all the laws passed and the regulations promulgated and enforced, success in food production ultimately depends on the wisdom of the decisions made by the farmer and the ability of farm workers to carry them out.

16

The way ahead

The modest objective of the previous chapters has been to outline the major factors that affect agricultural production and to give some indication of how they act and interact. We have no intention of assuming the role of prophets and trying to foresee the future course of events. This book is not intended to be a crystal ball in which all will be revealed.

Until the dreams of scientists are as consistent and as meaningful as those of Pharaoh, their interpretations by economists as accurate as those of Joseph, and the consequent administrative judgements as wise as those of Solomon, we believe that long-range predictions are futile.

All that we can do is to comment on the present state of affairs concerning the various factors we have discussed, and to make some suggestions for future action which seem likely to be more of a help than a handicap.

Weather and climate

Weather in the short term, and climate in the long term, are likely to continue to play dominant roles in regard to future food production, as they have done in the past. We cannot see that there is any convincing evidence indicating that any widespread catastrophic change in world climate is imminent. The climate of any part of the world will always tend to vary slightly over the generations, and even a continued trend in one direction of change will probably merely transfer the most favourable areas of production from one part of the world to another.

There does not seem to be any economic possibility of any successful man-made modifications of climate to the advantage of agriculture except on a very restricted scale. With the possible exceptions of the provision of shelter or irrigation, the attempts of man to control the weather for the growth of his crops has always been an expensive operation, and such costs are not likely to decrease in terms of money or energy. The effects of increasing atmospheric carbon dioxide will have to be carefully examined.

The better adaptation of biological material to the conditions of existing climates is likely to continue. This may well enhance productivity, but it will only minimally increase the choice of available farming systems, and it will only marginally reduce the uncertainties in yield due to the variations of the weather.

The interactions of climate, soil and the local environment will always determine the degree of choice available to a farmer in regard to what crops he should grow or which animals he should rear. This interaction also determines the potential yield of any commodity in a given year on a given site, although the possibilities of reaching such a potential depend on other factors.

Although we may become more accurate in our appreciation of the capability range of different localities and their relative levels of potential production, it seems most unlikely that we will be able to reduce such disparities to any great extent. Variations in farming skill or in available scientific and technological aids may sometimes obscure these fundamental differences, but they do not make them disappear. No matter to what extent the influences under the control of man are improved in his favour, there will always remain limitations on the choice of farming systems, and variations in the potential outputs will persist in different environmental conditions.

The changing nature of the annual weather patterns will continue to cause fluctuations in output on local, regional and global scales. There seems to be little chance that long-range weather forecasting will become sufficiently accurate in the near future to enable these yield variations to be predicted. In the absence of such advice, it is impossible to take counter-measures against future adverse conditions or to take advantage of the reliable prospect of forthcoming future weather. The challenges of the environment will have to be met as and when they occur.

It therefore follows that the world yields of most food commodities must be subject to a degree of fluctuation. Surpluses of storable commodities produced in good years must be accepted as an essential part of the system, and should be used to balance the shortfalls in the lean years; they should not be regarded as an embarrassment to be got rid of at any cost.

More thought should be given to the extent of the reserves required of the major commodities so as to provide a reasonable insurance against the risk of future shortages. The location and cost of storage and the degree of loss incurred during the storage period should be considered in relation to the amount of independence required. This will involve some difficult agroclimatological and political assessments on the availability of alternative sources of supply.

Unwanted organisms

It is highly probable that our understanding of the unwanted organisms (pests, diseases and weeds) will continue to improve and that methods of controlling them will become more efficient. Progress along such lines may indeed offer the best prospects for any increase in the total world food production. Experience has already suggested that the most cost-effective application of sciences such as meteorology to agriculture is in the identification of the environmental factors in epidemiology.

It is also probable that the costs of the necessary prevention or control operations will also continue to rise, and similar or even greater rises are to be expected in all other production costs. If land prices continue to escalate, then the necessity of maintaining or, better still, increasing output also rises, so that an increase in the premium to insure against the losses to unwanted organisms becomes acceptable to the farmer. It follows that in the end the consumer will have to meet these costs by paying more for food.

No final solution to the problem of controlling pests, diseases and weeds can be hoped for, any more than medicine can be expected to find a cure for all human disorders. Some of the problems may apparently disappear, but there is no guarantee that changes in the pathogens or in the environmental conditions will not cause a subsequent resurgence. Biological systems under severe stress seem capable of rapid diversification to minimise the effects of the stress.

It thus seems likely that there will always be unsolved problems or new threats emerging to fill the space created by the elimination of the old enemies to food production. It is often a difficult decision to make as to whether a farmer should relax or abandon precautions that have been so unsuccessful in the past that it seems that the threat has vanished; it may only by lying in wait. It therefore appears that in addition to the costs of regular precautions, the farmer must also be prepared to pay for a continued programme of research and development.

The biological forces acting against maximum food production are far too powerful, persistent and capable of continual modification for them ever to be finally defeated. The very most that scientists and farmers can hope to achieve is to restrict their influence. This will involve a constant vigilance, continued scientific investigation, and a series of critical decisions.

The value of progress

It is difficult, if not impossible, to state in precise financial terms the benefits that have accrued from any one development or innovation.

Except under very strictly controlled experimental conditions, it is rare for only a single factor to change and for everything else to remain unaltered. Even if such conditions are imposed, the results are likely to vary in magnitude at different locations and in different seasons.

As we have already indicated, complex interactions may result from one apparently simple change. The prediction of the benefits to be expected from yet undiscovered innovations is a venture into the realms of science fiction. What does seem certain is that such innovations will continue. New discoveries and inventions have helped to enhance agricultural productivity since the beginning, and it is very unlikely that the flow of ideas will cease suddenly in the coming years.

The difficulty for any controlling authority is in deciding how much money can be spent on research and development, and in what way such expenditure is most efficiently deployed. An even greater difficulty arises in the problem of putting the results of such effort into full working operation at the food production level.

There still exists in some quarters a kind of illusion that the addition of the adjective 'scientific' to the word 'research' produces a combination with an in-built guarantee of success. In practice, the expenditure of money on scientific research is an act of faith, not unlike investing on the Stock Exchange or betting on football pools or racehorses. Past form may give some guide to future performance, but only too often the next step forward is taken by unknowns who have had great difficulty in obtaining the initial financial support. Nobody really knows where the next successful idea will spring from, and the important felicity is the ability to recognise it when it emerges.

Much is spoken of the freedom of research, and indeed a very strong case could be made out for a system wherein the best scientists are selected, given as much money as can be spared, and then trusted to do their best to get on with the search for new knowledge. The only man who really can tell whether a problem is about to be solved is the man doing the work. The director of research may have a sound suspicion that something is about to break, but a research committee can be completely out of touch.

In days of financial stringency and a clamour for the solution of important problems, there is an increasing tendency for the holders of the purse-strings to inflict more and more restrictive controls on the research workers, sometimes with far from the best results. A point of absurdity can be reached if the size of a research grant is exceeded by the costs of its administration, or if more time and effort is spent in writing prospectuses and reports than in considering the problem. In any case, scientific problems tend to yield to gentle pressure, not brute force. Nature prefers seduction to rape, and seems to choose her own time for the revelation of her secrets.

Research planning

The question that now arises is whether the present systems are the most likely to produce useful results, or whether there is any room for improvement. Too often in many countries research in agriculture has been subjected to a stop–go system unrelated to the state of the industry or the demand for its products, but governed by the amount of tax contributed, the budget surplus or deficit, and by the philosophy of the government in office.

Research is not an instant process which can be switched on or off at will. Inspiration may come in a flash, but this is only the beginning of a chain of events. New ideas rarely arrive by accident, and are more likely to emerge slowly over a period of time. Private thought and mutual discussion may give birth to a new line of approach, but only experiment and experience can test it thoroughly in an open-ended process of trial and error.

The difficulty, and in some cases the impossibility, of curtailing the length of time required for plants and animals to complete their life cycles, plus the need for a repetition of experiments and tests over a range of environmental conditions, make it imperative that agricultural research programmes should be planned over a period of time. Once a technique or product worthy of test under field conditions has emerged, it is to be expected that it will usually take at least three years before any possible verdict can be given.

The sensible planning of research programmes is thus dependent on a stable supply of resources in terms of both manpower and materials. This might be best achieved if the national expenditure on such research were a fixed percentage of the gross agricultural output averaged over five years to allow for the inevitable fluctuations. This would ensure a predictable supply of funds which would be largely unaffected by inflation, but which would be automatically geared to the expansion or contraction of the industry as a whole.

The allocation of such funds would be subject to a periodic review, so that money could be apportioned to commodities according to whether they exceeded or fell short of demand. Although other factors, such as the emergence of promising ideas or new products, have to be taken into account, it seems reasonable to invest more on research into products which are in short supply than into those of which there is already an embarrassingly large surplus.

There are some topics in which private enterprise can, and should, supplement government-sponsored research and in many ways they are the more appropriate agencies. This applies especially to the discovery and development of new chemicals or crop-protection products and in the design of new machinery. In practice, the high and increasing costs of research and development tend to channel the efforts of commercial firms into searches for products which are likely to have a large selling potential, preferably on an international scale.

This is particularly true in regard to new chemicals, where the understandable concern about their potential dangers to the environment in general, as well as to the consumers of the products to which they are applied, demands the production of satisfactory evidence of their safety before they can be put on the market. The heavy cost of providing this evidence is too great for it to be incurred for commodities with only a limited demand or for the extension of the use of existing products to less widely grown plants or reared stock.

These 'minor' commodities may be extremely important to the economy of individual farmers or to a number of growers in a region of specialised production, so that in such circumstances it may be desirable for state research to complement the activities of commercial firms in the interests of both the producers and the consumers. This may also involve the acceptance of legal liability by the state for damages if any unforeseen adverse side-effects eventually emerge in field use.

The cost and complexity of the buildings and equipment needed by research scientists are constantly increasing, so that there is a tendency to concentrate their activities in fewer but larger establishments to make the maximum use of these expensive facilities. This has a number of obvious advantages, one of which would be that by assembling workers in different disciplines under one roof, it would be hoped that cooperation between them would be improved. Proximity should provide the opportunity to stimulate discussion, criticism and help, and thus engender the desirable cross fertilisation of ideas.

In practice, these hopes are not always realised. The increasing degree of specialisation by scientists at an early stage in their careers tends to produce a greater number of small disciplines, each speaking its own specialised language. It thus becomes easier for one specialist to communicate by long-distance telephone to a fellow member of his restricted subject in a foreign country than to hold a useful discussion with a member of a different discipline in the room next door.

Present trends in postgraduate education or in career structure do little to produce the polymaths who are capable of understanding and coordinating the efforts of the super-specialists, and yet there are few problems which can be solved satisfactorily by the exclusive use of one scientific discipline. The extent to which consultation and cooperation can occur will greatly depend on the personalities of the scientists involved, and on the traditions of their university or research establishment. Many obstacles can be overcome if there is a will to do so, and informal lines of communication are often more efficient than carefully planned liaison.

Another handicap to progress has been called the 'ivory tower' syndrome. The seclusion of bright intellects within any one close-knit community, be it religious, philosophical or scientific, can induce an introspective attitude creating resistance or even hostility to ideas generated elsewhere, particularly if the inmates of such enclaves are recruited at an early age and remain there for the rest of their working lives. However much a deep seclusion may be conducive to clear thought, it may be difficult at the same time to be aware of the rapid changes taking place in the outside world, so that too much effort may be spent on solving the problems of yesterday instead of facing up to those of tomorrow.

For steady useful progress, there must be a two-way exchange of information between the research station and the practitioner. Not all the new ideas originate in the laboratory, and not all the common practices are due for replacement. Above all, each wing of the farming army should be aware of the strengths and limitations of the others.

Location of research

Some of these fundamental or self-induced difficulties may be overcome by the wise and tactful actions of professors or research directors, but a more intractable problem is met when deciding where to locate a research station, and the answer is not always easy to find which will meet all requirements. All countries have to make decisions of this type at some stage of their development, and the answers they arrive at will vary greatly according to the local and national circumstances. Some of the principles involved may be illustrated by considering the situation in the British Isles.

The sites of some of the earliest and most distinguished research institutes in Britain were a consequence of the enthusiasm and generosity of local pioneers, who donated land for their foundation, often in the areas in which they lived. The result of this choice by chance process is that some of them are not now situated in the most appropriate areas to serve the current needs of agriculture.

Although some of these sites might have been well chosen for their original purpose, most of these old establishments have widened or even completely changed their scientific and agricultural interests, with the result that the problems now being studied are often those occurring in farming areas some considerable distance away. Changes in the pattern and distribution of farming systems, such as the migration of vegetable production towards the east coast, have produced a similar separation by distance of research and practice.

The present state of affairs is that the most productive area of large-scale arable farming, lying along the drier eastern side of the country from East Anglia through the Plain of York to the fertile valleys of Northumbria, contains no major research station catering for its special needs, with the possible exception of the Plant Breeding Institute and the National Institute of Agricultural Botany located on its extreme southern edge at Cambridge. The counties on the wetter western side of the country with larger areas of grass and the highest concentrations of livestock are no better served in regard to animal research institutes.

More appropriate sitings occur in other aspects of the subject. The Glasshouse Crops Research Institute is situated in the high sunshine belt on the south coast, which is eminently suitable for the growing of protected crops. The major fruit research station, at East Malling in the southeastern county of Kent, is near the heart of the largest concentration of top fruit growing in the British Isles, but regrettably a large proportion of its plantations are subject to late spring frosts, causing the loss of experimental results. It thus cannot be regarded as fully representative of the type of climate in which fruit is likely to be successfully grown in competition with other EEC areas of production.

If research is carried out entirely within laboratories or climate chambers, the location of the institute is not of major importance, but if the findings are to be put to practical use, then new ideas have eventually to be tested under field conditions. This subsequent stage of development is much easier to carry out if the suitable fields are close to the laboratories.

We have already explained that the physical environment is of critical importance in determining the potential growth and development of crops and stock, and that it also decides the extent and intensity of the unwanted organisms which hinder them from reaching their full potential. It would be quite unrealistic to expect to find a site representative of all the conditions under which a single commodity is produced, but it is obviously desirable that the ambient conditions under which trials and experiments are carried out should be as similar as possible to those prevailing in the main production areas.

With only a limited number of years available for field trials, it is often difficult to experience a fair sample of seasonal weather and so be able to predict the reproducibility of experimental results, but the uncertainties so produced should not be increased by carrying out trials under conditions of soil and climate which are known to be different from those with which commercial growers have to contend.

The importance of dialogue

Proximity, accessibility, and the increased chances of informal personal contact between research workers and the farmers whose problems they are investigating are important for another reason. The farmer seldom passes a clearly defined problem to the research worker and subsequently receives in return an ideal solution which can be adopted without doubt or reservation. Usually there is a series of dialogues between the two sides which leads to a succession of changes or improvements which can be incorporated into the farming system. This is best illustrated by an example.

A county agricultural adviser in England was concerned about the wide variability of often low profitability of winter wheat crops on one estate within the area for which he was responsible, and sought the advice of a number of specialised scientists to investigate the problem. The estate was on an exposed limestone ridge rising to some 300 m above sea level, with an annual average rainfall of about 825 mm, and a limestone soil of fairly good structure.

The farming systems were similar on all farms within the estate wherein grass leys (used predominantly for milk production) were ploughed in rotation to give a sequence of cash crops such as winter wheat, spring barley and sometimes a root crop. The team of specialists carefully studied all the fields with low yields of wheat, and put forward a large variety of plausible explanations. Agronomists cited poorly prepared seed beds and wrong choice of varieties; soil scientists blamed inadequate and ill-timed applications of fertilizer; plant pathologists and entomologists identified numerous damaging diseases and pests. All these possible reasons occurred in a bewildering number of combinations, but there did not seem to be a single common factor applicable to all the problem fields.

It was then suggested that, with the assistance of the various farmers involved, as much information as possible should be collected regarding the fields with the highest yields. There was again no uniformity in crop variety, in fertilizer usage, in pest and disease populations, but there was one common factor. All the high-yielding crops were drilled in autumn on a date which was far earlier than was customary for the area, and never later than the first week in October.

In an exposed upland site, where winter comes early and spring arrives late, early drilling might seem, with hindsight, an obvious logical step to take to secure good establishment of the germinating crop and lengthening of the growing season, but the early drilling dates which appeared to be so significant were much earlier than the optimum dates suggested as the result of drilling experiments carried out at lower altitudes. If the results of such trials had been interpreted in terms of soil temperatures and not in terms of calendar date, the recommendations might have been more helpful, but in the case under survey the early drilling was due to chance and not design or intent.

Some of the farmers on the estate were so convinced by the importance of early drilling that they began to plan deliberately to do so, but this meant changing their grassland management, and grass was the keystone of their farm profits. Instead of taking a hay crop after a field had been grazed, one farmer changed over to silage so that the ley could be ploughed earlier, usually in July, giving him adequate time to prepare a good seed bed before he was heavily engaged in the harvest of the current cereal crop. On one occasion when such harvesting was delayed by bad weather, another farmer employed a field contractor to meet the deadline of early drilling while he was still engaged with his combine harvesters in other fields.

The success of the practice of early drilling allowed the farmers to benefit from the introduction of high-yielding wheat varieties and more generous applications of fertilizers in a way that had not been previously possible. The earlier drilling of the first cereal crop after the grass break almost always resulted in an earlier harvest, so that it was then possible to follow it with a second crop of winter wheat which was more profitable than the customary spring barley. Where oats could be planted, the adoption of other research results led to a pattern of alternating winter wheat and winter oats, with higher yields of both crops. Lower disease risks permitted this sequence to be continued indefinitely, and this further increased the profitability of the whole system because the leys did not have to be ploughed up and reseeded so often, thus reducing costs.

This simple success story on a small scale contains many lessons with a far wider scale of possible application. A multidisciplinary team of specialist scientists identified a factor limiting productivity in a given environmental situation; the removal of this limiting factor enabled other new technologies to be introduced. The whole satisfactory solution was only made possible by the farmers providing the essential data and then being prepared to change their systems to test and profit from the findings of the scientists. This person-to-person collaboration is essential, and has to be based on mutual trust and mutual respect. In the final resort, it is the farmer who decides what modifications he is willing and able to accept, and which are useful enough to be retained until they can be supplanted by something better.

The role of the farmer in research and development is not always fully appreciated. He is in the key position to provide an early warning system of the emergence of a problem which may inhibit further advances in productivity. In addition, because of his intimate knowledge of a commodity, he may well be able to put forward ideas of his own, which will require developing and testing before they can be fully exploited. The brain of the scientists should be able to use the eyes of the farmer.

Every year the crucial testing of new techniques and materials is only made possible by the farmers offering the use of valuable land, equipment and labour, free of charge to the experimenters. Admittedly, the farmer may provide these facilities in the hope that the results will be of benefit to him, but he is also fully aware that the findings will be equally available to his competitors. There have been occasions, fortunately rare, when the experiments have gone sadly astray. The important fact is that without the co-operation of the farmer there would be no hope of adequate field testing, and without the exchange of facts and ideas between practice and theory there would be a very much slower rate of reliable progress.

Dissemination of research

In addition to his traditions, his experience and his native wits, the standard of education of the farmer is of the greatest importance in the furtherance of technological progress. He cannot be expected to be an expert in all the different sciences involved in modern farming, but he must have sufficient understanding of their aims and methods to be able to talk to research workers and advisers.

Besides being aware of what they can do for him, he must also be able to offer them advice and guidance on what is possible and what is impracticable under working conditions on a farm. He must be able to grasp the significance of their results, their possible limitations, and make an assessment of the possibilities they offer in terms of his own farming system and situation.

When new ideas are adopted and put into practice, it is the money and resources of the farmer which are put at risk, but the price and amount of future food supplies depend on the making of correct decisions by the producer. The path ahead is a difficult one, with a precipice on one side for the incautious enthusiast and a bog on the other for the ultra-conservative.

Every country has its own system of passing new ideas and information to the farmer, which depends to a large extent on sociological and political structure; there is no ideal system which would be suitable for all countries. Great Britain is fortunate in being better served in agriculture than in many other industries with the provision of education facilities and methods of circulation of farming information of technical importance.

In addition to universities and agricultural colleges providing degree and national diploma courses, there is also a chain of county

agricultural and horticultural institutes offering general and specialised courses of instruction covering almost every system of land use to
be found in Britain. One of the main functions of the governmental
Agricultural Development and Advisory Service is to keep the
farming community informed of new technological advances.
Instruction in practical skills is provided by courses run by the
Agricultural Training Board.

For study at home, there are the annual reports and special
publications of the agricultural research council institutes, technical
communications from the commercial firms offering services to the
industry, and technical articles in the farming press. For operational
guidance, up-to-date information regarding weather prospects or on
pest and disease risks are available on recorded messages through the
use of a telephone or the appropriate television data service system.

Meetings and conferences are organised by almost every official
organisation and by private societies, large and small. Commercial
firms exhibit their wares at all major agricultural shows and at special
'open days', when more is offered than mere blandishments and
enticements to buy. There is thus no shortage of opportunity to learn,
and all that is needed is the time and ability to digest the varied
mental fare.

There is perhaps a risk that the farmer may be on the receiving end
of too much information from too many sources for him to be able to
assimilate it all. At a time of rapid progress, there is an increasing
difficulty for the training establishments, even those concentrating on
a small number of enterprises, to keep abreast with the equipment
which is required for the most sophisticated and expensive technology. Even if the instructors are aware of the new methods, they
have little hope of demonstrating them.

A similar problem occurs on state experimental farms, where the
field equipment is sometimes almost obsolete compared to that used
on the more progressive farms. Government finance officers are
seldom in favour of continual capital expenditure, and often forget
that a farm director can feel a fool following a field he is supposed to
lead. There may thus be needed some rationalisation and reorganis-
ation of the system of initial and refresher education.

The scope for improvement

It seems to us that the identification of the factors limiting productivity, the research aimed at eliminating such factors, the testing and
development of new ideas, and the exchange of information and
advice amongst academics, scientists, technologists and farmers or
growers are not separate functions, but facets of a single process

which should be integrated as far as possible in aim and action in a way which will still leave room for individual initiative. Much may be said in favour of traditional structures, but more may be gained by smooth processes of evolutionary change, holding on to what has proved to be good and replacing it when possible with something that is likely to be better.

It therefore seems logical in Britain to combine the Agricultural Research Council, the Agricultural Development and Advisory Service, the county agricultural and horticultural institutes and the Agricultural Training Board into a single research, development and educational service. Its policy would be one based on coordination at all levels, and not under any circumstances a rigid system of control with no delegation of authority, which would be a sure recipe for heart break, stagnation and failure. Consideration should also be given to the inclusion of the semi-independent National Institute of Agricultural Botany, whose role in the testing of any new cultivars is an integral part of any system aimed at improving biological production.

If the political obstacles could be overcome, it would be a great advantage if similar organisations in Scotland and Northern Ireland were integrated into this aggregation.

A further improvement would be for arrangements to be made for closer co-operation and efficient exchange with similar climates and agricultural problems, such as Ireland, Denmark and the Netherlands. This process of improved liaison could indeed be extended throughout all the countries within the EEC to their mutual advantage. The present system, of collaboration based mainly on personal friendships and casual encounters at international scientific meetings, works very well to a limited extent, but it surely could be helped by overt encouragement. One of the simplest methods with the least danger of administrative impedance would be for a number of travelling scholarships, whereby scientists or advisers on paid leave from their regular employment could tour other countries, and in so doing act both as catalysts and pollinators of new ideas.

The suggested amalgamation in Britain would allow for a redeployment of existing staff and resources and offer the possibility of staff exchanges on a temporary basis. This would lead to all concerned having a much better idea of what was happening elsewhere, enabling them to perform their own duties in a more efficient manner. New ideas leading to widespread improvements often originate in small personal discussions, rather than within the costive atmosphere of committees.

Some research centres would still have a national role in two distinct ways. First, they would carry out research programmes under controlled conditions where external environmental factors are not likely to modify the results. Secondly, they would provide a support service of specialised staff, equipment and services for other research stations, thus reducing the need for replication of some sophisticated and expensive laboratory and computer equipment and the highly trained personnel necessary for its operation. Above all, such a system should not be throttled by complicated arguments about payment for mutual help. While it is essential to avoid the waste of public money, it is nonsense to employ unproductive clerical staff to transfer government funds from one pocket to another.

Most of the field research, development and educational effort could be organised on a regional basis, with a much greater local autonomy than exists at present. The regions should be defined on the basis of environmental factors and types of farming in preference to fitting in with existing local administration boundaries. Furthermore, because of the complexity of the farming pattern, it is very desirable that the boundaries of these functional regions should be flexible, especially in regard to the planning of field trials.

It is interesting to note that the latest official publication giving details of the agricultural climate of England and Wales refers to some 60 separate areas delineated in terms of their farming pattern and not by county boundaries. Following the same principle on a broader scale, we would suggest, as a basis for discussion, the following agricultural regions as a possible framework on which to build a rational subdivision of the country.

(1) The Northern Uplands of England: the Pennines, the Border Hills and the Lake District.
(2) The West Pennines: the relatively high rainfall areas of dairy farming in Lancashire and Cheshire, and also the high sunshine belt on the north-west coasts with a production potential as yet unfulfilled.
(3) The East Pennines: the lowland valleys and plains of Northumbria and Yorkshire.
(4) East Anglia: including Lincolnshire and the Fens, the main areas of large-scale arable farming.
(5) East Midlands and Central England: including the Thames Valley, with mixed farms, many of which are under pressure from other industries and urbanisation.
(6) West Midlands: including the lowlands in the Welsh border counties and the Severn Valley.
(7) South-east: including the main fruit- and hop-growing areas and the main concentrations of growing under glass or plastic.
(8) South: typified by chalk downland farming.
(9) South-west: an area with a great potential for early production, with the exception of the upland moors.

Other regions would, politics permitting, deal separately with the upland and lowland regions of Wales, Scotland and Northern Ireland.

Staff and resources would be allocated to each region, taking into account its present and potential output, the type of farming and the complexity of its problems. Each region would have a central research and educational centre dedicated to the improvement of the productivity of the enterprises suited to the area, and local agricultural interests would be strongly represented on its governing body. Sub-centres would have to be located at appropriate places to cater for particular specialist needs. Land and resources would be rented on a temporary basis to investigate problems where and when they occurred, and promptly relinquished when the need had expired.

General practitioners in agriculture and horticulture would be stationed throughout each region to maintain day-to-day contact with the farming community, dealing with their immediate questions and identifying the problems which might require further or future investigation. Such staff would not be employed on statutory or policy implementing functions. It is not wise for a man to wear two hats, one indicating a sympathetic adviser, the other a strict law enforcement officer.

As in the present structure, the general advisers would be supported by science and husbandry specialists at the regional and satellite centres. The number and nature of these specialists would depend on the needs of the region, but should always include one dealing with agricultural meteorology. A few professional meteorologists were attached to some centres of the advisory service in Britain soon after the last war, but their numbers did not increase rapidly. The reason for this was not that they were not needed, but that no one could decide which government department should pay their salaries. It is pathetic that a financial system designed to save public money should result in the waste of public brains. As the weather conditions are the major uncontrollable factor limiting food production, no research or advisory service to agriculture can function at its highest efficiency without access to the best possible advice from specialists in the subject. A critical environmental factor which may elude the biologist can often be obvious to someone trained in the physical sciences. It is not a question of ability, but merely the fruit of experience.

It is surprising how often in the past the biosphere has been treated as a bio-hemisphere. Due attention has been paid to the biology, soil physics and soil chemistry, but the questions arising from consideration of atmospheric physics and chemistry have been treated with less care than they deserve, and few specialists in this branch of science are to be found on the staff of research or experimental stations. Far too many experiments have been carried out without adequate record of the environment, and fewer still have been analysed with a satisfactory interpretation of the weather factor. We would hope to see more use made of mobile, interdisciplinary task forces which could be deployed to investigate the many interacting factors affecting growth, pest and disease incidence, or even the complete working of a farming system. A degree of flexibility must be incorporated in the planning, and the composition of the teams and their duration of work on any one problem should be suited to the task in hand.

There should also be greater flexibility and interchange of personnel amongst research, development and educational establishments, according to the needs of the time and the talents of the individual. As things stand at present, recently qualified graduates tend to be selected for one or other of these branches of the same tree before they, or anyone else, have had sufficient opportunity to assess their full aptitudes and abilities. Opportunities rarely arise for the switch from one vocation to another, and few posts exist which enable the holder to combine three types of mental agility to the benefit of all.

A research worker, in the proposed system, with the necessary inclination and ability would have the chance of bringing his research results to fruition in the farming system by direct communication with students and farmers. Similarly, the adviser with a promising new idea or line of approach to a problem could be seconded to a research team to help in the necessary testing and development. Much would depend on the personality and character of the individuals concerned; for some, such a switch in scientific ambience would be impossible, but for others it would prove a stimulating experience.

We would hope that in a pliant non-rigid organisation such as this there would be close links with all sections of the rural community, and that there would be quick reactions to the constantly changing needs of the agricultural industry. A considerable degree of regional freedom of action would be required to permit this, although a national hierarchy would have the task of maintaining uniformly high standards in all departments and in all regions. The central authority would also have to ensure that there were neither significant gaps nor unnecessary overlapping in the programme as a whole. This central body would be responsible for decisions regarding agricultural research, development and education policies, without any of the present problems concerning role demarcation, and free from the tangled network of communication channels which so often involve a multiplicity of time-consuming committees, large in membership, long in deliberation, but short in useful comment or decisive action.

We would hope that this would both simplify and accelerate the process of decision making, and might result in a considerable saving of highly paid staff. This would produce a secondary, but by no means negligible, advantage in that fewer technical staff who had gained prominence by their achievements in the laboratory or the field would be taken out of their scientific surroundings to fill purely administrative posts. Instead of having to generate and circulate endless series of reports and minutes of meetings (a task for which they have neither the enthusiasm nor the aptitude), they would be able to use their technical and scientific skills. This does not imply that a first-class scientist should be paid any less than a first-class administrator, but that as far as possible every man should be placed in a job that suits his talents. The job should be made to fit the man, and not the man to fit the job, and, most important of all, the highest remunerations should be adjusted to the ability of the person, not the title of his post.

Land utilisation

Although the socio-economic factors are under the control of man and originate from his opinions and reasoning, this does not make them any the more predictable than the weather. A group of experienced and learned authorities has recently put forward cogent and convincing arguments for the existence of a national land utilisation policy in Britain. The response in terms of interest, let alone action, from any major political party has been conspicuous by its absence.

Any *laissez-faire* policy for land use is incompatible with the aim of maximum home food production. The conflicting needs of agriculture, other forms of industry, transport, housing, recreation and conservation are not easily resolved, but this is no excuse for ignoring them and hoping that they will solve themselves or go away. There is even less excuse for piecemeal pragmatism. Far too many interested parties are involved, each of which may be able to advance sufficient elements of truth in their arguments to justify to themselves their political, commercial, administrative, ecological or emotional viewpoints and to convince the credulous, but none of them is sufficiently impartial and competent to produce a solution which will stand the test of time. Even the finest brains cannot make correct decisions without facts, without an ability to understand what such facts imply, and without a sense of the significance of the orders of magnitude involved. In some cases it is better to be numerate than literate.

This growing problem underlines the urgent need for the preparation of detailed, accurate maps and supporting information concerning land utilisation and land potential, so that the present position and future prospects can be fully understood in terms of work, space, amenity and food production. The longer the delay, the less the amount of land available; the greater the competition for its use, the more difficult will be the task of making the final decisions, with less and less hope of them being the right ones.

Within a given available area of agricultural land, the size and type of farming enterprises have an important bearing on productivity. The impossible ideal is a structure in which the type and size of each farm business are graduated to match precisely the ability and ambitions of its owner. No system of nationalised land allocated by the wisest of governments is ever likely to approach this Utopian state of affairs. No computer, however well programmed, could ever solve the equations quantifying the infinite variety of reactions due to the imponderable skills of farmers responding to the ever-changing and unpredictable circumstances.

Nevertheless, the governing powers may have to intervene to prevent the structure becoming so distorted in the proportions of its subdivisions that future output is threatened. As we have already indicated, the main dangers appear to lie in a preponderance of holdings that are either too small or too large. It is difficult to envisage legislation which will effectively control the fragmentation or amalgamation of holdings, or which will stabilise land prices at a level which will enable those with small capital but great farming skill to compete successfully for its acquisition against those with more capital but less ability.

Even so, some steps may be necessary to enable men of talent and ambition to set foot on the farming ladder and to climb the lower rungs. One possibility is for the state to buy land on the open market and, in viable units, either lease it for a predetermined period or sell it over a similar timespan to suitable applicants. Another is to provide capital with low or zero interest charges to those with proven skill and experience.

We have indicated previously that at the other end of the scale there may be potential dangers if too much land and bargaining power are concentrated in the hands of too few farming companies. Such a state of affairs may hamper change, as well as exacerbate the social problems or rural depopulation. Some restrictions on excessive expansion may have to be imposed, either directly by legal limitation or indirectly by fiscal measures. As a general principle, it can be said that loose systems of land structure last longer and work better. A complicated system can go wrong in a number of unforeseen ways, and the larger the system, the greater is the probability of an unexpected failure.

Farm prices

The amount and quality of land available for food production have a very obvious bearing on the amount of food produced and its cost. Such costs (as indicated earlier) are not solely determined by the laws of supply and demand, but are also influenced by the economic and political strategies of the government.

The basic problem facing the administrators is to help to create a prosperous and efficient food industry which produces sufficient food of the right kind and quality at the lowest price to the consumer at a regular, reliable rate. Although the demand can be calculated to a fair degree of accuracy, supply is subject to unforeseeable and uncontrollable variations. It is in this context that an attempt has to be made to devise a system of remuneration to the farmer which is as fair as possible to both him and the consumer. It is in the interests of all to provide the maximum possible stability in both supply and price.

The cash returns to the farmer must not only cover his total costs with a margin of profit to give him a satisfactory standard of living, but also allow him to have sufficient money for investment in new equipment and new technology. It is also necessary to encourage the production of the commodities which are in short supply and discourage the expansion of products which are already in surplus.

An unrestricted free trade system relying simply on the laws of supply and demand to achieve a satisfactory equilibrium does not offer a viable solution. The risk of a serious interruption in supplies from other nations, caused by political, economic or meteorological reasons, makes it politically untenable. At best it could only produce an unsatisfactory pendulum swing from gluts to scarcities, with supplies vainly trying to catch up with the oscillations in demand.

The Common Agricultural Policy of the EEC, though highly commendable in intention, has so far failed lamentably in execution. Payments for the production of unwanted surpluses have been an extremely costly operation, and it appears improbable that some of the member countries will continue to subscribe so liberally to satisfy the demands of farmers in other countries. There seems to be an illusion that somewhere in Brussels is located an Aladdin's cave; the future may show that it also could be the residence of Mother Hubbard.

A return to the farmer subsidy system operated in Britain before entry into the EEC is hardly likely to be politically acceptable. In any case, it did little to direct production into the commodities most needed by the consumers, and in some respects it may have assisted in the survival of some of the least efficient farmers. It therefore seems that a new approach to the difficult problem is overdue.

If the total annual outputs of the main commodities produced from the land, such as cereals, milk, meat, potatoes, and sugar beet, are examined, it is clear that there are considerable fluctuations from year to year, and this applies also to the outputs per unit of land. However, if the ten-year running means are plotted on a graph, then the successive points lie along almost straight lines, rising gradually over the decades, giving clear evidence of the increasing efficiency of the farmers. This indicates that farmers have a great ability to overcome collectively the setbacks inflicted upon them by the vagaries of the weather, pestilential attacks or political influences. They are not easily diverted from their overall strategies by minor fluctuations in demand or return.

It must be realised that the farmer is the final arbiter in regard to planned production. Accepting this, it seems logical that governments should enter into contracts with the farmers for the quantities and types of food product that they require, rather than try to influence them by indirect and uncertain methods.

Before dismissing this idea as unrealistic, it should be realised that it is merely an extension of the increasing practice of the buyers acting for large supermarket chains and food processors, who not only define the exact amounts of the commodity they require, but also define the exact specifications of what they refer to as quality and demand definite delivery dates. The supermarket idea of quality refers to age, size, uniformity and appearance; it may have little to do with taste.

A contract system

The operation of a contract system would require a central buying authority for each of the major foodstuffs, with regional offices to maintain close contact with the farmers. Contracts would be made at an agreed price for a period of, say, five years, although the length of the contract could be longer for permanent or semi-permanent systems and perhaps shorter for crops for which there is little need for large capital investment. Such contracts would be reviewed annually in regard to price and quantity, so as to take into account any changes in demand, rates of inflation, or catastrophes caused by weather, pests or diseases, but they would only be allowed to vary between previously determined limits.

Such a system would enable a government to have much more precise forward budgeting, better control over production levels, and therefore provide more stable prices, permitting a greater influence on the social and environmental problems of the countryside. There would not necessarily be a single uniform price level for all producers in all areas. If it was thought necessary to encourage production of a commodity in areas where the conditions were less than ideal or where the geographical position increased the transport costs, a higher price could be offered.

If a commodity was being produced in excess of current requirements, priority in awarding contracts would be given to farmers who, because of environmental or economic factors, had no alternative viable farming system available to them. An upper limit could be placed on the size of the contract granted to any one individual or company, or there could be a sliding scale with the price diminishing as the quantity rose above a certain level. Such a system might be necessary to avoid the development of monopolies, which would give too much bargaining power to a few individuals.

Another disadvantage in reducing the number of farmers producing one or more commodities to a low level is that farming involves the taking of unavoidable risks, the outcomes of which are largely unpredictable. If the critical decisions are taken by only a few farmers, each responsible for a large proportion of the total output, then this total is liable to vary greatly according to whether their judgements are right or wrong, unless they have taken the precaution of spreading the risks. If the decision making is shared by a greater number, then the odds on them being all right or all wrong in the same year are much smaller, so that the seasonal variations in production will be less. Stability of production, even at a level below the maximum, is far preferable to large year-to-year fluctuations.

Consideration should also be given to the dangers of very large contracts which might cause unacceptable depopulation problems in some rural communities. Moreover, the granting of some contracts might include conditions regarding the proper precautions that must be taken to avoid air or water pollution or the creation of other environmental problems.

Close coordination between the several buying authorities would be essential in order to maintain a sensible balance of production. Each authority would also need to create and maintain buffer stocks as an insurance against unavoidable shortfalls in output. There would also be a need for a system of quality controls, with price bonuses or forfeits for divergencies from agreed standards.

The major factors in the determination of price levels would be the costs of production and the need for continual investment in new technology. The state of the world markets would also have to be taken into consideration, and the degree of competition for the contracts would be a factor which might influence the agreed prices.

Opponents to any form of state control would suggest that experience of the errors of Crown Agents and the track record of nationalised industries (which, it was promised, were to put an end to all labour troubles and production problems), indicate that no government is fit to be trusted with the running of a stall at a jumble sale. More charitably, it could be suggested that it would be too difficult for anyone to allocate contracts which would be fair to all concerned. Farmers might object on the grounds that it would increase suffocating bureaucratic controls and would restrict their freedom of choice and action in responding to the changing circumstances which are beyond their control and yet with which they have to contend.

Prejudice apart, it is doubtful if these objections would stand up to close scrutiny, and at very least it could be argued that the alternatives might be a great deal worse. Concern for the environment, supported by legislation or by pressure of public opinion, already place constraints on the activities of the farmer and are likely to tighten with time. Economic pressures have always existed, and although they may be tempered by the present EEC policies, the high cost of such controls are bound eventually to result in some modifications which will be unlikely to make more money for farmers available from Community funds.

With this suggested contract system, the main difference would be that the objective would not be to achieve the maximum possible output from a farm, but to reach a target set by the farmer himself over the period of the contract. He could make his own choice of which commodities to grow and the amounts he intends to produce or, if he preferred, he could opt to produce luxury foods or commodities other than those subject to the contract system.

The farmer would have several years to balance out the fluctuations in production due to weather and weather-induced influences. If, at the end of the contract period, the farmer had a surplus of output over and above the amount contracted for, he would have several options still open to him. He could store it at his own expense as an insurance against any future shortfall, he could sell it on an export market, or use alternative outlets such as the conversion of food material to animal foodstuffs or fuel; he could even dispose of his surplus to another farmer who had failed to reach his own target figure. He would receive full payment for his contracted quantity and any extra revenue from whatever source would be a productivity bonus. His biggest risk would be if over the period of the contract he failed to produce the required amount. Not only would his income be below the amount he had budgeted for (unless he could complete his contract by buying the surplus of another farmer), but also his target figure for the next period would be liable to be reduced unless there were unusual extenuating circumstances.

There would be obvious advantages to smaller farmers in the formation of co-operative production and marketing groups. Contract obligations would be easier to meet by the balancing of surpluses with deficits within the group. The only major difficulties would be when all the farmers in the group produced more than they expected, or when they all produced less than the contract required. It would be possible to have greater diversity of the range of products within the group. This would again tend to smooth out the annual range of fluctuation in yields and income, because weather factors are seldom favourable or unfavourable to all types of enterprise in the same year. The costs of handling, grading, storage and distribution of the produce could be reduced below those incurred by the independent actions of the individual farmers. Furthermore, the voice of the co-operative would be likely to have more impact than that of each member acting alone when the contract prices were revised and the quantities to be supplied were negotiated. One of the reasons why some co-operatives have foundered in the past has been that farmers wanted to be in the co-operative when prices were low, but outside when prices were high. Under a contract system with an agreed price, this factor would not apply.

For small and large farmers alike, there would be the opportunity to develop farming systems which were the most suitable to the environment in which they operated and best fitted to the skills they could command. The systems and cropping programmes would be adjusted to a foreseeable sale and income, so that the costs incurred in modernising methods and equipment would become a matter for careful arithmetic rather than a hopeful gamble.

The contract system would in many ways be less complicated than that by which the payments made to farmers are at present determined. It would require modern electronic data storage and retrieval equipment to record the continual changes of quantity and quality of available stocks and their location. This information would have to be continually reviewed for the efficient operation of supplies and transport, but this in essence presents no greater problem in logistics than those solved by multinational chain stores.

A system based on contracts of this nature may never be perfect, but at least it has a chance of success if it is competently and honestly run. It has the great advantage of being a system which could be introduced gradually, starting with one or two major commodities and being extended to others as confidence and efficiency grew with experience. No initial plan can be free from snags, and crucial variables are often discovered by accident rather than foresight. Provided that modifying changes were introduced when they were found to be necessary, and complications reduced to a minimum, it might bring stability and justice to an industry beset for far too long by economic and production worries. When it is difficult enough to produce the food, at least the disposal of the end-products should be made as trouble free as possible.

Energy problems

The prime purpose of agriculture is to produce energy for man in the form of food, but to do this it has to consume energy in other forms besides that of the radiation from the Sun. The more technically efficient and productive it becomes, then the greater is its use of brought-in and bought-in energy. It must therefore compete with other users for its share of energy supplies. Its only claim to priority is that, until alternative ways of producing food are discovered, it is of vital importance to the survival of the human race.

It would therefore seem that it is just as important to develop an energy utilisation policy as a land utilisation policy. This would involve questions of the continuance of supply and of the costs involved. It is difficult for any industry to compete effectively if its competitors receive subsidies for energy either used directly for production or indirectly for the supply of new materials, handling, storage, transport or marketing. If energy supplies begin to be limiting to human activity, agriculture must be given fair treatment commensurate with its importance.

More research is needed to determine, in energy terms, the most effective of the present production methods, and to devise improvements which would reduce the consumption of energy. The possible development of new crop varieties, or even new species, which would be more efficient in the conversion of Sun energy into food energy deserves careful attention. Any review of energy use would have to take into account both the amounts and types of energy consumed on the farm and also the consumption off the farm, which in some cases would be the greater total amount.

Taking into account the inevitable length of time which must elapse from the inception of a new idea to its full implementation, the search for alternative energy sources must continue and grow in intensity. This search should include the possible exploitation of an extensive scale of the farmer's own by-products, as well as the use of waste energy from other industries. There are few climates in which the Sun is a reliable source of power, and most of these are outside the major agricultural areas, but modern engineering might make it possible for a reversion to the economic use of wind and water as local power sources on farms, a process that would be much easier if there could be found a more convenient method of storing electricity than is available at present.

The discovery of oil under the seas and the promise of as yet undiscovered resources of coal may suggest that there is no great urgency regarding future energy supplies, despite the steeply increasing costs of extraction and distribution. The whole problem poses immense difficulties, and it may be many years before satisfactory answers are given to all the questions. If these answers are not available when the critical energy need arises, then the survival of our descendants could be in jeopardy. In a world apparently unable to control its birth rate but becoming more adept at reducing its death rate, time is not on our side.

Envoi

We hope that we have shown that the forces controlling agricultural output and productivity are complicated and sometimes unpredictable in their effects, and that their interactions create an ever-changing situation which cannot be explained in a simple fashion. Over the centuries, man has improved his performance as a provider of food, and we see no reason why he should not continue to do so. We have tried to emphasise the importance of the farmer himself as the maker of the critical decisions which affect the ultimate outcomes, and make no apologies for considering him to be the key to any future success.

There are no easy solutions or facile answers. We would rather liken the situation to an esoteric game of multi-dimensional chess in which man, at the very least, has to gain the verdict of a draw. We started this book with an adage, let us therefore end it with an allegory.

The Red King of Famine is supported by the Red Queen who represents the powerful adverse factors of the environment; the Red Rooks or Castles are the competitors for land and energy use; the Red Knights are the unwanted biological organisms which move in so odd a fashion; the Red Bishops represent the social and economic pressures, and the Red Pawns stand for the demands for each farming food commodity.

Opposing them, fighting for our lives, is the White King of Plenty assisted by the White Queen representing the collective skill and industry of the farming community; the White Castles are the sensible and effective policies for land and energy use; the White Knights are armed with the new technology; the White Bishops preach the gospel of information and education, and the White Pawns represent the supplies of each agricultural product.

The game is complicated far beyond the mathematical fantasies of Lewis Carroll, as it is almost impossible to remove any piece from the board, although the White Pawns are often in danger. On both sides the different pieces move simultaneously and are controlled by more than one player. Some of the rules of the game, those of biology, chemistry and physics, are unalterable, but may be beyond our complete understanding; other rules seem to change as fancy dictates.

We do not believe that our present knowledge makes it possible to predict the final result of this contest with any accuracy, still less that we are in a position to do so. We do, however, plead that none of the white pieces is brushed off the board by the careless wave of an ignorant hand.

To end on a note of optimism, we would like to trust in our belief in the power of human intelligence, and to suggest that the chances of avoiding defeat by the red forces can be improved by carefully noting the moves of all forces, white or red, and then, with due thought, coordinating the moves of the white forces to the best possible advantage of mankind.

Those of our readers who have had the patience to follow us through to the end may by now disagree profoundly with some of our arguments or conclusions. If, however, in this process they have considered more deeply the manifold factors which influence productivity in agriculture, we shall have achieved the first of our objectives. If as a result of such thought they are inspired to actions which will increase food production, we will have achieved the second.

All we can do is to study and compare, and not be too hasty in our opinions, lest we be judged very severely by those that come after us.

Hendrik van Loon

Suggestions for further reading

The lists given below do not pretend to be either comprehensive or even fully representative of the vast amount of literature devoted to the many varied facets of agriculture. They attempt to offer suggestions of suitable entry points into further study in depth of those areas which are of particular interest to the reader. In many cases the works cited contain numerous additional references in their own bibliographies, so that by their use the search for information can be prolonged indefinitely.

The inclusion of a book in these lists does not imply that we always agree with all or even any of the information and opinions it advances. It is essential that each book should be read critically; statistics must be valued according to the source and methods by which they have been derived; figures and diagrams should be queried if they are unaccompanied by evidence of their accuracy; facts must be distinguished from opinions, and the latter must be considered with an open mind bordering on scepticism, no matter how eminent the author. Factual errors have a long survival potential; they tend to be quoted and requoted with little or no check on their accuracy, especially if they appear to support the opinions of the author.

For anyone especially interested in British agriculture, a careful study of the agricultural statistics stretching back to 1868 provides a very good picture of the pattern and rate of change of land use and yields. Comparison of the most recent editions of standard works such as *Fream's elements of agriculture*, *Farm mechanisation*, *The pesticide manual*, and *Pests of field crops* offer more readable information on this process, and also reveals how much or how little the future trends were foreseen in the earlier editions.

The book by E. C. Large entitled *The advance of the fungi* gives a very salutary account of the emergence of the new agricultural sciences and the frustrating obstacles to truth (including apathy, stupidity and incredulity) which had to be overcome over a century of slow progress to reach the present state of knowledge. Similar obstacles are probably still to be encountered in each and every science.

Part I   The meteorological factor

AGROCLIMATE

1962   G. Trewartha. *The world's problem climates*. London: Methuen.
1965   C. G. Johnson and L. P. Smith (eds). *The biological significance of climatic change in Britain*. London: Academic Press.
1968   Unesco. *Agroclimatological methods*. (Proceedings Reading Symposium). Natural Resources Research, vol. 7. Paris: Unesco.
1970   C. V. Williams and K. T. Joseph. *Climate, soil and crop production in the humid Tropics*. Oxford: Oxford University Press.
1976   L. P. Smith. *The agricultural climate of England and Wales*. Ministry of Agriculture, Fisheries and Food, Technical Bulletin no. 35. London: HMSO.

1977   R. A. Bryson and T. J. Murray. *Climates of hunger. Mankind and the world's changing weather.* Wisconsin: University of Wisconsin Press.

1977   K. Takahashi and M. Yoshino (eds). *Climate change and food production.* Tokyo: University of Tokyo.

1979   M. R. Biswas and M. K. Biswas (eds). *Food, climate and man.* Chichester: Wiley.

1979   T. F. Gaskell and M. Morris. *World climate, environment and man.* London: Thames & Hudson.

1981   W. Bach, J. Pankrath and S. H. Schneider (eds). *Food–climate interactions.* Dordrecht: Reidel.

1981   S. W. Burrage and M. K. V. Carr (eds). *Climatic change in European agriculture.* Centre for European Studies Study Paper no. 12. Ashford: Wye College.

1981   L. E. Slater and S. K. Levin (eds). *Climate's impact on food supplies. Strategies and technologies for climate-defensive food production.* Boulder, Colorado: Westview Press.

1981   C. D. Smith and M. L. Perry (eds). *Consequences of climatic change.* Nottingham: Department of Geography, University of Nottingham.

1982   K. Blaxter (ed.). *Food, nutrition and climate.* Barking, Essex: Applied Science Publishers.

1982   V. J. Kilmer. *Handbook of soils and climate in agriculture.* Boca Raton, Florida: CRC Press.

1983   D. G. Johnson *et al. The world's grain economy and climate change to the year 2000. Implications for policy.* Washington DC: National Defense University Press.

WEATHER, PLANTS AND ANIMALS

1969   C. V. Smith. *Meteorology and grain storage.* World Meteorological Organisation Technical Note no. 101. Geneva: WMO.

1971   G. W. Hurst and R. P. Rumsey. *Protection of plants against adverse weather.* World Meteorological Organisation Technical Note no. 118. Geneva: WMO.

1972   C. V. Smith. *Some environmental problems of livestock housing.* World Meteorological Organisation Technical Note no. 122. Geneva: WMO.

1973   R. O. Slatyer (ed.). *Plant response to climatic factors.* (Proceedings Upsala Symposium). Ecology and Conservation, vol. 5. Paris: Unesco.

1974   J. L. Monteith and L. E. Mount (eds). *Heat loss from animals and man.* London: Butterworths.

1975   J. L. Monteith (ed.). *Vegetation and the atmosphere.* London: Academic Press.

1980   D. M. Gates. *Biophysical ecology.* Berlin: Springer-Verlag.

1980   J. Shejbal (ed.). *Controlled atmosphere storage of grains.* Developments in Agricultural Engineering, vol. 1. Amsterdam: Elsevier.

1981   J. A. Clark (ed.). *Environmental aspects of housing for animal production.* London: Butterworths.

1981   A. H. Fetter and R. K. M. Hay. *Environmental physiology of plants.* London: Academic Press.

WATER SUPPLIES AND IRRIGATION

1973 V. A. Kovda, E. Van der Berg and R. M. Hagen (eds). *Irrigation, drainage and salinity*. Rome: FAO. Paris: Unesco.

1973 J. V. Lovett (ed.). *The environmental, economic and social significance of drought*. Sydney: Angus & Robertson.

1973 H. C. Pereira. *Land use and water resources*. Cambridge: Cambridge University Press.

1975 Anonymous. *Drought and agriculture*. World Meteorological Organisation Technical Note no. 138. Geneva: WMO.

1976 M. Falkenmark and G. Lundh. *Water for a starving world*. Boulder, Colorado: Westview Press.

1978 Anonymous. *World water balance and water resources of the Earth*. Paris: Unesco.

1981 V. E. Hansen *et al*. *Irrigation principles and practice*. 4th edn. Chichester: Wiley.

POLLUTION

1968 E. I. Mukammal *et al*. *Air pollutants, meteorology and plant injury*. World Meteorological Organisation Technical Note no. 96. Geneva: WMO.

1975 W. W. Murdoch (ed.). *Environment, resources, pollution and society*. London: Freeman. Cambridge, Mass.: Sinauer.

1979 Anonymous. *Agriculture and pollution*. 7th report of the Royal Commission On Environmental Pollution. London: HMSO.

1980 Anonymous. *Inorganic pollution and agriculture*. Ministry of Agriculture, Fisheries and Food. ADAS Reference Book no. 326. London: HMSO.

1982 M. M. Benarie (ed.). *Atmospheric pollution 1982*. Studies in Environmental Science, vol. 20. Amsterdam: Elsevier.

1982 W. C. Clark (ed.). *Carbon dioxide review*. New York: Oxford University Press.

1982 M. H. Unsworth and D. P. Ormrod. *Effects of gaseous air pollution in agriculture and horticulture*. London: Butterworths.

GENERAL

1962 L. P. Smith. *Weather and food*. Freedom from Hunger Campaign Basic Study no. 1. Geneva: WMO. Rome: FAO.

1972 L. P. Smith. *The application of micrometeorology to agricultural problems*. World Meteorological Organisation Technical Note no. 119. Geneva: WMO.

1973 J. L. Monteith. *Principles of environmental physics*. London: Edward Arnold.

1975 L. P. Smith. *Methods in agricultural meteorology*. Developments in Atmospheric Science, vol. 3. Amsterdam: Elsevier.

1980 G. W. Robertson. *The role of agrometeorology in agricultural development and investment projects*. World Meteorological Organisation Technical Note no. 168. Geneva: WMO.

Part II   The land factor

LAND AND SOILS

1961   T. Wallace. *Mineral deficiencies in plants*. London: HMSO.

1969   J. S. Bibby and D. Mackney. *Land use capability classification*. London: Soil Survey of Great Britain.

1972   D. Hillel (ed.). *Optimizing the soil physical environment towards greater crop yields*. London: Academic Press.

1974   D. Mackney. *Land use capability classification*. Ministry of Agriculture, Fisheries and Food Technical Bulletin no. 30. London: HMSO.

1974   J. Von Schilfgaarde. *Drainage for agriculture*. Agronomy Monographs no. 17. Madison, Wisconsin: American Society of Agronomy.

1975   Anonymous. *Soil physical conditions and crop production*. London: HMSO.

1976   L. F. Curtis, F. M. Courteny and S. Trudgill. *Soils in the British Isles*. London: Longman.

1976   L. P. Smith and B. D. Trafford. *Climate and drainage*. Ministry of Agriculture, Fisheries and Food Technical Bulletin no. 34. London: HMSO.

1977   J. S. Russell and E. L. Graecon (eds). *Soil factors in crop production in a semi-arid environment*. Brisbane: University of Queensland Press.

1978   K. J. Beck. *Land evaluation and agricultural development*. Wageningen: International Institute for Land Reclamation and Improvement, Publication no. 23.

1978   D. B. Davies, D. J. Eagle and J. B. Finney. *Soil management*, 3rd edn. Ipswich: Farming Press.

1978   D. H. Foth. *Fundamentals of soil science*, 6th edn. Chichester: Wiley.

1980   D. Hillel. *Applications of soil physics*. London: Academic Press.

1980   L. F. Molloy (ed.). *Land use and the role of research*. Wellington: New Zealand. Department of Scientific and Industrial Research.

1981   D. Dent and A. Young. *Soil survey and land evaluation*. London: George Allen & Unwin.

1981   D. J. Greenland and M. B. H. Hayes. *Chemistry of soil processes*. Chichester: Wiley.

1981   S. G. McRae and C. P. Burnham. *Land evaluation*. Oxford: Oxford University Press.

1984   J. R. Archer. *Fertilization of crops*. Ipswich: Farming Press.

EROSION

1980   M. Holy. *Erosion and the environment*. Oxford: Pergamon Press.

1980   M. J. Kirkby and R. P. C. Morgan. *Soil erosion*. Chichester: Wiley.

1981   R. P. C. Morgan. *Soil conservation. Problems and prospects*. Chichester: Wiley.

1981   G. C. Schwab *et al. Soil and water conservation engineering*. Chichester: Wiley.

1982   D. Zacher. *Erosion*. Developments in Soil Science, vol. 10. Amsterdam: Elsevier.

Part III   The biological factor

PLANTS AND ANIMALS

1971   P. F. Wareing and J. P. Cooper. *Potential crop production.* London: Heinemann.
1972   G. C. Evans. *Quantitative analysis of plant growth.* Oxford: Blackwell.
1975   D. M. Gates and R. B. Schmerl (eds). *Perspectives of biophysical ecology.* Berlin: Springer-Verlag.
1977   J. J. Landsberg and C. V. Cutty (eds). *Environmental effects on crop physiology.* London: Academic Press.
1979   J. C. Bowman and P. Susmal (eds). *The future of beef production in the EEC.* The Hague: Martinus Nighoff.
1979   F. L. Milthorpe and J. Moorby. *An introduction to crop physiology.* Cambridge: Cambridge University Press.
1979   H. Russell and R. C. Staples (eds). *Stress physiology in crop plants.* Chichester: Wiley.
1979   T. K. Scott (ed.). *Plant regulation in world agriculture.* New York: Plenum Press.
1980   P. S. Carlson (ed.). *The biology of crop productivity.* London: Academic Press.
1980   W. Holmes (ed.). *Grass productivity and utilization.* Oxford: Blackwell.
1981   Anonymous. *Agricultural yield potential in continental climates.* Bern: International Potash Institute.
1981   S. B. Johnson (ed.). *Physiological processes limiting plant production.* London: Butterworths.
1981   C. R. W. Spedding (ed.). *Vegetable productivity.* London: Macmillan.
1981   C. R. W. Spedding, J. W. Walsingham and A. M. Hoxey. *Biological efficiency in agriculture.* London: Academic Press.
1981   N. C. Stoskoff. *Understanding crop production.* Reston, Virginia: Reston Publications.
1982   H. Kilhara. *Wheat studies.* Developments in Crop Science, vol. 3. Amsterdam: Elsevier.
1982   R. D. Politiek and J. J. Backer (eds). *Livestock production in Europe.* Developments in Animal and Veterinary Sciences, vol. 8. Amsterdam: Elsevier.
1983   B. L. Nestel (ed.). *The development of animal production systems.* World Animal Science, vol. A2. Amsterdam: Elsevier.

UNWANTED ORGANISMS AND THEIR CONTROL

General
1964   I. Taylor and J. Knowlsden. *Principles of epidemiology*, 2nd edn. London: Churchill Press.
1967   P. H. Gregory and J. L. Monteith. *Airborne microbes.* Cambridge: Cambridge University Press.
1974   W. W. Fletcher. *The pest war.* Oxford: Blackwell.
1976   H. Sinneker. *General epidemiology.* New York: Wiley.
1982   D. E. Pedgeley. *Windborne pests and diseases.* Chichester: Ellis Horwood.
1983   J. B. Brooksby (ed.). *The aerial transmission of disease.* (Proceedings of a

Royal Society discussion meeting, February 1983). *Phil Trans R. Soc. B*
302 (1111), 437–604.

Weeds
1978   J. C. Fryer and R. J. Makepeace. *Weed control handbook*, vol. 2.
       Recommendations, 8th edn. Oxford: Blackwell.
1981   M. J. Samways. *Biological control of pests and weeds*. Institute of Biology,
       Studies in Biology no. 132. London: Edward Arnold.

Animal diseases
1967   D. Sainsbury. *Animal health and housing*. Eastbourne: Baillière Tindall.
1970   L. P. Smith. *Weather and animal diseases*. World Meteorological Organ-
       isation Technical Note no. 113. Geneva: WMO.
1975   B. Halpin. *Patterns of animal disease*. Eastbourne: Baillière Tindall.
1978   T. E. Gibson (ed.). *Weather and parasitic animal disease*. World Meteoro-
       logical Organisation Technical Note no. 159. Geneva: WMO.
1980   W. H. Parker. *Health and disease in farm animals*, 3rd edn. Oxford:
       Pergamon Press.

Plant diseases
1934   W. C. Moore, A. Smith and G. Pethybridge. *Fungal and other diseases of
       crop plants*. London: HMSO.
1943   W. C. Moore. *Diseases of crop plants*. London: HMSO.
1952   G. Ordish. *Untaken harvest*. London: Constable.
1958   E. C. Large. *The advance of the fungi*. London: Jonathan Cape.
1959   W. C. Moore. *British parasitic fungi*. Cambridge: Cambridge Univer-
       sity Press.
1972   J. J. Baker. *Diseases of crop plants*. London: HMSO.
1973   H. Martin. *The scientific principles of crop protection*, 6th edn. London:
       Edward Arnold.
1974   J. Kranz. *Epidemics of plant diseases. Mathematics, analyses and modelling*.
       Berlin: Springer-Verlag.
1978   P. R. Scott and A. Bainbridge (eds). *Plant disease epidemiology*. Oxford:
       Blackwell.
1979   D. L. Ebbels and J. King (eds). *The scientific basis for administrative control
       of plant diseases and pests*. Oxford: Blackwell.
1979   B. Schippes and E. Gams (eds). *Soilborne plant pathogens*. London:
       Academic Press.
1980   P. S. Teng and S. V. C. Krupa (eds). *Crop loss assessment*. University of
       Minnesota Agriculture Experiment Station, Miscellaneous Publica-
       tion no. 7.
1982   J. Dekker and A. Georgopoulos (eds). *Fungicide resistance in crop
       protection*. Wageningen: Centre for Agricultural Publishing and Docu-
       mentation.
1982   J. L. Hatfield and I. J. Thomason. *Biometeorology in integrated pest
       management*. London: Academic Press.
1983   Anonymous. *Agricultural chemicals approval scheme. Approved products for
       farmers and growers*. London: HMSO.
1983   R. B. Austin (ed.). *Decision making in the practice of crop protection*.
       London: British Crop Protection Council.

1983   C. R. Worthing (ed.). *The pesticide manual*, 7th edn. London: British Crop Protection Council.
1984   F. G. W. Jones. *Pests of field crops*, 3rd edn. London: Edward Arnold.

Part IV   The human factor

TECHNOLOGY

1968   W. J. C. Lawrence. *Plant breeding*. Institute of Biology Studies in Biology, vol. 12. London: Edward Arnold.
1980   R. G. Hurd, P. V. Biscoe and C. Dennis (eds). *Opportunities for increasing crop yields*. London: Pitman.
1981   C. Culpin. *Farm machinery*, 10th edn. London: Granada.
1982   B. Butterworth and J. Nix. *Farm mechanisation for profit*. London: Granada.
1982   T. H. Thomas (ed.). *Plant growth regulators – potential and practice*. London: British Plant Protection Council.

ENERGY

1975   L. C. Ruedisili and M. W. Firebaugh (eds). *Perspectives on energy*. Oxford: Oxford University Press.
1976   G. Leach. *Energy in food production*. London: IPC Scientific and Technical Press.
1979   B. A. Stout *et al. Energy for world agriculture*. Rome: FAO.
1980   W. Bach, J. Pankrath and J. Williams (eds). *Interaction of energy and climate*. Dordrecht: Reidel.
1980   D. Pimental (ed.). *Handbook of energy utilization in agriculture*. Boca Raton, Florida: CRC Press.
1982   A. Blanc-Lapierre (ed.). *Mankind and energy; needs, resources, hopes*. Studies in Environmental Science, vol. 16. Amsterdam: Elsevier.

SOCIO-ECONOMIC FACTORS

1974   Anonymous. *New agricultural landscapes*. London: Countryside Commission.
1975   D. K. Britton and B. Hill. *Size and efficiency in farming*. Aldershot: Saxon House.
1977   Anonymous. *Land use. Lowland farming*. Nature Conservancy Council. London: HMSO.
1978   Anonymous. *Report of a MAFF scientific working party on manurial residues*. London: HMSO.
1978   Anonymous. *Agriculture and the countryside*. London: HMSO.
1979   C. S. Barnard and J. S. Nix. *Farm planning and control*. Cambridge: Cambridge University Press.
1980   K. Blaxter. *Food chains and human nutrition*. Barking: Applied Science Publishers.
1980   T. Giles and M. J. Stansfield. *The farmer as manager*. London: George Allen & Unwin.
1980   M. H. Omar. *Economic value of agrometeorological information*. World

Meteorological Organisation Technical Note no. 164. Geneva: WMO.
1980   J. M. Powell (ed.). *Socio-economic impact of climate.* Information Report NOR-X-217. Canada: Northern Forests Research.
1981   I. Carruthers and C. Clark. *The economics of irrigation.* Liverpool: Liverpool University Press.
1982   A. E. Blackwell *et al. The costs of the Common Agricultural Policy (CAP).* Beckenham: Croom Helm.
1982   L. B. Curzon. *Land tenure in Great Britain. Land law.* Plymouth: Macdonald & Evans.
1982   F. Sturrock. *Farm accounting and management,* 7th edn. London: Pitman.
1982   M. F. Warren. *Financial management for farmers.* London: Hutchinson.
1983   C. H. Hanf and G. Schiefer (eds). *Planning and decision in agribusiness; principles and experiences.* Developments in Agricultural Economics, vol. 1. Amsterdam: Elsevier.

General reading

1962   D. L. Stamp. *The land of Britain. Its use and misuse.* London: Longman.
1963   A. N. Duckham. *The farming year.* London: Chatto & Windus.
1963   W. H. Pawley. *Possibilities of increasing world food production.* Freedom from Hunger Campaign Basic Study no. 10. Rome: FAO.
1964   J. T. Coppock. *An agricultural atlas of England and Wales.* London: Faber & Faber.
1968   H. A. Steppler (ed.). *The food resources of the world.* Montreal: Agriculture World Press.
1969   G. Wrigley. *Tropical agriculture and development of production.* London: Faber & Faber.
1975   F. Suringh *et al. Computation of the absolute maximum food production in the world.* Wageningen: Department of Tropical Social Science, University of Wageningen.
1979   G. W. Cox and M. D. Atkins. *Agricultural ecology. An analysis of world food production systems.* San Francisco: W. H. Freeman.
1979   M. Schnapf (ed.). *Farmland food and the future.* Ankeny, Iowa: Soil Conservation Society of America.
1979   C. R. W. Spedding. *An introduction to agricultural systems.* Barking, Essex: Applied Science Publications.
1980   Anonymous. *Perspectives in world agriculture.* Farnham Royal, Slough: Commonwealth Agricultural Bureaux.
1980   N. Tracy. *Agriculture in Western Europe. Challenge and response.* London: Granada.
1983   C. R. W. Spedding (ed.). *Fream's agriculture,* 16th edn. London: John Murray.

SOURCES OF INFORMATION

1981   J. R. Blanchard and L. Farrell (eds). *Guide to sources for agricultural and biological research.* Berkeley: University of California Press.
1981   G. P. Lilley (ed.). *Information sources in agriculture and food science.* London: Butterworths.

1981　A. W. Moore *et al.* (eds). *Information system for soil and related data.* Wageningen: PUDOC.

DATA AND BIBLIOGRAPHIES

1868–1904　*Board of agriculture returns England and Wales.* London: HMSO (Annual Volumes).
1909–84　*Agricultural statistics England and Wales.* London: HMSO (Annual Volumes).
1984　　　Government publications, sectional list no. 1. *Agriculture and food.* London: HMSO.
1984　　　Ministry of Agriculture, Fisheries and Food publications. *Agriculture and food catalogue.* London: HMSO.

The last two titles are the lists of British Government publications dealing with many aspects of food and agriculture, which are obtainable from MAFF (Publications), Lion House, Willowburn Estate, Alnwick, Northumberland NE66 2PF. The lists are usually revised annually, and the publications range from short (free) leaflets concerning practical problems to longer (priced) booklets and bulletins dealing in greater detail with particular topics. Although there is some variation in their quality and extent of detail, they are prepared by authors who are often recognised as experts in their subjects. They may not always be revised frequently enough to keep pace with the rate of change within the industry, but even so they are worth consulting by anyone searching for information on most aspects of British agriculture.

SCIENTIFIC PAPERS

There are a very large number of scientific papers on relevant topics being published in a variety of journals. For example, the 'Recently published papers' section of *Agricultural Meteorology* (Amsterdam: Elsevier) contains over 3000 titles annually on only the meteorological aspects of the subject.

The best reference sources are the series of monthly abstracts published by the Commonwealth Agricultural Bureaux, Farnham Royal, Slough SL2 3BN, England, including publications dealing with subjects such as: agricultural engineering, animal breeding, dairy science, field crops, forestry, herbage, horticulture, plant breeding, entomology, plant pathology, soils and fertilizers, veterinary research, weeds and world agricultural economics. They also publish annotated bibliographies on special subjects, compiled from the entries in these publications.

Subject index